WITHDRAWN
HARVARD LIBRARY
WITHDRAWN

TOWARD THE ESTABLISHMENT OF LIBERAL CATHOLICISM IN AMERICA

Joseph A. Varacalli

UNIVERSITY
PRESS OF
AMERICA

LANHAM • NEW YORK • LONDON

Copyright © 1983 by

University Press of America,™ Inc.

4720 Boston Way
Lanham, MD 20706

3 Henrietta Street
London WC2E 8LU England

All rights reserved
Printed in the United States of America

Library of Congress Cataloging in Publication Data

Varacalli, Joseph A.
    Toward the establishment of liberal Catholicism in America.

    Bibliography: p.
    1. Catholic Church–United States. I. Title.
BX1406.2.V37   1983   282'.73   82-23811
ISBN 0-8191-2974-7
ISBN 0-8191-2975-5 (pbk.)

All University Press of America books are produced on acid-free paper which exceeds the minimum standards set by the National Historical Publications and Records Commission.

DEDICATION

This work is dedicated to the memory of Henry J. Browne (1919-1980), a great Catholic scholar and an even greater Christian.

TABLE OF CONTENTS

Preface. vii

Introduction xi

PART I

INITIAL CONSIDERATIONS FOR THE ANALYSIS OF THE BICENTENNIAL PROGRAM AND MOVEMENT

Chapter One
An Introduction to the Facts 1

Chapter Two
An Overview of the Major Issues. 7

Chapter Three
The Forces of Modernity. 19

PART II

THE HISTORY OF THE BICENTENNIAL PROGRAM AND MOVEMENT

Chapter Four
The Description of the Bicentennial
Program and Movement 27

Chapter Five
Criticisms of the Bicentennial
Program and Movement 99

PART III

THE PRESUPPOSITIONS OF THE BICENTENNIAL PROGRAM AND MOVEMENT

Chapter Six
The Cultural Presupposition:
The American Civil Religion and
the Theology of Vatican II 115

Chapter Seven
  The Formal Organizational Presupposition:
  The Machinery of the American Catholic
  Church 165

Chapter Eight
  The Social Organizational Presupposition:
  The Development of the "New Catholic
  Knowledge Class" 189

Chapter Nine
  The Sociological Social-Psychological
  Presupposition: The American Catholic
  Social-Psychological Revolution. 213

PART IV

CONCLUSION AND EVALUATION

Chapter Ten
  The Institutionalization of the
  Liberal Catholic Perspective in
  America: A "System of Checks and
  Balances", A Theological Pluralism,
  and a Developing Theology of
  Pluralism. 241

Appendix A - The 182 Proposals of the
             Call to Action Assembly 263

Appendix B - The Call to Action Assembly
             Delegate Profile. 295

Bibliography 299

PREFACE

Toward The Establishment of Liberal Catholicism in America is a re-edited, shortened, and slightly updated version of my Rutgers University doctoral thesis, *The American Catholic Call for Liberty and Justice for All: An Analysis in the Sociology of Knowledge*, successfully defended in December of 1979. Let me immediately extend my thanks to my dissertation committee members for their assistance and criticism: Joseph B. Maier, Louis H. Orzack, Peter L. Berger, Edward A. Shils, and especially, Henry J. Browne. I also owe my thanks to four specific members of the Catholic intellectual community apart from Professor Browne. They are Frank Butler, the Executive Secretary of the Bicentennial Committee; Mr. James Finn, then editor of *Worldview* magazine and a member of the Bicentennial Committee; Professor David J. O'Brien of Holy Cross College, the "official" historian of the Bicentennial Program and also a member of the Bicentennial Committee; and finally, Bishop Joseph Francis of Newark, Chairman of the *Bishops' Ad Hoc Committee on The Call to Action Plan*. The first three gentlemen provided me with important interviews. Mr. Finn, in addition, turned over to me his complete file of both published and unpublished material. Mr. Butler continually mailed to me any program material available at the United States Catholic Conference. He also arranged permission for me to attend the "mini Call to Action" follow-up held in Washington, D.C., in March of 1979. Professor O'Brien kindly gave me permission to examine his complete file of material during a visit to Holy Cross College, including his general and as yet unpublished history of the Bicentennial Program, *A Call to Action: The Church Prepares for the Third Century*. Bishop Francis kindly mailed to me his committee's report, *The Diocesan Implementation of "To Do The Work of Justice: A Plan of Action for the Catholic Community in the United States"*. The results of this valuable survey have been incorporated into this updated version of my thesis. To these individuals and to the all too numerous to cite members of the Catholic intellectual community who were of assistance to me, I offer my profound thanks.

vii

Last but not least, let me acknowledge my debt to the Tears and Motichka families for their assistance in the technical preparation of the manuscript: to Mary for her proofreading, to Mary Ann for her typing, and to Mike for his babysitting while Mary Ann was typing.

Given its central importance, one substantive issue will be addressed here at the outset. It involves a widely-held interpretation, within liberal Catholic circles, that the overall Bicentennial Program was more a failure than a success. In his "Toward An American Catholic Church" (Cross Currents, Volume XXXI, #4, Winter, 1981), David J. O'Brien represents, quintessentially, such a view when he states:

> Many Catholics have been disappointed with the Bishops' efforts to promote shared responsibility . . . . Most dramatically, the Liberty and Justice programs of regional hearings and diocesan discussions, climaxing in the national Call to Action Conference of 1976 in Detroit, aroused high hopes for collaboration and cooperative action which were for the most part disappointed. While some of its recommendations were implemented by existing committees, many of its calls for vigorous efforts to implement existing positions on social issues died of neglect or lack of resources, while more controversial recommendations for Church reform were rejected out of hand. Worst of all, no substantial effort was made, on the basis of the enthusiasm generated by the program, to build new forms of cooperation either among organized national constituencies of religious, clergy, minorities, and apostolic movements, or among the Bishops themselves. In the long run, the Bishops must build effective forms of consultation and shared responsibility but they will not do so until they have a clearer sense of the mission of the National Conference of Catholic Bishops.

The analysis offered in the following pages is not overly sympathetic to Professor O'Brien's general conclusion that the Bicentennial was a failure from the perspective of the liberal cause.

There are two reasons for this. The first, and less important, reason entails making explicit just what a "successful" Bicentennial Program would entail from the perspective of socialist-leaning Catholics like O'Brien. It would entail nothing less than the American Catholic Church identifying totally with what Avery Dulles has referred to as the "servant" model of the Church. It would also necessarily entail a great deal of power and authority shifting away from the diocesan level and towards the national level in the form of a much expanded and highly centralized national episcopal conference. And it would also necessitate the institution of fraternal and democratic procedures of decision-making in a Church that is constitutively autocratic in its essentials. When guaged against such a standard, the program can be termed a failure. However, when guaged against the empirical reality of the manner in which the hierarchy of the Church has responded either historically to the vision of liberal Catholicism or comparatively to the various non-activist oriented wings of a very pluralistic contemporary American Catholic Church, the program must be evaluated as successful from the perspective of the advocates of liberal Catholicism in America.

The second, and more important, reason for not sympathizing with the general assessment of O'Brien "holds constant" the question of the success of the ten year program sponsored by the Bishops. The Bicentennial process must also be viewed as a social movement whose life and vitality cannot be measured solely by the response of the Bishops to the 182 proposals that emanated from the 1976 Detroit Call to Action Conference over a short period of time. Whatever the final impact of the Bicentennial Program (which officially ends in 1983), one thing is clear: the Bicentennial movement, which created the program and then fed off of it, is clearly gathering steam as the American Catholic Church approaches the turn of the twenty-first century. Indeed, since the completion of my dissertation such distinctly liberal issues that surfaced during the Bicentennial Program as the threat of nuclear war, American involvement in Latin America, opposition to what is now called Reaganomics, and a host of human rights concerns, among many others, has coalesced many Bishops, clergy, religious, and laity into an effective, if not dominant,

force within both the Church and society today.
Program or no program, the Bicentennial movement is
alive and thriving.

INTRODUCTION

This work offers a sociological interpretation of the significance of an American Catholic program and movement for both American and world Catholicism. The movement is a liberal, social-activist one that predates, is inextricably intertwined with, and will ultimately long outlive the "Liberty and Justice for All" American Catholic Bicentennial Program sponsored by the American Bishops.

It is important to make the point that the Bicentennial <u>Program</u> must be distinguished from the Bicentennial <u>movement</u>. The program can be viewed as the formal response of the American Church hierarchy to implement certain features of a Vatican II theology in the United States. The program represents a marked recognition on the part of the American Church hierarchy of both the reality, and to a lesser degree, of the legitimacy, of the dispersion of charisma, "of God's gift of grace", throughout a Church defined as the "people of God". The success of the program, from the viewpoint of the advocates of a liberal Catholicism, was not unqualified. The more radical proposals for both structural and status/authority changes in the Church were clearly rejected by the hierarchy. The latter, while clearly recognizing the democratizing trend of modern life, insists that the trend operate within the boundaries of the institutional Church and not be allowed to preempt the role of the hierarchy.

The movement, however, goes much deeper behind the American Catholic scene. It entails the ongoing historical attempt, initiated by a certain wing of the Church long before Vatican II, to institutionalize a liberal agenda in the United States. The actors involved in the movement needed the legitimation of Vatican II to be able to move effectively in this direction. Their support of the program is seen as one important way to move in this direction. The program, then, should not be viewed, at least sociologically, as an end in itself. The movement is clearly the most successful in the history of the liberal social activist wing. The movement that was so intimately involved with the program is analyzed as straddling the distinction of either being coopted fully by the hierarchy or coopting the hierarchy herself. This work simultaneously analyses the effectiveness of both the program and movement. Sociologically speaking, however, one must not too closely identify the degree of success of one with the other. As will be documented, the results of the program, from the viewpoint of its advocates, were mixed; the movement, however, has considerably strengthened itself due to the very reality of the program itself.

The analysis offered here will document just what were the theological-cultural, formal-social organizational, and social-psychological "presuppositions" for the creation of the program and the increased strength of the movement; how successful the program was; and the meaning that the program has for the cause of liberal Catholicism in the United States; and what the movement signifies for the Church Universal vis-a-vis developments within world Catholicism. The Bicentennial movement also provides a convenient opportunity to locate and highlight the present state of American Catholicism against the more inclusive matrix of American society. The movement is by no means representative, in and by itself, of the present state or future course of events of American or world Catholicism. However, a sociological investigation can help pinpoint just what the movement does represent and what it doesn't and just why and how this is so. In addition to the not insignificant groups supportive of the movement, there are many Catholics who accept the movement only on a qualified basis, and others who are either opposed, or indifferent, or simply unaware and excluded from the movement and that which it signifies.

In order to properly assess the success of the Bicentennial Program and movement one must analyze the development on the part of the hierarchy of a system of "checks and balances" that constantly moves the various wings of the Church towards "la via media" as one method of attempting to keep rather disparate groupings under one roof. Such a system may eventually encourage the development of a fully articulated "theology of pluralism". At the same time, such a system of checks and balances allows various Catholic groupings to move, within certain parameters, away from an ecclesiastically-defined Catholicism. The movement is seen as only one direction (a politicized, intellectualistic direction) that this is taking place within American and world Catholicism. It is within this developing reality of pluralism and of the need of the Bishops to minimally meet the needs of many divergent Catholic groups, that one can argue that liberal Catholicism has succeeded in firmly establishing itself as one of several alternate and authentic Catholic paradigms.

PART I
INITIAL CONSIDERATIONS FOR THE ANALYSIS OF THE BICENTENNIAL PROGRAM AND MOVEMENT

CHAPTER ONE

AN INTRODUCTION TO THE FACTS

The elaborate three stage, ten year (1973-1983) American Catholic Bicentennial Program which focused on the theme "Liberty and Justice for All" was sponsored by the Church's national episcopal conference and official national level bureaucracy, the National Conference of Catholic Bishops/United States Catholic Conference. It was initiated by its Advisory Council which had been created only as recently as 1970, fought for and protected by the liberal social activist wing of the Church located within the confines of N.C.C.B./U.S.C.C., and monitored throughout the first two stages by the Bicentennial Justice Committee. The program was quite deliberately linked to Pope Paul's Apostolic Letter, A Call to Action, (1971), which concerned itself with the need to translate Catholic theological principle into Catholic activity devoted to questions of social justice. It was also spurred on by Paul VI's 1967 statement On The Development of Peoples which argued the need for justice in the relationship between developed and Third World countries. Perhaps most inspirational was the Synod of Bishops' document Justice in the World published in 1971 which pronounces that "action on behalf of justice and participation in the transformation of the world fully appear to us as a constitutive dimension of the preaching of the Gospel, or in other words, of the Church's mission for the redemption of the human race and its liberation from every oppressive situation". That American Catholics have a theological imperative to actualize such sentiments is made clear by Archbishop Gerety in his pastoral letter The Day of Peace Restored (1973). For the powerful supporter of the Bicentennial Program:

> We must also admit that we have not listened very carefully to Pope John's teaching or the teaching after him and of the Second Vatican Council, of Pope Paul VI and of the Synod of Bishops, on matters of justice and peace. Inescapably they require American Catholics to consider what it means to be the Church in our society.[1]

1

As J. Bryan Hehir of the Bicentennial Committee put it, the two purposes of the program are "to stimulate a process of reflection, examination, planning and action by the Catholic community in the United States on the topic of freedom and justice in our society and in the global community" and "to allow us to pass from a knowledge of principles to a level of practice . . . (this) second objective . . . flows from the first. If we carry out the process of moving from principles we will be carrying on a kind of dialogue with the structures, systems of power organization, influence and wealth in our country and in the globe today".[2]

The Bicentennial Program consisted of three, more or less, distinct stages. The first "grass roots" stage included, in this order: (1) the collection of over 830,000 individual responses from approximately half the nation's dioceses that solicited which issues on the part of Catholic parishioners were perceived to be vital to the contemporary Church; (2) numerous parish and diocesan meetings; (3) seven regional "justice hearings" in which over 500 Catholic clerical and lay leaders presented testimony; and (4) using as a base the individual responses, the justice hearing testimony and Church writings, eight writing committees prepared working papers and proposals along eight separate themes. The overall theme of "Liberty and Justice for All" was investigated in the following eight different areas of activity that confront the Church's relationship to society: Church, ethnicity and race, neighborhood, family, personhood, work, nationkind, and humankind.

The second stage consisted of the national Catholic assembly held in Detroit in October of 1976, the Call to Action Conference. The conference debated, voted, amended, and eventually passed an enormously large list of recommendations along each of the sub-themes--a total of 182--which were to be considered by the National Conference of Catholic Bishops at their subsequent May meetings from 1977 through to 1981.

The conference was attended by 1,340 delegates from 150 out of 170 dioceses of the country. It was composed of approximately 47% laity and 53% clergy including 110 of the nation's 300 Bishops. There were present, in addition, 94 national Catholic organizations with voting privileges. Over 1,000 non-voting observers were also in attendance. Over two-thirds of

2

the voting delegates were employed by the Church and over 90% claimed heavy involvement in various Church organizations.

The third period of the overall "Liberty and Justice for All" program (1977-1981) was designated by the Bicentennial Committee as a time of "follow-up", that is, to study, discuss, and implement appropriate-- from the viewpoint of the Bishops--Call to Action recommendations. At their May 1977 meeting, the Bishops responded initially to the Call to Action proposals by (1) issuing a pastoral statement addressing some of the more controversial Detroit recommendations and (2) assigning each recommendation to a Bishop's Committee within the N.C.C.B./U.S.C.C. It was then the task of each respective committee to evaluate each of its assigned resolutions a directive to either (1) study, (2) act immediately, (3) support existing activities or (4) "respond in light of the universal law of the Church." (Given their invaluable use throughout the forthcoming analysis, all 182 proposals with their N.C.C.B./U.S.C.C. designation are listed in Appendix A). The pastoral reply also created a Bishops' Ad Hoc Committee on The Call to Action within the N.C.C.B./U.S.C.C. under the chairmanship of a liberal prelate, Archbishop John Roach. The task of the committee would be to serve as a strong monitoring committee, complete with funds and staff, and which was authorized to receive regular progress reports on the implementation of acceptable proposals.

The 1978 May meeting of Bishops produced the "Call to Action Plan", later entitled To Do the Work of Justice. The plan proposed a six prong attack on the theme of "Liberty and Justice for All" through its sections on human rights; economic justice; the Church as people, parish and community; family life; education for justice; and world hunger. Unsatisfied merely to mandate, the plan called for a review of national accomplishments and pitfalls in 1983 (thus adding to the Bicentennial Program an additional two years). The year 1978 also saw the creation of a permanent secretariat within the national level bureaucracy, that of the Secretariat for the Laity, which would be of special assistance to the Call to Action Bishops' Committee.

In March of the following year 1979, the Ad Hoc Committee on the Call to Action Plan, in conjunction with both the Secretariat for the Laity and the staff of the U.S.C.C., held a "mini-Call to Action" follow-up in Washington, D. C. At this three-day conference over 300 Bicentennial diocesan coordinators reported to each other the progress, or lack thereof, in the implementation at the local parish level of the Call to Action proposals. This information was then gathered by the staff of the U.S.C.C. and later disseminated to the various dioceses throughout the country.

In November of 1979, the Ad Hoc Committee on the Call to Action Plan indicated that it would formally survey and report on the follow-up activity in the dioceses to the directives in To Do The Work of Justice. A total of 106 dioceses completed the survey by the requested return date of July 15, 1980. This figure represented 62.3% of the nation's dioceses. Based on these survey results, the Committee, now chaired by another liberal prelate, Bishop Joseph Francis, produced the report, The Diocesan Implementation of "To Do The Work of Justice: A Plan of Action for the Catholic Community in the United States". A final report on diocesan implementation of Bicentennial related directives will take place sometime after the completion of the program in 1983.

FOOTNOTES

[1] Quoted in *Liberty and Justice for All: A Discussion Guide* Washington: Committee for the Bicentennial/United States Catholic Conference 1975, p. 24.

[2] *Ibid.*, p. 5.

CHAPTER TWO

AN OVERVIEW OF THE MAJOR ISSUES

The importance of the American Catholic Bicentennial Program can perhaps be best illustrated when highlighted against the sober remarks of the American Catholic historian, Thomas T. McAvoy. In the very last paragraph of his monumental A History of the Catholic Church in the United States completed in 1969, the scholar noted:

> looking over the two decades since World War II, we see that . . . despite the fact that most of the arguments in the Catholic press have been about Catholic intellectual efforts and the participation of the layman in the government of the Church, there has been no real change in the status of either question.[1]

Father McAvoy characterized the years immediately prior to Vatican II as follows:

> a scrutiny . . . at the end of the decade of the fifties shows that American Catholicism was prosperous but unexciting. There was practically no national Catholic movement outside of the usual fraternal and social organizations. Even the National Catholic Welfare Conference (the predecessor to the N.C.C.B./U.S.C.C.) exercised little influence because of the supremacy of diocesan government and the general conservatism of the hierarchy. The role of the Catholic layman was discussed, but no one offered a solution to the lack of lay leadership.[2]

The years immediately following Vatican II did give evidence of the beginnings of a liberal Catholic movement through the creation of organizations such as the Catholic Committee on Urban Ministry (1967), the Center of Concern (1971) and Network (1971) which eventually would play such a strategic role throughout the Bicentennial program. Nonetheless, it held true that McAvoy could still conclude in 1969 that:

7

. . . to say when the . . . spirit of Pope
John and his council first affected American
Catholics in some force is at present impossible. Future generations . . . will have
to determine when the movements stirring in
American Catholicism first joined up with
the aggiornamento.[3]

Only four years after Father McAvoy's
observations, the wheels of the most impressive,
large-scale, systematically constructed social activist
program were to be set in motion by the Advisory
Council of the N.C.C.B./U.S.C.C. Even in the year 1969,
however, Father McAvoy was astute enough to recognize
the most likely vehicle through which any concrete
application of Vatican II would eventually actualize
itself. As he put it:

> One of the major changes . . . for the
> United States has been the formation of
> the Bishops Conference. The decrees of
> the Conference were at first minor . . .
> but unlike the National Catholic Welfare
> Conference the new Conference has power
> and with Papal approval can make decrees
> binding on the American Church. There is
> here the major force for interpreting the
> further changes decreed by the Council or
> demanded by the American phase of aggiorna-
> mento.[4]

The first major document which was issued
by the National Conference of Catholic Bishops was
the pastoral, The Church in Our Day, published on
January 21, 1968. It represents the American
hierarchy's interpretation and application of the
constitution of the church as propounded in Vatican
II's most seminal document, Lumen Gentium, "On the
Church". In Lumen Gentium, the chapter on "the people
of God" comes before that on the hierarchial structure,
thus highlighting "officially" the increased status of
the laity and, by implication at least, the decreased
status of the clergy. The very reality of the American
Catholic Bicentennial Program can be interpreted, in
part at least, as the Church hierarchy's recognition of
the need for a more continuous, articulate, and vital
relationship between itself and the "ordinary" Catholic.
That this was the interpretation of the meaning of the
Bicentennial Program by the Bicentennial Committee is

8

made clear by its report sent to the N.C.C.B. just after the completion of the program's second stage, the Call to Action Conference. As the report states:

The Church in the U.S. has been experimenting since Vatican II with structures of consultation at the national level, one of the most successful of which is the Advisory Council of the N.C.C.B./U.S.C.C. Continuing in this tradition many felt the need to invite laity, religious and clergy to participate in setting goals for the Church at the national level. The justice conference, known later as the Call to Action Conference, seemed to be a good opportunity to try to see if a process of broad consultation could be used to establish goals and enlist the support of the Catholic people in working for these goals. While clearly advisory in nature, the justice conference and the consultation which preceded it were given unusual significance by the Bishops' commitment to develop a plan of action for justice based upon its results. Thus, the bicentennial program was to be a process giving the Catholic community an experience of consultation and shared responsibility, and to produce a product, i.e., a five year pastoral plan for justice. On that basis the Committee began its efforts to carry out the plan for the consultation.[5]

The Bicentennial movement is indicative of the aspiration of a liberal Catholicism that has historically been ever present within American Catholicism but which required changes in American culture, theological legitimation, formal and social organization and in the social-psychology of at least a significant segment of the Church to emerge as a permanent force. The development of an American Civil Religion in which "all men of good will" and "one nation under God" acknowledge that "God's work must truly be our own" and who submit to the demands for "liberty and justice for all" served to foster the ecumenical activity of the Bicentennial participants and advocates. Vatican II theology, in turn, served to reinforce and legitimate, at least in the minds of the Bicentennial advocates, the very same American Civil Religion which represented the religious dimension most meaningful to American Catholic liberalism in the pre-Vatican II twentieth century. The creation and function of the Advisory Council as serving as a liaison between the Bishops and the American Catholic population-at-large is but a small part of the formal and social organizational change taking place within the American Catholic Church. There has occurred within the framework of the Church, especially at the national and diocesan levels, a dramatic increase in bureaucratization, professionalism, and specialization. This change results partly out of the necessity of a Catholic Church claiming universality to keep pace with the rationalizing tendencies of the outer world society. Catholic "specialists" and "professionals" are needed to create "Catholic social policy" and to represent the "Catholic position" to the secular elites within government, scientific, educational, and cultural organizations at the national, regional, and to a lesser degree, local level.

The professional segment of the Church is here being termed the "New Catholic Knowledge Class". The New Catholic Knowledge Class is a group of highly educated, professionally-oriented social activists and bureaucrats from the ranks of both the laity and lower-echelon clergy and religious who occupy the bulk of the various Catholic national and diocesan level bureaucracies and organizations and other entities like campus ministries, universities and colleges, research institutes, publishing houses, etc., who are concerned with the creation, manipulation, and implementation of socio-religious knowledge, symbols, and ideas and with the social policy and programs that emanate from such. The American Catholic Bicentennial program presupposed the existence of a significant base of social activists with professional expertise in the humanities, social sciences, business fields, and theology, and also a reasonably coordinated network of organizations from which both to recruit supporters and to attempt to implement and institutionalize the thrust of the program. Regarding the former point, that of its social organization, it has only been recently that one could claim that the American Catholic Church has become a middle-class one with its concomitant vanguard of "professionals" and "experts". Regarding the latter point, the fact remains that, only as recently as the period immediately prior to the opening session of Vatican II, the American Catholic liberal wing had lacked the necessary formal organizational machinery to attempt to initiate

10

the program. While the creation of the National War Council in 1917, the predecessor of the N.C.C.B./ U.S.C.C., provided a sort of "sanctuary" for liberal Catholicism--a rather precarious one supported mainly by a selective interpretation of Rerum Novarum and Quadragesimo Anno--it was really not until after Vatican II that the concept of a national episcopal conference became fully accepted and that the formal organizational network of liberal Catholicism could expand and become dispersed enough "downwards" to attempt a truly national level program that systematically organized and brought together the parishes and dioceses of the country. Vatican II called for the creation (or, as in the U.S. case, the strengthening) of national episcopal conferences with some autonomy from Rome in the implementation of national Catholic social policies and also with the creation of diocesan-level priests' senates and pastoral councils that include representation from the laity. Such structures represent the "official" formal organizational vehicles through which the democratizing ideals of the Bicentennial Program were originated from and are attempting to be institutionalized through.

These social and formal organizational changes share a fundamental affinity with a Vatican II theology with its emphasis on "the Church as the people of God" (and not defined solely in terms of its hierarchy and of Papal Authority) and with its emphasis on the role of the Bishops as "servants of the servants of God" (as contrasted to a more authoritarian leadership position). Such theological legitimation encourages and makes plausible to a certain Catholic constituency the need for national episcopal conferences run by "specialists" (who need not be higher echelon clergy) with some autonomy from Rome and for the institutionalizing of "democratizing" procedures within the national Church like those called for throughout the Bicentennial Program.

The successful institutionalizing of democratic procedures also requires a "democratization" at the individual social-psychological level. Such an orientation is one that feels free to incorporate--to attempt to make "Catholic"--ideational components not hitherto considered to be within the parameters of orthodoxy. Indeed, one of the hallmarks of a "liberal" religiousity--Catholic or otherwise--is a "forward", optimistic orientation to the world that is constantly attempting to "make sacred" elements of the universe hitherto considered "profane".

It is the New Catholic Knowledge Class that stands at the intersection of those changes at the levels of culture, society and personality. It is a class that represents strengthening of hitherto unorganized elements of American liberal Catholicism that crystallized during the Bicentennial Program and that constitutes the human capital for the movement. Thomas Fox, writing just after the conclusion of the Call to Action Conference in October of 1976, hints at this conclusion:

> What began two years ago as an effort to find out what troubled Catholics and what they wanted Church leaders to do in areas of social justice had, by the time the conference ended, snowballed. The conference became a national forum for priests, sisters, and laypersons to call for radical change, taking the Bishops call and Church teachings as the ground for that change.[6]

The American Catholic Bicentennial Program has provided the forum and means of communication through which lower echelon clergy and laity of "professional" or "specialist" status occupying "middle-management" positions within an ever increasing Church bureaucracy have organized themselves and are attempting to implement structural and theological change within the Church. Proposed structural changes involve the expanding of Church bureaucracies at all levels to implement many of the "liberty and justice for all" proposals. Theological changes involve a switch in emphasis from what Max Weber[7] has termed the "traditional authority" of the Bishop (as it is couched in ostensibly "legal-rational" terminology) to the "rational pragmatic" authority of the "professional Church bureaucrat" as discussed by Paul Harrison.[8] Perhaps even more dramatically, the Call to Action was a call for the extension of "legal-rational" authority to the lower-echelon clergy and laity. From the viewpoint of Edward Shils,[9] such a movement entails a "dispersion of charisma" to individuals hitherto standing beyond the pale of the Church"s "centre", of that locale that generates and defines the moral, political, and theological universe. Viewed either way, such a transition points to a possible, although not inevitable, "crisis of authority" between and among the Pope, American Bishops and the New Catholic Knowledge Class along the classical Marxian conception of "class", i.e., an individual's or a group's relationship to the "modes of production". "Production" in this case, again, refers much more to the creation of knowledge, ideas and symbols than it does to material factors.[10]

The list of proposals coming out of the Detroit Call to Action Conference is indicative of this possible "crisis of authority". Both the nature of many of the proposals and of the social interaction evident throughout the program is illustrative of the attenuation of deference granted to the Pope and American Bishops by the delegates. This attenuation seems to be the case not only in terms of the layman's (or lower echelon clergy's) relationship to a Bishop, but also to that of a Bishop to Supreme Pontiff. It can be plausibly argued that what Vatican II represented to the American Bishops and to their national episcopal conference in their relationship to Rome, the Bicentennial Program represented to the individual Catholic in his relationship to his Bishop or diocesan leadership. "Collegiality", in so many words, is constantly entended ever more centrifugally.

The Bicentennial movement, following the intellectual tradition of Richard Hofstadter[11] and Joseph Gusfield,[12] is more a "symbolic crusade" than it is an economic one. The movement represented the vehicle through which the voice of an historically suppressed, or at best ignored, liberal social activist wing has come bellowing out of the Church's socio-theological wilderness. While the proposed changes of the Call to Action Conference are no doubt motivated to a great degree out of sincere theological conviction and a religio-humanitarian concern for the poor, they remain, as matters of fact, self-serving, both "materially" and more importantly for most, in terms of "status". The Spirit moves and builds within society and through human nature with the result that, as ever, motives are mixed. Both the Bicentennial Program and movement must be analyzed through an awareness of the inevitability of religion's partial accomodation to society, of what Max Weber has referred to as the "routinization of charisma".[13]

13

The fact that material and status considerations becomes more compelling factors over time does not exhaust the meaning of the "routinization of charisma" as it applies to the case of the program and movement. Routinization results just as much from a lack of expedient means for the constant refueling of the charismatic force as it does from the simple bad faith of individuals. Simply put, there is an uneven development of formal organizational structure throughout the Church which hinders the successful institutionalization of the program's "charismatic ideals" throughout Catholic America. Where there is no structure, there simply isn't any procedure through which the Call to Action proposals can be mediated "downwards" from the national level to the population-at-large.

The reality of an uneven institutionalization constitutes, from the viewpoint of the more zealous supporters of the Bicentennial Program, a serious problem. These supporters are those who insist that the criterion of success of the process and movement is the degree to which the Church's approach to the question of social justice becomes a centralized, systematic and rational one. Such advocates are doomed to disappointment given several sturdy facts. First of all, according to canon law, the Church is run by Bishops who have, for the most part, autonomous or "Ordinary" power over the official Church activity within their own dioceses. Thus an unsympathetic Bishop can conveniently ignore the exhortations from the national level inspired and run program. And second of all, there were and are many segments of the overall Catholic population that are either hostile or indifferent to the type of Catholic expression that the Bicentennial Program represents. To demand that the success of the program rely solely on its ability to transform the whole Church in its image is to guarantee a negative evaluation. On the other hand, the opposite position, i.e., that the program has completely failed, is equally a useless evaluation. The facts are that the N.C.C.B./U.S.C.C. has a great deal of moral suasion, that it is a strong supporter of programs consistent with the liberal, "social" nature of much of Vatican II theology, and that much voluntary and "unofficial" activity sympathetic to the program and movement can proceed unabated and undisturbed by the local Ordinary. Such considerations make the analysis of the routinization of the charismatic ideals of the Bicentennial Program either presently, or in the near future, an exceedingly difficult and problematic task.

The fact that the Bicentennial movement is a class-specific one located within the confines of national and regional Catholic bureaucracies points to another important element of our overall analysis. Simply put, the case may very well be that the social policies and programs of the New Catholic Knowledge Class are incongruent with the wishes of the local parishioner, priest or Bishop. This incongruence derives from the tendency for the "local" Bishop, priest, and parishioner to stress the "integrative" functions of providing solace, support, and mediating a sense of the transcendent versus the tendency of the more national or "cosmopolitan" oriented individual to emphasize an interpretation of the Gospel that is one of "immanance" and one calling for the radical and prophetic alteration of existing social structural arrangements.[14] The New Catholic Knowledge Class, aided considerably by the existence of the professional staff of the U.S.C.C., is oriented toward the national level and with this more prophetic interpretation.

One final issue involved in an overall interpretation of both the Bicentennial Program and movement entails an understanding that the Catholic Church is developing a system of "checks and balances" that recognizes a multitude of perceived partial truths regarding the nature of authority within the Church, the nature of the Christian message, and the proper role of the Catholic vis-a-vis his "earthly" versus "spiritual" involvements. Such a system of "checks and balances" protects the integrity of a variety of forms of Catholic expression and, at the same time, constantly moves the Church toward "la via media". The Bicentennial Program can best be analyzed as the Church hierarchy's qualified acceptance of the liberal wing of the American Church as one of other equally legitimate Catholic movements within the Church today. The dispersion of authority that is concomitant with the development of "checks and balances" moves various Catholic groups centrifugally away from an ecclesiastically defined Catholicism without granting any one group a complete autonomy from the Magisterium or, conversely, without having the Magisterium "move out" solely to any one group, thus overidentifying with it, and in fact, being completely coopted by it. The American Catholic Bicentennial movement is seen as only

CHAPTER THREE

THE FORCES OF MODERNITY

Sociologically speaking, the American Catholic Church must be viewed as an entity that is being affected not only by developments within world Catholicism and American society but, even more fundamentally, by the world-transforming global processes associated with modernity. The latter impign upon the American Catholic Church and force some sort of reaction on the part of its various segments. Given that the Bicentennial movement represents the avant-garde wing of the American Church, its response to the global forces of modernity has been a positive one. It is the liberal wing of the Church that constantly attempts not only to meet modernity "head on" but to make it Catholic.

One important angle in interpreting the significance of the program and movement is to analyze it in light of what Edward Shils claims to be the modal movement in history, that of the "dispersion of charisma". It is a movement which describes the process of the greater inclusion of hitherto peripheral groupings into central decision-making arenas of modern life.[1] Such a discussion is an extraordinarily useful one in describing the "collegial" tendencies of world Catholicism, as evidenced by the theology of Vatican II and some of its concrete applications, i.e., the creation of the Synod of Bishops, the internationalization of the College of Cardinals, the greater autonomy given to regional and national episcopal conferences and the creation of priests' senates and pastoral councils, the latter including representation from the laity. Of more specific relevance for our study is that the program represents a marked recognition on the part of the American Church hierarchy of both the reality, and to a lesser degree, of the legitimacy, of such a dispersion of "God's gift of grace".

Edward Shils' general discussion of the "dispersion of charisma" can be broken down into three independent but interdependent social forces. They are the processes of democratization, pluralism and civility. Each one of the processes can be

19

fruitfully applied to the analysis of the Bicentennial Program and movement.

The Bicentennial Program marks the first serious--and certainly "systematic" and "rational"-- attempt to democratize the American Catholic Church. This attempt was initiated by a numerically small but anything but uninfluential left-wing segment of the Church hierarchy. It sought out, found, and meshed together the not-so-unusual coalition, among both lower-echelon clergy and laity, of intellectuals, church bureaucrats, social activists, and non-white ethnic "minorities".

Democratization can most generally be defined as the increased demand on the part of the "mass" of any society's population for recognition in decision-making concomitant with the recognition on the part of that society's elite core--as grudging and partial as it may be--of the validity of such demands.[2] Central to this overall process of democratization on the part of individuals once isolated from those political arenas from which, following Erving Goffman,[3] "the action emanates", is a more marked display of individualism and an increased concern with abstract and theoretical issues not previously considered, either on the part of the elite or mass, to be the proper domain of the "little man". From the viewpoint of the elite, democratization acknowledges the growth and manifestation of that "spark of divinity" latent within the soul of each and every individual. Put another way, democratization entails a gradual, but by no means complete, shifting of the locus of charisma, from those who possess it by virtue of their encumbered office within elite institutions to individual "citizens" who, in a stumbling, inarticulate, and incomplete manner, have increasingly come to believe in the reality of their own charisma. Translated into something more relevant for American Catholicism, democratization entails an increased "say" on the part of priests, religious and certain groups of laity within the Church at the partial expense of the Bishops, i.e., those who hold their authority by virtue of the concept of "apostolic succession".

An analysis of the Bicentennial celebration also exposes the reality of a great deal of pluralism both outside of and within the Church. The modern situation, following the general thrust of Peter Berger's[4] work, fosters open systems of knowledge which are both in competition and communication with each other. Every religious community in the modern world becomes, literally, "heretical", i.e., it is forced to choose among, or react in some way to, many differing systems of knowledge. Both the Bicentennial Program and movement attracted numerous and disparate "interest groups" representing women, blacks, hispanics, American Indians, the disabled, homosexuals, the divorced, among others. An analysis of the Bicentennial movement is particularly interesting in that it exposes both a pluralism within the liberal, social activist wing of the Church as well as delineating its most general and common features, thus helping to set it off against the present situation of the Church Universal.

Democratization encourages pluralism and pluralism in turn, fosters a sense of democracy. Both, in turn, breed disagreements over both the goals and means of worship and action. Put simply, the incorporation of once peripheral elements in the American Catholic Church into its central decision-making arena inevitably entails disruption and disagreements among an ever increasing number of factions. A radical pluralism, obviously, could lead to the destruction of the Church. A less radical pluralism, in which at least a few constant themes are agreed upon by at least most parties--the "rules of the game" so to speak--, need not lead to chaos but, instead, to an increased display of tolerance. While the Bicentennial Program was openly criticized by both "left" and "right" wing factions, the fact remains that, for the most part, the discussion remained within the structures of the Church institutionally defined, thereby granting those structures a legitimacy as "the appropriate locales where things must be ironed out". As Lewis Coser[5] has forcefully argued, such a form of conflict can actually serve a positive function: to restructure existing forms instead of destroying them altogether, in the face of the growing perception on the part of at least a significant minority that the existing patterns of relationships are, in some sense, "outdated".

The interdependent processes of democratization and pluralism are concomitant with yet another interrelated world-wide development that has had its effect on both the world and American Catholic Church, to wit: the spread of civility. Civility results from the attenuation of primordial and sacred ties.[6] It is a positive force in history that fosters a sense of tolerance and restraint towards ideational positions not one's own, thus allowing for communication, compromise, and possible synthesis. The spread of civility in the American Catholic Church can no more be magnificently illustrated than by reference to the inclusion of groups in advisory positions throughout the Bicentennial Program which, in a pre-Vatican II Church, would have been absolutely unthinkable, and indeed, theologically sacrilegious.

As a matter of fact, and despite the reality of the fluid position of the American Church as evidenced by the controversy surrounding the Bicentennial, one can say at the same time that the American Catholic Church is today much more of a "civil" or "consensual" Church than at any previous time since at least the beginning of the mass migration of immigrants in the 19th century. It is more consensual or civil in that, more so than ever, it is at least listening to and asking the opinions of large groups of people hitherto ignored politically (although, perhaps, never spiritually or materially). It is more consensual precisely because it is starting to recognize the reality of the "dispersion of charisma", of "God's gift of grace", among the mass in a democratic and pluralistic setting like that of the United States. The American Catholic Church of the present day is simultaneously at its most fluid and consensual periods in its 200 year history. That this is even perceived to be the case at the level of world Catholicism has been recently stated by Pope John Paul II in his first encyclical, <u>Redemptor Hominis</u> ("The Redeemer of Man") as follows:

> In spite of all appearances, the Church is now more united in the fellowship of service and in the awareness of the apostolate. This unity springs from the principle of collegiality, mentioned by the Second Vatican Council. The principle of collegiality showed itself particularly relevant in the difficult post-conciliar period, when . . . it helped dissipate doubts and at the same time indicated the correct ways for renewing the Church in her universal dimension.[7]

Indeed, the American Catholic Bicentennial Program is a beautiful example of a exercise that serves to "dissipate doubts"--only one of several collegial developments--in the contemporary Church. The American Catholic Bicentennial movement is illustrative of the dialectical relationship between the forces of conflict and consensus operant in the Church today. As Archbishop John Roach in his "Doing Justice: Some Reflections on The Call to Action Plan" put it in 1979:

> On one hand, the Bicentennial process highlighted the serious differences within the Catholic community. Many dedicated Catholics expressed strong reservations about some features of Church life. Yet on the other hand, (it) would provide dramatic evidence of the unity of the Church, the enthusiasm and power of its people, and their care for one another.[8]

FOOTNOTES

[1] Edward A. Shils, *Center and Periphery* (Chicago: University of Chicago Press, 1975.

[2] Edward Shils, op. cit., 1975.

[3] Erving Goffman, *Interaction Ritual* (N.Y.: Doubleday, 1967.

[4] Peter L. Berger, *The Sacred Canopy* (N.Y.: Doubleday, 1967); Peter L. Berger, *A Rumor of Angels* (N.Y.: Doubleday, 1970); Peter L. Berger, *The Heretical Imperative* (N.Y.: Basic Books, 1979).

[5] Lewis Coser, *The Functions of Conflict* (Glencoe, Illinois: Free Press, 1956).

[6] Edward Shils, op. cit., 1975.

[7] John Paul II, *Redemptor Homis*, 1979 (Boston: St. Paul Editions).

[8] Unpublished paper presented to "mini Call to Action" assembly in Washington in March of 1979 by Archbishop John Roach entitled "Doing Justice: Some Reflections on the Call to Action Plan".

PART II

THE HISTORY OF THE

BICENTENNIAL PROGRAM AND MOVEMENT

CHAPTER FOUR

THE DESCRIPTION OF THE
BICENTENNIAL PROGRAM AND MOVEMENT

The idea to convene a national Catholic assembly came in the year 1973 from the Advisory Council of the National Conference of Catholic Bishops/The United States Catholic Conference (N.C.C.B./U.S.C.C.). The Advisory Council consists of a total group of 60 members composed of Bishops, priests, sisters and prominent Catholic laymen whose task it is to meet before every meeting of the National Conference of Catholic Bishops, to review the agenda of the meetings and to offer advice and criticism. The Advisory Council is a recent creation, founded in 1970 by John Cardinal Dearden, then President of the N.C.C.B., to serve as a mechanism to broaden the channel of Catholic opinion to the Bishops.

Specifically, the idea for a national Catholic assembly came from Sister Augusta Neale of Emmanuel College who had suggested to her colleagues on the Advisory Council that it would be appropriate to hold a national pastoral council in the United States. After investigation, the Council vetoed the suggestion given its awareness of the uneven development of the parish and diocesan pastoral councils throughout the country. However, the idea of the need for a general consultation was retained. Suggestions were put forth to the effect that several national assemblies might be held on subjects of broad interest. Sister Augusta proposed that the first be held on the subject of justice, which would be timely given recent promulgations on the subject by Pope Paul VI and the Synod of Bishops. This advice was passed on to the N.C.C.B. and was approved by that body. A Bishops' Bicentennial Committee composed of Bishops, members of the Advisory Council, clergy, religious and professional lay people was created to sponsor a program that would have as its focal point the October, 1976 "Call to Action" Assembly held in Detroit.

The assembly, the Bishops followed, would attempt to be as representative of the American

Catholic population as possible. Furthermore, its specific task would be to suggest to the Bishops ways and means by which the Church in America could respond to both Pope Paul's Apostolic Letter A Call to Action (1971) and to the Synod of Bishops declaration, Justice in the World (1971). In the former statement, Pope Paul specifically concerns himself with making urgent the need for each national Church community to translate Catholic principle into more specific forms of social action. As Pope Paul put it:

> It is up to the Christian communities to analyze with objectivity the situation which is proper to their own country, to shed on it the light of the Gospel's unalterable words and to draw principles of reflection, norms of judgement, and directives for action from the social teachings of the Church.[1]

In Justice in the World, the Synod of Bishops declared that "action of behalf of justice is a constitutive element of the preaching of the Gospel". The key word here is "constitutive". A concern with the institutionalizing of justice in this world would now be granted an equal, not (as previously interpreted) "derivative", status with the worship of the One God and the spreading of the Good News of Eternal Salvation in the next world.

Combining the principal concerns of these two recent and influential documents, one comes up with not only a call for action on behalf of the theme "Liberty and Justice for All" but also for a certain freedom from Rome on the part of the American hierarchy in the implementation process. Both concerns represent a part of the not yet fully developed legacy of the Second Vatican Council. And both concerns historically represent "constitutive" elements of the American liberal Catholic agenda.

David J. O'Brien, a member of the Bishops' Bicentennial Committee, noted an important move in the "Liberty and Justice for All" program. The move entailed a shift from one of "consultation as a means to an end", the "end" being a series of formal statements of Catholic positions on justice, to that of "consultation as an end in itself", a call for the "average Catholic "to speak up". As O'Brien puts it:

While there was a basic continuity in the emphasis on the theme of justice, the goals of the program gradually shifted over the course of two years (1974-76). Initially, the purpose had been to popularize Catholic social teachings, give them flesh in the life of the American Church, and produce a rather formal statement to the broader society. The desire to involve large numbers of people in order to give the program credibility and impact, however, resulted in a growing emphasis upon the discussion program in the parishes and broad participation in the regional meetings. This reflected a changing understanding of the product of the program, from a statement to a pastoral plan of action. It reflected, too, a shift in process, from a rather formal and scholarly study of the concept of justice to the articulation of needs through the invitation to "speak up". Consultation as a means to an end gradually gave way to consultation as an end in itself.[2]

According to O'Brien, Brian Hehir of the U.S.C.C. Division of International Justice and Peace, had originally suggested that the Bicentennial Program model itself after the 1968 Medellin Conference of Latin American Bishops, which was sympathetic to a "theology of liberation" perspective. Two crucial interventions by another member of the Bicentennial committee, Michael Novak, were decisive in the shift of emphasis in the program. First of all, Novak suggested that instead of handing down an agenda to the Catholic community, the program should be looked upon as an opportunity to invite the Catholic community to express its own agenda for change within and outside of the Church. Second of all, Novak suggested that the program not focus on specific social issues, but on what he called "social organisms", i.e., those of the family, neighborhood, ethnic and racial groups, personhood, nationhood, Church and humankind, a list to which work was subsequently added.

Michael Novak's call for a broad process of consultation among Catholic Americans was accepted. The Bicentennial Committee then took it upon itself to author a "Discussion Guide" booklet, the subject matter of which was to be the "social organisms" as outlined by Novak. Nearly a score of individuals, principally members of the Bicentennial Committee, contributed to the text of the document. For instance, Michael Novak and Geno Baroni explored the bicentennial theme as it related to ethnic groups in America; Monsignor George G. Higgins, Catholic expert on labor affairs, examined the bicentennial subtopic on work; David J. O'Brien, wrote on the subject of the changing relations of American Catholics to American society; Peter Henriot, of the Center for Concern and Dr. Jorge Dominguez of Harvard University's School of International Affairs, discussed the responsibility of the American Church to those who struggle for freedom and equality in other parts of the globe; David Tracy of the University of Chicago Divinity School wrote on the many meanings and functions of the Church; and Rev. Jesus Garcia Gonzalez, Director of the Social Secretariat for the Church in Mexico, offered a "Latin American view of the Church in the U.S."

J. Bryan Hehir and Francis J. Butler, Executive Director of the Bishops' Bicentennial Committee, in the documents' introductory pages, provided the background material outlining the proposed examination of the process and presented the details of the planned activities leading up to the 1976 Call to Action Assembly. A series of essays were written on all eight bicentennial subtopics as well as on a series of special topics such as the situation of the Spanish-speaking and the Native American in the United States. In addition, participants of a two-day consultation of more than 50 national Catholic organizations were called together on September 20-21, 1974, by the committee to discuss the newly proposed consultation process and to contribute ideas to the Discussion Guide.

A series of questions were included in the document to both guide and stimulate discussion of these topics. These materials were discussed at the local parish level in 1975 during Lent. "Feedback" sheets were prepared on which participating parishioners could record the major issues they felt the Church should address. On any one particular issue, room was allowed for up to five possible "priorities for action".

In order to carry out the proposed parish level consultation, as well as for purposes of coordinating any other related bicentennial activities in the future, the Bicentennial Committee devised a plan designed to appoint a person in every diocese as a "bicentennial coordinator". The plan was in great part accomplished through the influence and prestige afforded by a letter sent by the chairman of the Bicentennial Committee, John Cardinal Dearden, to each and every diocese requesting this courtesy. Numerous meetings were held in Washington, D. C. involving more than 100 diocesan coordinators. These meetings were led by Bishop Rausch, then General Secretary of the N.C.C.B./U.S.C.C., by Rev. J. Bryan Hehir and Mr. James Jennings of the U.S.C.C. Division of Justice and Peace, as well as by the rest of the Bicentennial staff as occasion and need dictated. In addition to the local "bicentennial coordinators", the Bicentennial Committee appointed a "national staff coordinator" for each of the eight justice sub-themes. Sister Margaret Cafferty was in charge of personhood; Monsignor Francis J. Lally for family; Mr. Kevin Farrell for neighborhood; Dr. Frank Butler for ethnicity and race; Mr. John Carr for work; Ms. Kathleen White for nationhood; Rev. Bryan Hehir for Church; and Mr. James Jennings for humankind.

The Bicentennial Committee also proposed the remaining broad stages of the Bicentennial Program as it was then envisioned. A series of six regional "justice hearings" would be held during 1975 to gather testimony which would supplement the data emerging from the parish discussions. (As it turned out, a 7th justice hearing was added). The national conference would then follow in 1976, publishing as a matter of course the results of the two-year investigation. The conference would also recommend to the Bishops appropriate programs for the Church to implement and, finally, produce a major document on behalf of the American Catholic population.

The Parish Consultations

Slightly less than half of the nation's dioceses participated in this phase of the overall program, and the phase closest to being termed as "grass roots". More exactly, 79 out of the nation's 162 dioceses sent back their feedback sheets to the national office in Washington, D. C. This figure is somewhat deceptive given the fact that in many dioceses the program participation was minimal

with only a few parishes participating within many
dioceses or with only a few parishioners participating
within a larger percentage of a diocese's parishes.
The report of the Bicentennial Committee, however, was
somewhat more positive. As the report follows:

> While not every diocese participated in
> this program, some activities already underway
> related to the Bicentennial effort. For
> example, the Indiana State Catholic Confer-
> ence had already initiated a "speak out"
> program similar in intent to the bicentennial
> consultation; therefore the five Indiana
> dioceses did not submit materials for the
> computer. However, a complete report, with
> recommendations for action, was submitted to
> to the bicentennial office and made available
> to the committees preparing the working papers
> for the Detroit assembly. In all, some
> seventy dioceses submitted materials ranging
> from reports of alternative bicentennial
> programs conducted in their area to complete
> transcripts of deanery or diocesan wide hear-
> ings. Fifty-one of these dioceses were also
> counted among the seventy-nine feeding into
> the computer process. In total, then, 107
> dioceses contributed materials for the consulta-
> tion process . . . . Finally, a wide variety
> of additional material was received from
> individual parishes in dioceses which had no
> program and from many national Catholic
> organizations.[3]

In terms of the eight sub-themes, the aggre-
gate distribution of the over 800,000 individual returns[4]
was as follows: 20% of the total responses were concerned with questions categorized by the Bicentennial
staff coders as primarily dealing with internal Church
matters, while approximately 14% were listed under
the headings of family, nationhood and personhood, and
only 8% described under the category of work and race
and ethnic relations. Far more telling is the information on "priorities for action". The overwhelming
response fell on those issues that were "closest to the
life of the participants--family, church and parish,
youth, the old, and the needs of the poor".[5] The
information provided by both O'Brien and a study by
the Center for Concern indicate that the "average
Catholic" was most incorporated into the Bicentennial

Program at this stage. It is important to point out that even here it was a certain type of Catholic who "spoke up". The type of lay Catholic who participated was one who took the institutional Church, its teachings and its organizational appendages "in a serious manner".

Those Catholics that did speak up did so, unsurprisingly, on many immediate and practical considerations, considerations that were concrete and touched on their everyday round of existence. This fact surprised the Bicentennial Committee who wrote that:

> . . . the issues uncovered in this wide consultation ranged from local parish finances to world hunger. Unexpectedly perhaps, the focal point came to rest on questions of family life, internal Church matters and local neighborhoods. Doctrinal matters were addressed only in an indirect fashion where they seemed to be at the foundation of moral questions and Church discipline.[6]

David O'Brien lists the top 34 "priorities for action" as follows:

1. no action given

2. make a real commitment to the neighborhood

3. provide continuing adult education on marriage and family life

4. improve communications between Bishops, priests, and laity

5. provide parish facilities, programs and support for young people

6. promote family unity through activities like home Masses

7. provide family life programs

8. Church identification with the poor by communicating their needs

9. encourage parents to listen to their children

33

10. provide professional counseling service
11. support family life education
12. promote right to life in every phase of life
13. emphasize Gospel values in everyday life
14. share Church resources with the poor
15. assist communication of the values of the family
16. take a more realistic position on birth control
17. better communication with Church teachings
18. Bishops and priests to teach need for persons to make moral decisions
19. promote equal opportunity
20. assist fight against crime
21. act on behalf of aging
22. provide continuing education programs
23. develop community spirit in Church
24. denounce injustice in work wherever found
25. work for acceptance of all races
26. help develop good self-image in persons
27. promote liturgies which express ethnic and racial values and traditions
28. oppose infringement of basic human rights
29. women should be free to perform all ministries
30. help raise consciousness on the needs of humankind

31. expand the role of the laity

32. reorder priorities toward human needs

33. make celibacy optional for priests

34. ordain women as deacons.[7]

David O'Brien ventures forth what is probably a safe generality regarding the question of just what kind of Catholic groups did participate (and, conversely, did not participate) at this stage of the program:

> The consultation technique called forth certain types of persons, willing and able to engage in discussion, interested in the corporate life and work of the church. Middle class Catholics, involved in one way or another by choice in the Church; poor people looking to the Church to help meet concrete human needs, people convinced of the importance of the social ministries of the Church, all of these were attracted to the program. People alienated from the Church or with only a casual relationship to the Church, people from working class backgrounds uncomfortable in discussion groups, people generally satisfied with the parish, people indifferent to the social ministries, such persons were far less likely to choose to take part in a program of this sort.[8]

The Center for Concern's evaluation, <u>Detroit and Beyond</u>, generally concurs with O'Brien. As the report puts it:

> The concern with family is high. So also is the need to explore women's role. Likewise the sense of outwardness or social concern for the poor, the aging, youth, orphans, widows, the alienated, and global justice. Finally, as inevitable, the Church figures strongly, although very little in the top 15 items. The world comes first; the Church second. One could make the conclusion, therefore, that the parishioners represented here are family-centered people,

quite willing to explore women's role, high in social concern, and supporting an outward-oriented Church which does not put itself first.[9]

It is important to point out that it was only at this stage that one can say that "the world comes first; the Church second". Subsequent stages of the Bicentennial Program were clearly in the hands of Church professionals, specialists and bureaucrats who converted general calls for action into calls for action through the various agencies of the Church. As Detroit and Beyond put it, "structure" was added to "issues". The Center for Concern publication follows:

> Undoubtedly this reflects the significant role played here by people with middle range policy responsibility in the Church and social insitutions. While many testimonies simply call attention to the fact of painful issues and make moral appeals to conversion or for "someone to do something", the more sophisticated "middle-management" voices of the Church are better targeted institutionally. Consistently they call for creation, enlargement, or support of an office, commission, or committee entrusted with their particular concern. Such structures, they insist, over and over again, are to be centered in a national body with regional and local echoes at lower institutional levels.[10]

The Justice Hearings

The second stage of the Bicentennial Program consisted of a series of national justice hearings, seven in all, which were held in various major cities across the nation. Each hearing was to focus on one or more of the "social organisms" as developed by Michael Novak. In reality, however, each hearing was more or less open to questions and discussion that ran the gambit of all the various sub-themes as well as just about any issue that an informed Catholic would want to discuss in a 5 to 15 minute presentation.

The first meeting was held in Washington, D. C., during the days of February 3-5, 1975, on the subject of "Humankind". The second was held in San

Antonio on April 3-5, 1975 on the subject "Nationhood". The third hearing was held in the St. Paul-Minneapolis area during June 12-14, 1975, on the subject of "The Land". The fourth, at Atlanta during August 7-9, 1975, focused on the subject "The Family". The fifth, on "Work", was held in Sacramento during the days of October 2-4, 1975. Newark was the site of the sixth justice hearing centering on "Ethnicity and Race", December 4-6, 1975. The final hearing was held in Maryknoll on the subject "Global Justice", July 14-16, 1976.

The format was that of a "congressional-style" hearing in which a total of 521 individuals took an active part. A total of 381 witnesses presented testimony before a rotating panel (140 in toto) comprised of N.C.C.B. Bicentennial Committee members, Bishops, and other clergy and lay consultants. As John Cardinal Dearden, in the opening speech in Washington put it, "in the bicentennial effort which we are beginning today, the Bishops of the U.S. invite others to join in the widest possible sharing of assessments of how the American Catholic community can contribute to the quest of all people for liberty and justice".[11] And contribute the testifiers did, in over a thousand pages of small and closely printed testimony divided into seven separate volumes.

The concerns that were expressed in Washington ranged from global ones--world hunger and unemployment, the needs of the Third World, the role of multinational corporations and U.S. foreign policy in world affairs--to the more earthy and concrete problems of day-to-day survival among illegal aliens, migrant groups, ghetto residents and the urban elderly poor. Various representatives of women's groups testified to the effect that discrimination against women pervades every area of life, the Church included.

At San Antonio each of the hearings was divided into two sessions. The first was devoted to testimony by specialists in the areas of immigration, education, economics, sociology, history, and labor. These experts made rather studied observations on complex national problems, with their presentations both documented by statistics and generally reflective of an understanding of the "broad social picture". The other portion of each day's activity was devoted to testimony from the local community, with witnesses ranging from illegal aliens and local community organizers to members of the San Antonio Archdiocesan Council of Catholic women. The explicit strategy employed here was to make the dry, academic issues of the first session more "real" and "alive" when followed by local testimony, especially when the local testimony came from, to use a favorite bicentennial phrase, the "victims of injustice". This format was found so successful in its dramatic results that it was followed throughout the remainder of the justice hearings.

The third Bicentennial hearing was held in the Twin Cities. Attention was focused primarily on the problems facing those who live in rural areas of the country and on Native Americans. In addition, a considerable portion of the hearings also focused on the internal Church question of freedom and equality in its own affairs.

Atlanta was the site of the fourth in the series of meetings. This meeting highlighted social justice concerns centering in on family life. Witnesses presented testimony on the concerns of Black and Hispanic families, families in Appalachia, and middle-class family problems. A great deal of the testimony attempted to analyze both the positive and negative effects that contemporary social, economic, political, and technological developments have on the quality of family life. A question that was also raised was on the possible ways in which the family can act as a transforming agent in the Church and society.

During the Sacramento hearing on Work, the questions of the Church's role in assisting laborers in their right to organize and in helping the unemployed were discussed. Other subjects such as unionization in Catholic sponsored institutions, job discrimination and retirement were also brought up.

Testimony on the subject of Race and Ethnicity was heard during the sixth hearing held in Newark. Issues such as the role of the parish in the neighborhood, the positive and negative effects of strong ethnic identification, redlining in neighborhoods, assimilation and acculturation, the Church's insensitivity to blacks, hispanics, and white ethnic cultural traditions, urban plight and urban disinvestment, among many others were brought to the floor.

Upon the completion of the six hearings of 1975, the Bicentennial Committee was concerned that insufficient attention had been given to such international issues as world hunger, disarmament, human rights and especially the economic relations between industrialized and less industrialized "third world" countries. A special convocation was organized in the summer of 1976 in Maryknoll, New York. This hearing featured the testimony of invited guests from organizations and government agencies concerned with foreign policy, as well as the testimony of Church leaders from Africa, Asia and Latin America.

Despite the fact that there was a not inconsiderable amount of testimony presented by "local" or "neighborhood" Catholics, some themselves "victims of injustice", there was a marked difference in the quality and type of justice hearing testimony when contrasted to the parish outpourings. While the latter could be characterized as centered in on issues of the "everyday round of life", the former, at least in good part, could not. And even in those cases in which everyday issues were addressed by "local" people, it was clear that such local types were not representative of their communities, at least in terms of linguistic ability, in terms of their degree of social activism, and in their advocacy of social scientific intervention into the affairs of the everyday.

The fact remains that the justice hearings gave evidence of the mark of the specialist, the professional, the theoretician. In most cases, the material was presented in a systematic, logical manner, showing the ability to think in the abstract, to manipulate language and ideas, to make a "proper presentation of self", and to make "connections" (whether accurate or not) between societal forces at large as they impinge on the everyday life of the individual. Most of even the "local" participants gave evidence of thinking in a "social scientific" manner, in terms of what C. W. Mills has aptly termed the "sociological imagination".[12] This held true, once again, even for the local community organizers--only less so, as illustrated nicely by their more than occasional misuse and "popularization" of certain theoretical concepts. Not only did most think sociologically, or social-scientifically, but they presented their testimony in a language betraying the uneven influence of social science in everyday thought and activity. The following sample of notables, from both the Catholic and non-Catholic world, gives evidence of the wide range of issues that complex thinkers attempt to tackle, the mental connections between different social units that complex thinkers attempt to make, and the elitism of this second stage of the program.

During the Washington, D.C. hearing[13] the President of Notre Dame, Reverand Theodore Hesburgh, could state the "200 years after the Declaration of Independence, America and the rest of the world need a Declaration of Interdependence". Catholic theologian, Avery Dulles, could implore that when facing the "double dilemma" between that of abstract and concrete commitment, and between secular and religious roles, the Church should search for "la via media". Rev. Phillip Murnion, then Director of Pastoral Research for the Archdiocese of New York, could state bluntly that "the fundamental moral question we face . . . is whether we can as a people counter systematic injustice with a systematic response of teaching, relationships, and actions that ground mutual responsibility as the highest accomplishment of humanity". Author Gary MacEion could criticize Pope Paul's Populorium Progressive as "lacking a true global vision". For MacEion, "it reflects the historic conditioning of a people who view the world's economic history as conterminous with the society of modern capitalism and view it from the emotional standpoint of its beneficiaries". Father Silvano Tomasi could make the analogy of the Church's teaching that "We, though many, are one body in Christ and individually members of one another" (Rom. 1, 2) to the present day reality of cultural pluralism within the American Catholic Church. Sister Elizabeth Carroll, a staff associate of the Center for Concern was one of the many women who testified during the hearing. For Sister Carroll, "The Gospel message is one, simple, whole truth applicable to male and female alike. Yet a double standard has been derived from it. The Church, along with society, has too readily divided the world into two moralities; one for the woman and one for the man". In the opening presentation, Cardinal Dearden even referred to the socialization process of fellow Catholic Bishops. As Dearden follows, "speaking as a American Catholic Bishop, I assure you that the Bishops do not stand apart from the Catholic community in the U.S. We are products of that community, formed and influenced by the same history that has molded the rest of the Church in this country. Because this is so, we look to our fellow Catholics and our fellow Americans to help us determine how best we can perform our service of leadership and fulfill our responsibilities in these times."

At the San Antonio meeting,[14] Mr. Jesus Zapata, a social worker, spoke on the reality of "an unequal distribution between rich and poor parishes". Father Edmundo Rodriquez called for a more "systematic" involvement of the N.C.C.B. in matters of funding social justice programs, a shift that would entail a move from the more ad hoc nature of "crisis funds available in organizations like the Campaign for Human Development . . . to program funds, which constitute the regular way we support our churches and the regular way we support everything". For Sister Mario Barron, "perhaps the Church's response is going to have to consist of an examination of our economic system . . . the things we are saying is that there is something wrong with that system". Father Virgil P. Elizondo, President of the Mexican American Cultural Center, called for an effort to "conscienticize entire seminary faculties to the needs of the Spanish speaking of the West Coast, the West and Southwest". Historian Jesus Chavarria of the University of California at Santa Barbara claimed that "if we were to ask those Chicanos . . . how they feel toward the bicentennial, they would reply simply that we have little to celebrate for our revolution has not yet come . . . today the Catholic Church as an institution still has to make a decisive commitment to the redress of historical wrongs".

The St. Paul-Minneapolis meeting[15] saw Burt Evans, Professor of Economics at the University of Nebraska, label our current economic system as a "corporate ceremonial waste system of economic behavior . . . which is fostered by multinational corporations." The then-Senator Walter Mondale quoted the Coleman Report which "found that native Indian children more than the children of any other minority group believe themselves to be below average intelligence". Mr. Gene Fox of Catholic Social Services declared that those suffering must be put into the position to "define their own reality. In the words of Paolo Freire, they must be acting subjects, not objects who are acted upon". For Mr. Marvin Manypenny,

Executive Director of the Near Southside Receiving Center, "the ramifications of alcoholism have to be looked at as sociological, cultural, physiological, psychological, and spiritual impediments". Jan Belland of the Minneapolis Public Schools spoke on the dangers of our "chemical dependent society". Historian James Hitchcock, speaking on the concerns of middle Americans, "warned that it would be a mistake of the first order to interpret the problems of society in exclusively economic terms, and that the Church will miss a crucial opportunity if the statements which finally emerge from these hearings concentrate wholly on economic problems, important though those are". Hitchcock then urged the Bishops to include in their consideration of justice issues the threat to family life today, the role of moral values in education, contemporary anti-Catholicism and the problem of violent crime. The hearing was also the scene of an interesting exchange on the subject of "justice in the Church" between Bishop Rausch, then General Secretary of the N.C.C.B./U.S.C.C., and theologian Rev. Richard McBrien, former President of the Catholic Theological Society of America. McBrien had taken the position that before the Church can address the world on issues of justice, justice must first be institutionalized within the Catholic community. For Bishop Rausch, however, "we simply cannot wait upon our personal perfection in an unjust society, while another generation of children passes into a limbo of uncertainty, an abyss of deprivation . . . . Unless we are prepared to purge our ranks of all who disagree with us and become a self-righteous sect, we must look both inwardly and outwardly . . . we must . . . deal with racism and economic justice, both in our own house and in that broader society whose life we share".

At the Atlanta meeting,[16] Dr. Robert Staples, graduate director of the University of California at San Francisco sociology department, made a call for a "national commitment to family support systems". Dr. Murray Bowen , Clinical Professor of Psychiatry at Georgetown Medical Center, delivered an analysis on recent "social regression in American society . . . judged by symptoms that are a product of anxiety, by man's maladaptive behavior". Rosemary Haughton, British journalist and lecturer, spoke on the functions of the family for first generation Catholic immigrants as a "refuge . . . as the only kind of protection against want, isolation, and exploitation". However, for Ms. Haughton, the "modern Christian family, though, has a special role to fulfill, a ministry of loving service . . . . Contrary to popular belief, the best marriages and happiest families don't happen because people concentrate first of all on the quality of their relationships, but rather when the couple and then the family as a whole, is involved in something bigger . . . the work of God".

At the Sacramento hearing,[17] Mr. Leon H. Keyserling, President of the Conference of Economic Progress, spoke on the subject of "The Moral Basis of Economic Policy", indicated his support of the Humphrey-Hawkins Bill and criticized the economic theory of Milton Friedman of the Department of Economics at the University of Chicago. Bayard Rustin, President of the A. Phillip Randolph Institute, called for a "redefinition of the meaning of work and the necessity of full employment". Cesar Chavez spoke on the recent passage of a bill in the California State legislature that gave farm workers the right to bargain collectively. Joseph Cunneen, editor-in-chief of Cross Currents, acknowledged "the need to recognize the widespread apathy and indifference to the Church felt by rank and file Catholics across the country".

In Newark,[18] Geno Baroni, then President of the National Center for Urban Ethnic Affairs, stated "the need to develop an urban policy that legitimizes ethnic, racial and cultural pluralism". For Michael Novak, American Catholics "having come of age . . . have a responsibility to begin to make our contributions . . . to America". History Professor Jay P. Dolan of Notre Dame spoke on the "demise of national parishes under the forces of Americanization". Steven Adubato of Newark's North Ward Cultural and Educational Center made a presentation on the "positive and negative consequences" of strong ethnic identification. Andrew Greeley, of the National Opinion Research Center, addressed the question of moral integration in American society and insisted that, if American cultural pluralism is to be viewed adequately from a theoretical perspective, it must be seen through the metaphor of a "mosaic with permeable boundaries". Catholic social historian Henry J. Browne spoke on the historically varying stances of "openness" of the Catholic hierarchy to lay initiatives. Monsignor

John Oesterreicher of the Seton Hall Institute of Judeo-Christian Studies, spoke on "Catholic-Jewish relations" in light of Vatican II. Dorothy Day, founder of the Catholic Worker Movement, spoke of the "greatest enemy of the Catholic Church today . . . as Catholic self-reliance on the State". Brother Joseph Davis, Executive Director of the National Office for Black Catholics, spoke on the "historic failure" of the American Catholic Church "to give its full commitment to something black". Mayor Ken Gibson acknowledged the help of Catholic organizations in attempting to "deal effectively with the needs of American central cities". Congressman Charles Rangel, of the House Ways and Means Committee and Chairman of the Congressional Black Caucus, spoke of the "political clout . . . that the Church ought to exercise on such moral issues like the passage of the Humphrey-Hawkins Bill".

At the Maryknoll meeting,[19] Archbishop Peter Gerety implored Catholics to become aware "of the need to integrate the Gospel message into the socio-economic and global structures which are becoming increasingly important in our interdependent world". Archbishop Marcos McGrath of Panama, speaking for the Latin American Church, stated "the need for a new international economic order". Likewise, Bishop James Sangu of Tanzania, representing Africa, argued that "the basic issue which causes a confrontation between the Third World and the industrialized countries is the unjust economic world order". For Bishop Francisco Claver of the Philippines "the micro and macro level of economics are connected as only Siamese twins can be". And finally, for Auguste Vanistendael, Chairman of the European National Justice and Peace Commission, "there should be a tremendous drive . . . to get Catholics more interested in public and international affairs".

A few observations regarding the hearings stage of the program should be made at this point. First of all, the hearings were heavily over-represented by people affiliated with and employed by various Church organizations. Secondly, many of the speakers and panelists were people with a great deal of education, social status, and occupational prestige. And while it is certainly true that the process of "middle-classification" is a real one for large segments of Catholic America, many of the speakers and panelists represent the "who's who of American Catholicism" and are not to be confused with the recent cadres of Catholic suburbanites. Many of this elite grouping who were not employed by the Church nonetheless were affiliated with governmental organizations, prestigious private institutes, and in the field of higher education.

Many of the "local" speakers without a great deal of education, social status, or occupational prestige were still employed by, or at least attached to, local Catholic organizations. Those "local" types, on the other hand, who were not directly involved with the Church had, in most cases, an indirect contact. They were most likely to be community and neighborhood organizers most visible to those Church officials dealing with the needs of the poor in any particular community.

On one hand there were many types of testifiers present at the justice hearings--in terms of status, income, education, linguistic skill, or simply, in terms of power and influence. They ranged from the highly educated Catholics who operate either the national or regional offices in the Church, government, or in the University to local social activists of one kind or another. On the other hand, however, what threads these various people together is their familiarity with the Church and her organizational network, a social activism that betrays an underlying taken-for-granted assumption that poverty and injustice are "social problems" that can and must be eliminated (or at least alleviated) and that the Church has a mission on earth and in human history that includes active involvement in such an endeavor. In terms of the unrepresentativeness of the justice hearings, there are many Catholics who are not familiar with or actively involved in the labyrinth of Catholic organizations or who believe that "the poor will always be with us" or believe that one ought not to "mix politics with religion."

It also should be noted that this stage of the Bicentennial Program included a series of voluntary, local meetings. Approximately 20 dioceses sponsored their own justice hearings or town meetings to identify justice issues in their own dioceses. Records of these meetings were submitted to the Washington based national headquarters of the Bicentennial Committee.

One must not underestimate the value of the Justice Hearings--from the viewpoint of the advocates of liberal Catholicism in America--in serving as a vehicle by which social activists hitherto in a fragmentary and inarticulate relationship, "discovered each other for the first time". As the post-Detroit report of the Bicentennial Committee put it:

> . . . the hearings were the center of attention of the bicentennial program during 1975. Testimony was often dramatic and moving; people of various backgrounds and interests discovered each other for the first time . . . . One significant result was simply the value of the hearing process itself. Each hearing provided a forum for persons often not heard in local or national life. It broke down barriers that often separate various groups.[20]

Writing Committees

The task of coverting computerized data, transcripts of national and local hearings, as well as other miscellaneous material into statements and recommendations that were to be discussed, refined, and voted on at the Detroit Assembly rested with a little over 60 individuals. These individuals were divided into eight writing committees, or "nuclear committees of specialists" as they were referred to by the Bicentennial Committee. Each committee was assigned one of the eight justice themes. The writing members were drawn from the fields of theology, social science, and social service. The committee started their work in March of 1976 and worked through August of that year. Periodic meetings among committee members and between committees allowed points to be shared, discussed and debated. By early September, eight documents were mailed to all Call to Action delegates, thus allowing the delegates approximately 5 weeks to study the resolutions in preparation for the Detroit conference.

Each committee was chaired by a Bishop, and each committee included priests, laity and religious. The "Church" committee was chaired by the then President of the N.C.C.B., Archbishop John Quinn and included, among others, such notables as Joseph

Cunneen; Rev. Avery Dulles; Rev. John T. Finnegan, President of the Canon Law Society of America; Dr. James Hitchcock; and Rev. David Tracy. The "ethnicity and race" committee was chaired by Bishop Rene Gracida of Florida and included, among others, Michael Novak; Timothy Smith, Professor of History at John Hopkins University; Dr. Jesus Charvarria; Rev. Paul Asciolla of the National Center for Urban Ethnic Affairs; and the now Bishop of Newark, Joseph Francis. The "Family" committee was chaired by Bishop Thomas Grady and included, among others, Mrs. Patricia Crowley of the Christian Family Movement. The "Humankind" committee was chaired by Bishop James Malone and included, among others, Dr. Jorge Dominquez and Ms. Eileen Egan, the latter the Project Supervisor for the Catholic Relief Services of the U.S.C.C. The "Nationhood" committee was chaired by Bishop Ignatius Strecker and included, among others, Rev. Ernest Bartell, President of Stonehill College; Mr. Steve Bossi, Director of Research and Policy Development of the National Catholic Rural Life Conference; and Dr. Dorothy Dohen, Professor of Sociology at Fordham University. The "Neighborhood" committee was chaired by Bishop Francis Magavero of Brooklyn and included, among others, Professor Henry J. Browne; Mr. Harry Fagan of the Commission on Catholic Community Action for the Diocese of Cleveland; and Ms. Peggy Roach of the Catholic Committee on Urban Ministry. The "Work" committee was chaired by Bishop Joseph Donnelly and included, among others, Mr. Matthew H. Ahman, Associate Director of Governmental Relations of the National Conference of Catholic Charities and Rev. Edward Ryle of the National Catholic School of Social Services of Catholic University. The "Personhood" committee was chaired by Bishop Bernard Law and included, among others, Sister Margaret Farley of the Yale Divinity School; Ms. Virginia Finn of Lenox, Massachusetts; and Sister Barbara Thomas, President of The Leadership Conference of Women Religious. David J. O'Brien coordinated the overall writing process and was the person finally responsible for insuring that the writing committees completed their documents containing the specific resolutions.

<u>The Final Preparations: Workshops and Delegate Selection</u>

Beginning in April of 1976, the Bicentennial Committee staff arranged a series of meetings or "workshops" in the existing twelve N.C.C.B. regions to prepare the delegates for the Detroit Justice Conference. At these meetings, the delegates reviewed the history and progress of the program to date through the use of video-tapes and slides of the national justice hearings and familiarized themselves with computerized summaries of findings from the parish discussions. The day-long workshops, under the general directorship of Sister Margaret Cafferty, were scheduled from April to June in 1976 and were strategically located throughout the country. Delegates were invited to attend the workshop closest to them. Over 55% of the actual delegates to the conference attended one of these workshops.

The purpose of these workshops were varied. First of all, it allowed the delegates time to familiarize themselves with the three-day series of activities to be held in Detroit. Less technical motives, however, were involved. As a Bicentennial Committee memo put it, these meetings also afforded the Bicentennial coordinators "an opportunity to orient the delegates to the Church teachings on social justice".[21] Additionally, the Committee hoped "that the exposure to delegates from other dioceses will motivate those from places where there has been no (local) program to start some reflection process in their own dioceses".

Delegate Selection

In a Bicentennial memo entitled, "A Proposed Plan for Delegate Selection", the fear was expressed that "judging from early returns from the 'Liberty and Justice for All' discussion program, middle-class white Americans constitute a heavy proportion of those who have been involved in the parish discussion program."[22] The memo followed, "to ensure somewhat of a balance in the Detroit Justice Conference, and to make sure concerns voiced during the regional hearings and numerous local hearings are represented, the following delegate selection process is recommended:

   1. Each diocese will be entitled to nine delegates. That number includes the Bishop and the diocesan bicentennial coordinator.

   2. In naming his delegates, the Bishops will be urged to use an "open

48

2. That the laity, constituting 47% of the assembly, were underrepresented, despite the fact that their voice at Detroit was, most probably, larger than in their home parishes.

3. That the middle-class "bourgeoise" suburban Catholic (16%) was less represented than what might have been expected.

4. That women (40%) and "minorities" (19%) while having a larger voice at Detroit than in their home parish or diocese, were nonetheless underrepresented.

5. That, unlike the majority of Catholics, the delegates were heavily (64%) employed by the Church and actively involved (90%) in various Church organizations.

David O'Brien summarized the importance of this last observation as follows:

the prominence of such a heavy proportion of Church workers is a factor of considerable importance. It helps account for the kinds of change which the delegates made in the resolutions, away from somewhat ambiguous generalities and toward clear assignment of responsibility to specific organizations, offices and agencies. While parish participants were often unaware of episcopal statements on Church teachings, delegates referred often to Church documents and pushed for their promotion and implementation. While parish participants were family and parish oriented; the former tended to ignore diocesan and national Church structures; the latter gave them high importance.[25]

Regarding the representativeness of the Call to Action Conference, Thomas Stahel claims that:

The Bishops have tapped . . . a middle-leadership echelon in the American Church--young clerics, women religious, chancery employees both lay and clerical, special activists--who are, by and large, liberal.

51

They may not exactly reflect the main
body of the Church now, but they are an
important part of the Church and show the
direction in which it is poised to move
in the next five, not to say, fifteen
years.[26]

As Thomas Fox[27] put it, the conference
"highlights a growing tension among . . . American
Catholics who, while raised to respect the nation's
democratic ideals, are within a Church which limits
decision-making". As James Finn, then editor of
Worldview, put it "the Detroit conference was a call
to action and the call was not only to the Bishops".[28]
Perhaps the spirit of the Call to Action was best
epitomized by Sister Margaret Cafferty, a key member
of the Bicentennial staff who constantly urged the
delegates not to be shy. As she put it:

. . . your Bishops selected you. Your
organizations selected you. It is not
necessary to be a theologian to take
part in these deliberations. You are
the people of God. You are the input.[29]

The Call to Action Conference

The "Call to Action" was held in Cobo Hall
in Detroit from October 21st through the 24th, in
1976. Before the conference was to end 182 proposals
were to be discussed, voted on, and eventually
passed. (Cf. Appendix A).

On October 21st, all 1,340 delegates were
addressed in plenary session by John Cardinal Dearden.
As Dearden stated, "we are trying to begin a new way
of doing the work of the Church in America. We may
fail, but let us try and let people in the nation say
of us that they cared enough to try".[30]

With the conclusion of Cardinal Dearden's
remarks, each delegate went to his assigned session
(e.g. Church) and then to one of the sub-sections
within the main section (e.g. for the "Church" section,
the subsection might be either "divorced Catholics",
"lay involvement in decision making", "Church finances",
etc.). Each delegate received a set of "white" working
papers containing the writing committee's voting proposals. Thomas H. Stahel lucidly summarizes the rest

of the three day process:

> The subsections were given nine hours to revise their proposals, add to them (almost always) or delete something (hardly ever). These revisions produced an entirely new set of "pink" working papers, which then became grist for the improvement of the whole section meeting together. The major sections made their substitutions and additions in a four-hour session that produced another new set of working papers, this time "yellow", which were destined to undergo the supposedly severe scruniny of the plenary council of the delegates in the last hours of the assembly.[31]

James Finn and Thomas Stahel offer complimentary explanations as to why the final plenary session was unable to exercise a moderating influence on many recommendations that were clearly unrepresentative of the massive Catholic middle. Both explanations involve criticisms of the assembly process itself which resulted in a certain shallowness of deliberation and short attention span expended on the proposals. For Stahel:

> One hour was allotted to each section in the final session and each section had three or four parts, and most of these parts had three of four voting proposals. As it turned out, the entire hour in every case was consumed in disposing of amendments and the inevitable parliamentary wrangles, so that the substance of the proposals never got seriously questioned by the conference as a whole . . . . Faced with a "yes" or "no" alternative on swatches of proposals, they choose never to exercise their veto.[32]

For James Finn:

> What I have termed the "weakness of generosity" occurred in the plenary session. Those who worked hard in the sections devoted to their special interests expected the assembled delegates to take that work seriously and not damage it by amendment and qualifications.

And they extended that same courtesy to
the delegates who worked in other sections.
Thus, without a suggestion of conspiracy
or insidious lobbying, some extreme statements were readily accepted by the plenary
group and now form the official statement of
the Detroit conference.[33]

Thomas Fox made another interesting observation on the process that might have encouraged the
"radicalness" of certain proposals. It involved the
evolution of the internal dynamic commonly called
"momentum". For Fox:

> Clearly, the three day gathering picked up
> a momentum of its own. Delegates shed
> initial hesitations, grew in confidence,
> expressed surprise at learning that other
> delegates from other parts of the nation
> harbored similar thoughts and feelings--
> that radical change within the church is
> required. A sense emerged among a clear
> majority that justice cannot be compromised,
> cannot be denied any person--if the Church is
> to be faithful to its teachings, if the
> Church is to be credible.[34]

As a matter of fact, the variable "momentum"
was operationalized through a "before-after" questionnaire study conducted by Dr. Frank Manning.[35] Dr.
Manning found that many Call to Action delegates prior
to the event were quite skeptical as to whether or
not their experiences and input would be taken seriously
at Detroit. After the event, however, those same
delegates were, for the most part, enthusiastic and
felt that the results of the conference had exceeded
their expectations.

Another evaluation, prepared after the
Detroit Assembly by the original writing committees,
offers a clue as to why the extremity of the some of
the proposals. The report claimed that the Call to
Action assembly was not characterized by the degree
of professionalism as were the writing committees
themselves:

> . . . in a few cases . . . the delegates
> had not paid sufficient attention to the
> results of the consultation as summarized

in Roman Catholicism could find strong theological support for their positions. Debates about ecclesiology and about the meaning of Vatican II and its teachings, long abstract and theoretical, now had a concrete, specific event on which to focus. The Bishops had encouraged this debate by making the event advisory, extraordinary, and voluntary rather than convoking a national pastoral council. All agreed that the Call to Action recommendations were advisory in nature; what was at issue was the weight which should be given to the advice and to the process which provided it. On these questions, the Bishops and their people were divided.[44]

It is interesting to point out that Frank [Mann]ing in his study indicated that "while the [deleg]ates were largely in accord with the process, [inte]nt and goals of the Call to Action, the bishops [were m]uch more conflicted in their reactions".[45] For [this] reason, it would be unfair to conclude that the line [of de]marcation was in all cases that of "delegate" [versus] "Bishop". Indeed, he concludes that "it is [prob]able that a kind of dialectical tension will [endur]e, especially with regard to theological/pastoral [contr]oversies which run headlong into longstanding [tradi]tions. Even so, there are so many dimensions of [social] justice on which hierarchical leadership and [ot]her sensitized leaders of the people of God [can work together].[46]

In his "Report on the Justice Hearing" John [Cardin]al Dearden reported that:

[Th]e results of the bicentennial process may [at] this point seem hasty, untidy, careless, [ev]en extreme. But on closer examination, [it] seems to me that far more often the [wo]rking papers and conference resolutions [de]monstrate a warmth and sympathy for the [pr]oblems of Church leadership on the part [of] our people, their enthusiastic affirma[ti]on of Christian faith and hope, their [sin]cere willingness to share in building [a s]tronger Church and their firm resolve to [ful]fill a Christian ministry to the world. [No] one expects us to endorse all that

58

in the working papers. The original recommendations were . . . more nuanced and carefully stated than was true of the final resolutions.[36]

In order to remedy this situation the writing committees called for "serious study and reflection on the results of the program" and the greater "utilization of the services of scholars . . . in consultation with Bishops and staff persons from the N.C.C.B./U.S.C.C."

Russell Kirk leaves no doubt as to his opinion of the obvious populism of the assembly and what it signifies, or doesn't signify, for the future of the American Catholic Church. For Kirk:

Call to Action converted itself into a one-man/one-vote National Assembly, all ranks and dignities comingled and confounded, after the French pattern of 1789 rather than after the American pattern of 1776. The majority of the delegates tumultuously endorsed resolutions instructing the Bishops to arrange promptly for ordination of women, marriage of the clergy, a fair deal for homosexuals, etc. . . . many other resolutions hastily adopted would alter the Church--and the Republic still more greatly, were they to take on flesh.[37]

However, Kirk noted:

The Bishops aren't fools, and the American public does not intend to demolish our existing structure of order and justice and freedom at the behest of an egalitarian utopianism. The silliness of the Call to Action soon will be forgotten; and we will have 13 years--until 1989, the really important date in our Bicentennial commemoration--in which to prepare for a call to thought.[38]

Russell Kirk's remarks--regarding the radicalness, if not the silliness, of the Call to Action--become even more interesting when taken in light of another study done by Dr. Frank Manning.[39]

55

Dr. Manning conducted a "content" analysis evaluating the changes made by the delegates in the action recommendations submitted to them by the writing committees. His study indicated that there was a strong continuity between the suggestions of the writing committees and the eventual Call to Action recommendations. According to Manning, in most cases, changes made in the initial recommendations tended toward specifying clear goals and assigning responsibility to particular offices. This led merely to a multiplication of requests for offices and structures, with the intention of making the recommendations more concrete, specific, and practical. Even the post-Detroit writing committee's evaluation, despite their reservations, indicated that none of their recommendations were reversed; but that many, indeed, were strengthened. As Frank Manning put it:

> The great majority of amendments which passed simply enlarged (in a few instances to a radical degree) on what was essentially present from the beginning. This trend was accompanied by extreme reluctance to defeat a recommendation once it had been approved at the writing committee level. Substantive additions were contributed at the section level, but existing recommendations changed relatively little.[40]

Thomas Fox made essentially this same observation:

> In most cases, except for the stronger use of language, the first recommendations were outgrowths of recommendations that delegates had received prior to coming to Detroit. The agenda was drawn up by Catholics working over the past two years. The Bishops, conference organizers, and delegates knew in advance what they were to consider and had adequate time prior to the conference to reflect on the agenda.[41]

The point, when combining Kirk, Fox and Manning, is that the forces of significant change within the Church extend, not just to those on the periphery of the Church's organizational structure, but to the highest levels. "At the top", perhaps, this sympathy is couched differently in terms of intensity and content. Bureaucratic-in (like many U.S.C.C. staff and writing c members), as compared to ideological-in (like many Justice Hearing testifiers) to have mastered the art of "diplomati as a strategy for the implementation o While the use of means between the bur ideological Catholic elites may differ ence, by no means, excludes a compatib and a commonality of vision. There is Pareto knew well, two ways to the top it is the way of the "lion" and, for the way of the "fox".[42] Whether the the Call to Action will soon be forgo there is no sympathy for the Bicenter movement within the higher levels o bureaucracy seems to be a far more p sideration than Russell Kirk allows editors of the *Christian Century* cla

> ... the recommendations on t women in the life of the Churc indicate future upheavels. Th call for the ordination of wom the priesthood may point to he cussions in the Church's highe Add to this the plea that sex be eliminated from the liturg Church literature--as well as to allow a married priesthood clear that American Catholic and administrative problems

David J. O'Brien spoke ambiguity, importance and problen Call to Action conference and wha the future of American Catholici

> The Call to Action conferer been a controversial event the content of its recomme process of consultation, t of representatives of the and the resolutions of dif democratic vote represente innovations in American C But those who found them certain areas of Church l who thought such procedur

transpired at Detroit. People do expect us to continue the process by responding with decisive action where it is called for, and with honest disagreement where that seems necessary. The key to our actions in the future is to continue the process, to build on the hopes that have been awakened, to act upon our clear responsibility for the unity, fidelity and vision of the Catholic community.[47]

The Great Wait

Throughout the three year process of discussions, committee meetings, hearings and the Call to Action Conference, participants were told that their suggestions and recommendations would provide advice to the National Conference of Catholic Bishops and would be taken into account in framing a five year pastoral plan on justice. It was constantly emphasized throughout the program by the Bicentennial Committee, that while the Bishops could not expect to meet every request, they would make a serious effort to respond to the various concerns expressed and the actions recommended.

In his "Report on the Justice Conference" (Nov. 9th, 1976), John Cardinal Dearden concluded with a brief outline of the process leading up to the May, 1977 N.C.C.B. meeting in which the Call to Action was to be evaluated by the American Bishops. He first announced that his Bicentennial Committee would be dissolved after preparing its final detailed report. Then he followed:

> At the meeting of the NCCB Administrative Committee on Saturday it was determined to have the president of the conference appoint a task force to review the report of the Ad Hoc Committee in consultation with existing NCCB/USCC office staffs. From this task force will come recommendations to be reviewed by the Administrative Committee at its meeting in February. What is approved then will be distributed to the Bishops for consideration and action at the May meeting of our conference. . . . This plan of action should allow us in an orderly and responsible way to respond to

59

the earnest faith-filled voices of our
people as they have addressed us in this
bicentennial year.[48]

The truth of the matter was that there was
precious little "order and responsibility" in the
maneuvers between "liberal" and "conservative" factions
among the Church hierarchy between the conclusion of
the assembly and the Chicago Bishops' meeting to be
held on May 23rd, 1977. The liberal-oriented Dearden
committee did go out of business at the end of the
year. The critical decision making body at this
point would then be the full body of Bishops and their
respective officers. Preparation for the May meeting
was handled personally by the then-President of the
N.C.C.B., Archbishop Joseph Bernardin. The task
force that was to receive the report of Dearden's
Bicentennial Committee and prepare for May was highly
conservative, and numbered some of the most outspoken
opponents of the Call to Action. In addition to
Archbishop Bernardin, the task force included Cardinal
Krol of Philadelphia, Cardinal Carberry of St. Louis,
Archbishop John Maguire of New York, Bishop Joseph
McNicholas of Illinois, Archbishop John Quinn of
Oklahoma City, Cardinal Baum of Washington and
Bishop William McManue of Indiana.

The conservative constituency of the
committee and the absence of Cardinal Dearden,
Archbishop Gerety or any member of their Bicentennial
Committee was a fact of great concern to Call to
Action advocates. Indeed, they had much to worry
about. The Bernardin task force did submit the first
draft of the Bishop's response to the February
N.C.C.B./U.S.C.C. Administrative Board as planned.
This secret draft, presented at a closed meeting,
was apparently terribly critical of the overall Call
to Action assembly and Bicentennial Program. In a
National Catholic Reporter article, "Cardinal Fights
to Save Call to Action Process: Infighting Follows
Task Force Recommendations", Mark Winiarski follows:

Cardinal John Dearden of Detroit has
been waging a behind the scenes battle
to rescue the "Call to Action" process
from dismemberment by other Bishops . . .
Dearden has circulated among select Bishops
a letter harshly critical of the treatment
afforded Call to Action by a task force

appointed to formulate the Bishop's response to the recommendations. (His) letter reportedly threatens public criticism of the task force at the Bishops meeting May 3rd through 5th in Chicago . . . . Call to Action proponents left the administrative committee meeting "terribly discouraged".[49]

However, Winiarski noted that "observers say the Dearden letter has forced the task force to redraft its response rather than risk a public floor fight at the Bishop's May meeting".[50] Despite this small concession to the Dearden wing, it was clear that Bernardin had acted immediately in other ways to establish control of the Detroit follow-up process. Frank Butler, the Executive Director of the program, was not invited to participate in any way for the May preparation. Neither was David J. O'Brien, who reassumed his duties at Holy Cross College. Perhaps most significantly, Sister Margaret Cafferty, who was originally scheduled to remain on the staff until May, left as of March 1st to become Executive Director of the Catholic Committee on Urban Ministry.[51] According to O'Brien, she left out of a feeling of frustration generated by a set of restrictions placed on her by the U.S.C.C./N.C.B.B. leaders. Among other things, she was forbidden to hold a series of scheduled meetings to assist in the local implementation of the Call to Action proposals and was forced to discontinue publishing the Bicentennial newsletter which had previously served as a vital source of communication for Call to Action organizers and sympathizers. The aim for the Bernardin supporters was to have the situation remain as "frozen" as possible until May when the Bishops would decide the fate of the program.

To the chagrin of the conservative camp, however, the lack of N.C.C.B./U.S.C.C. institutional support stood in marked contrast to local level interest. As Mr. Mark Winiarski reports:

> The hierarchial infighting comes at a time when "grassroots" interest and hope in the consultative Call to Action process is blossoming. The Quixote Center in Mt. Rainer, Md., has sold some 85,000 tabloid reprints of the Call to Action recommendations and many dioceses are conducting meetings to plan implementation

of resolutions that pertain to parish and diocese.[52]

The point that the Call to Action can serve as a vehicle to recover the lay apostalate "with or without the Bishop's help" was made in the form of an exhortation in an <u>America</u> editorial. As the editors put it in their "No Need for the Great Wait":

> (Possibly) militating against . . . (the) educational effort (of the Call to Action) . . . is an attitude of the "great wait": Let's see what the Bishops will do. The Bishops were the one's who called for the Detroit meeting in the first place . . . . It is not as if the Bishops were now required to validate what happened at Detroit. Not since Vatican II has the American Church experienced such enthusiasm as that generated by the Bishop's initiative in their Call to Action. It would be fatal if the parishes now waited to see what else the Bishops will do.[53]

While liberal social activists were working at the local level, the minority liberal Bishops' wing was doing what it could to best insure a positive response to Call to Action proposals in May. This activity was best indicated by a motion, supported by 65 Bishops, to postpone a vote on the formal approval of a Pastoral Letter at their November, 1976 Bishops meeting. The <u>Pastoral Letter on Moral Values</u> had been under discussion for four years and many of its concerns overlapped with those expressed at Detroit. The liberal Bishops feared that deliberation on many Call to Action proposals would be short-circuited before the May evaluation, causing bitterness and rancor among those who had worked so hard to promote the Bicentennial Program.[54] While the minority Bishops' motion was defeated, the 65 votes gathered indicated significant support among at least a certain wing of Bishops for the Bicentennial Program.

In many ways the content of the <u>Pastoral Letter on Moral Values</u> would reflect the eventual Bishop's evaluation of the Call to Action proposals. Both the letter and the Detroit recommendations indicated a strong support of national issues such as repudiation of abortion and racism, a call for full

62

employment, fair housing, and penal reform. Perhaps most importantly, both the college of Bishops and the Detroit delegates voted in such a way as to insist that the language of "obligation and justice" rather than that of "charity and aid" should govern the dealings of richer nations with poorer.

The divergence between the Detroit assembly, on the one hand, and the Pastoral Letter on Moral Values (and the eventual Bishop's evaluation of Detroit) dealt more on internal matters of faith, morals, and dogma. Specifically, the pastoral letter maintains the ban on contraception, rejection of divorce, pre-marital sex, and all homosexual activity whereas the Detroit delegates were much more apt to urge the "responsibility of the individual to form his/her own conscience in matters such as these".

The Bishops Meeting May, 1977

As the eve of the Bishop's meeting approached, James Finn wrote:

> The attention aroused by the meeting the American Catholic Bishops will hold in May is unprecedented. There have been, for example, more applications for press credentials than for any previous general meeting of the Bishops. And an impressive number of Catholic organizations and individuals have tried publicly to bring an outline of their own deep interests into focus with what they hope that meeting will accomplish. The reason for this surge of interest is not that the Bishops of this country have suddenly become more popular, but that they are going to consider recommendations derived from the Detroit Call to Action conference of October. . . . The participants understood that their advice would be seriously considered by the N.C.C.B. and that their work would help form and shape a five year pastoral plan on justice. . . . These recommendations are the consequence of a process that is itself unprecedented in American Catholic history, so that their May meeting the Bishops will not follow custom but will establish it. The attention concentrated

63

on that meeting is justified.[56]

The initial response of the Bishops was self-consciously declared as "partial" and "preliminary"; the Bishops would have more to say in the next few years, especially at next year's May meeting. At the 1977 May meeting, the Bishops' adopted a two-pronged response in the form of two documents which, they stressed, must be taken together. They were (1) a pastoral statement, The Bishops Pastoral Reply to the Call to Action, addressing some of the more controversial Detroit recommendations and intended as an initial response and (2) a chart assigning each recommendation to the appropriate committees of the N.C.C.B/U.S.C.C. for study, evaluation and action. In addition, and in an extremely important victory for the Dearden-Gerety wing, an "ad Hoc Committee on the Call to Action" was created within the N.C.C.B./U.S.C.C., composed of Bishops and members of the Advisory Council. The committee was charged with the development of the five year "pastoral plan of action" and with overseeing its implementation. It's task is to report its progress to each of the Bishops' general meetings in November for the next five years.

James Finn listed three problems the Bishops would have to confront when reviewing the Call to Action proposals. They are:

1. How will the Bishops assign priorities to the vast number of recommendations;

2. What plan will the Bishops devise to implement them; and

3. What understanding of the Church will underlie their deliberations and their planning.[57]

Regarding the first of Mr. Finn's questions, one can say that, theoretically, the Bishops did not assign priorities to the vast number of recommendations; each and every one of the recommendations was sent to an existing N.C.C.B./U.S.C.C. committee. Bishop Joseph McNicholas explained the rationale for the chart of committee assignments in this way:

> We want everyone in the country to know that we are responding to all recommendations, not sweeping any under the rug, but putting

all through the structures, the committees of the Conference where all proposals originate. We are thus exercising our listening role and our teaching role.[58]

It was then the task of the respective committee to label and evaluate its assigned resolutions a directive to either:

(1) study

(2) act immediately

(3) support existing local activity, or

(4) respond in light of the "universal law of the Church".[59]

In actuality, however, priorities were assigned. This strategy allowed the Bishops to immediately circumvent any prolonged discussion on "controversial" matters of faith, morals and dogma. Simply put, such issues as the ordination of women, a married clergy, the right of laicized priests to preach, birth control, democratic selection of Bishops, female altar service, equality in racial/ethnic distribution of hierarchy, etc., were, in effect, declared outside the domain of authority of the laity and lower echelon clergy. Each such controversial proposal was assigned to the number "4" category, thus ending any possible debate.[60] Predictably enough, the Committee assigned to handle such proposals was the powerful and conservative Administrative Committee on the N.C.C.B./U.S.C.C.

On the other hand, resolutions that supported the already existing activities of the Church were given "3's". Proposals such as calls for justice education and research, the development of Catholic public policy research, respect for life, etc., fit such a categorization. Many, from the viewpoint of the majority of Bishops, useful (and perhaps, disarming) proposals for the training of clergy, increased vocations, adult education, continuing education for the clergy, ministry to American Indians, the creation of a Diocesan Family Life Office, strengthening campus ministries, introduction of parent education and occupational counseling, helping to assist unorganized workers, and the teaching of social justice, were given "2's".

On the other hand many resolutions dealing with matters of internal organizational Church reform were given "1's". A few examples are the call for the establishment of a National Review Board, Affirmative Action within the Church, the establishment of a multiethnic office, Indian, Black, and Hispanic secretariats and seminaries, investigations of Church investments, divestment of Church properties, a Catholic Bill of Rights, U.S.C.C. equal employment program, and development of a "theology of work", etc. Such a categorization created the suspicion (held by many Bicentennial advocates) that many of the proposals that were "under study" could, in effect, be hopelessly "buried in bureaucracy".

The decision to direct each and every proposal to various committees allowed the majority bloc of Bishops to control the temper and flow of the Detroit "follow up" procedure. It effectively stifled the momentum of the Call to Action and disallowed the possibility that an inner dynamic would take off and promote rapid internal change within the American Church. Advocates of the Bicentennial movement, however, could take solace in the fact that their proposals were "alive" precisely in the sense of being located within the national bureaucracy. As time, energy, finances, and organizational effort allowed they could be brought up periodically for discussion, debate, and perhaps some day, for approval. As students of Max Weber's discussion of bureaucracy are well aware, one of the characteristics of such a form of formal organization is the constant review of procedures and decisions. Put crudely, the bureaucracy has indeed swallowed the proposals and may suffer from chronic fits of indigestion as a result. The more sober and realistic supporters of the Bicentennial movement realize that now "their foot is in the door" and, moreover, the primary forces of modernity, that of the spread of democracy, pluralism, and civility, are on their side. Put even more simply, the "traditional" authority of the Bishop might plausibly be expected to "last just so long" in a bureaucracy that is itself embedded in a wider cultural matrix that takes universalistic criteria for granted, and one that values highly the role of those in the possession of "modern" or "rational" forms of knowledge.

The second general question that Mr. Finn posed for the Bishops was "what was the Bishops plan for the implementation of the proposals? What are the structures through which plans will be carried out? Who is going to do what? And with what resources?" As Mr. Finn himself put it:

> When one listened, at the plenary session in Detroit, it was impossible not to feel that too much was being placed on the Bishops' desks. Much of what was recommended can best be carried out through national and diocesan organizations, religious communities, and issue-oriented organizations. Some of these have, in fact, already started working on plans inspired by the Bicentennial program. Outlining these distributed responsibilities is itself a necessary educational task of the Bishops.[61]

As the Bicentennial Committee noted:

> . . . this consultation demonstrated that the relationship of the N.C.C.B./U.S.C.C. to individual dioceses, national organizations and movements, and religious communities, must be clarified to enable all to understand the nature, functions and responsibilities of an episcopal conference and its proper role in suggesting actions and activities in the Catholic community.[62]

The answer to Mr. Finn's second question is that the Bishops initiated some modest activity within the national level structure itself; it created in 1977 the "Ad Hoc Committee for the Call to Action" whose task it would be to serve as a strong monitoring committee, complete with funds and staff, and which would be authorized to receive regular progress reports on the implementation of proposals through existing committees. In 1978, a permanent secretariat was created, that of the Secretariat for the Laity, which would be of special assistance to the Call to Action Committee. In 1979, a "mini Call to Action" assembly was sponsored by the Call to Action Committee, the Secretariat for the Laity and the U.S.C.C. to gather information on, and encourage further, the implementation of proposals at the diocesan and parish level.

      Despite this response, however, David J. O'Brien argues that national activity must be linked systematically to local programs in order to make the Bicentennial Program truly successful. O'Brien ponders a crucial point:

> What was unclear is whether the N.C.C.B would be prepared to reallocate resources and reorganize departments in order to better support the thrusts of the Call to Action resolutions toward shared responsibility, pastoral renewal and local social action. Each of these thrusts would eventually require serious change. The institutionalization of consultation and eventually of shared decision making at the national level would dramatically alter the work of the episcopal conference. National support for local efforts at pastoral renewal would require serious efforts to strengthen committees, staffs and budgets for the offices dealing with the laity, family life, pastoral practice and liturgy-- all of which are presently small and understaffed. Local programs of social action would require new efforts at outreach, consultation, and coordination by the offices of Social Development and International Justice and Peace. Also it would move the emphasis of these offices away from developing and communicating models of structures and programs for parish and diocesan justice and peace offices, and developing and evaluating educational programs. In short, implementation of the basic thrusts of the Call to Action would make the N.C.C.B./U.S.C.C. in key areas a center for stimulating, coordinating and assisting people at the local level, an effort that will require serious changes in established programs and attitudes.[63]

      Most Bicentennial advocates agreed with O'Brien and Finn that the issue of implementation would ultimately determine the success or failure of the program. As O'Brien makes perfectly clear, national level activity can be of limited effectiveness if not successfully coordinated at more local levels.

In terms of implementation, many Bicentennial advocates argued that the program was more a failure than a success. While the Bicentennial Program called for a truly national program, a truly systematic linking of national, statewide, diocesan and parish structures, the Bishops were, for the most part, unprepared to tamper with the basically "states rights" nature of the American Church. Such a decentralized organizational and authority structure is one which leaves each Bishop free to implement proposals as he pleases. Furthermore, such an arrangement, for all practical purposes, places each local Church, its "official" programs, and any programs generated by the laity that desire organizational assistance in the hands of its Bishop.

O'Brien, talking about the differing worldviews of "professionals" advocating the systematic and rational implementation of the proposals as contrasted to that of the local Bishop, put it as follows:

In contradistinction to the Bishops who want to insure that such national programs do not unduly disrupt their efforts to maintain the complex network of institutions for which they feel responsible, Church professionals, through such organizations as the National Federation of Priests Councils, the Leadership Conference of Women Religious, the National Catholic Educational Association and the National Conference of Catholic Charities, have a national rather than diocesan perspective. They look to the N.C.C.B./U.S.C.C. to take progressive positions on public policy issues; they expect the conference to articulate an American position on matters of universal Church life; they look to the conference as the only recourse for persons working in unprogressive or badly managed dioceses; they have nowhere else to look.[64]

O'Brien gloomingly concludes that the episcopal conference has limited power and that American Catholicism remains, more so than not, a "states rights Church". As he put it:

The conferences' leaders might be as personally responsible as anyone could ask and they would still not be able to do much about many matters of great concern to the (Call to Action) groups. The decentralized organization of the Church, the limited resources of the N.C.C.B./U.S.C.C. and the powerlessness of anyone save Rome to do much about pastoral or managerial problems of individual dioceses are inescapable realities in the contemporary American Church.[65]

       The <u>Bishop's Pastoral Reply to the Call to Action</u> did explicitly acknowledge the limited power of the episcopal conference to forcibly implement programs at the local parish level. As the <u>Pastoral Reply</u> states, "among matters which are beyond the competence of our conference as such to influence directly we note . . . themes concerning the parish which emerged from the consultation."[66]

       The modest structural change that has taken place at both the national and diocesan level left the more fervant supports of the Bicentennial movement unhappy. In an issue of <u>National Catholic Reporter</u> written immediately after the May 1978 Bishop's meeting which had more to say on the Call to Action, a despondent David J. O'Brien claimed that the Bishops "wrote the final chapter of this episode in U.S. Church history."[67] As "O'Brien continued, "the episcopal conference's failure to develop a truly national voice or to provide even minimal leadership for the U.S. Church reflects the broader erosion of what used to be called "liberal Catholicism."[68]

       One can argue with O'Brien's assessment. The truth of the matter is that, while many of the proposals are not being implemented either fully or in part, certain key areas of the N.C.C.B./U.S.C.C. do serve as a center for the constant generating of ideas and programs; ideas and programs that find a strong legitimation in at least a certain interpretation of Vatican II theology. It is interesting to note here that many of the changes called for by the Second Vatican Council have been, at best, only partially implemented. Just as it would be outrageously premature to claim that the legacy of John XXIII has reached its final form, so would it be equally premature to claim, at least from a sociological view, that "the final chapter of this episode in U.S. history has been written". Suffice it to say here that both the "causes" of Vatican II and the Bicentennial Program are to be found in world-wide, transforming social forces and not (primarily at least) in the conscious acts of individuals, Bishops included. Simply put, the reasons, the forces and the people behind both the Bicentennial Program and movement will not disappear overnight for the convenience of the conservative Bishops. The Bicentennial advocates may have engaged in a stalemated battle, but they "live to fight another day". Furthermore, many of the Bicentennial Program sympathizers hold high positions within both the Catholic hierarchy and cultural community; they are, so to speak, "already in the fortress" making future "siege" attempts much more likely to become progressively more successful. An adequate assessment of the impact of the Bicentennial Program must, again, take into account the fact that it has "fueled" a movement that will long outlive itself.

A hopeful, yet cautious, James Finn raises his third question about the nature of the Bishops' response to the Bicentennial:

> The third point--how the Bishops approach their task, with what attitude on the myriad issues placed before them, how they consider their responsibilities to other Christians in the community of faith--may be the most significant, indeed the crucial, point of the May meetings. Two documents of Vatican II, "The Dogmatic Constitution on the Church" and "The Pastoral Constitution on the Church in the Modern World" carry us some distance beyond the understanding of the Church that most Catholics had in the early 60's. Nevertheless, some people wish to regress to those earlier, apparently less-troubled times, to assert or to accept on the basis of authority what should be the result of collective thoughts, action and prayer.[69]

Was, then, the Bishops' deliberations, "open to new and greater exploration", the "result of collective thought, action and prayer?" Or did the

Bishops "regress to those earlier, apparently less troubled times, to assert or to accept on the basis of their authority?" It is clear that the majority consensus at the May meeting was a continuation of the historical assertion of the Bishops' teaching authority. This point is best illustrated by Archbishop Bernardin's opening address in which he bluntly declared that "amidst the controversy (of the Call to Action) people have forgotten that the role of the Bishop as guaranteers of the faith is to lead and to guide the rest of the Church".[70] Bishop Romeo Blanchette of Joliet even went as far as declaring that the faithful would be confused or even scandalized if those recommendations which conflict with Church teaching were even so much as referred to the various committees of the N.C.C.B./U.S.C.C. As Blanchette declared, "the Holy See has already spoken on these issues. We have just pledged loyalty to the Holy See. Our people will be confused and think we ourselves are not sure about those issues if they are referred to committees".[71]

      The May meeting was, more so than not, a victory for Archbishop Bernardin over Cardinal Dearden, of "charisma of the office" over the further dispersion of charisma, and that of historical practice over recent theological development. In this last point, however, the supporters of the Bicentennial movement can find comfort; the fact that a liberal interpretation of the Vatican II conception of the proper role of the hierarchy, as compared to "the people of God", has not been "successfully internalized" by the majority of Bishops themselves does not mean that it will never be. Put another way, symbols and ideas do count and may very well eventually have their impact on everyday thought and activity. Vatican II theology is a "social fact", has approached "thingness" in the precise Durkheimian sense. Its facticity constitutes an important weapon in the arsenal of the New Catholic Knowledge Class. Many sophisticated conservatives, perhaps, realize that in Vatican II, "the damage to the existing authority structure of the Church has been irreversibly done." Using a key insight of Edward Shils, one can point to the wisdom that "primordial" bases of allegiance, once destroyed, are terribly hard, if not impossible, to replace.[72] The days, in other words, in which Catholicism can be identified, tout court, with an ecclesiastical definition may well be over. The sociologically interesting question may be the nature of emerging compromise between ecclesiastical and "communal" forms of Catholicism.[73]

The *Bishops Pastoral Reply to the Call to Action*, interestingly enough, is consistent with the idea of partial democratization through its reference to Vatican II's *Lumen Gentium*. As the Pastoral states:

> The bicentennial program must be understood in light of what Vatican II has said about the Church . . . Fundamental to the theological vision of *Lumen Gentium* is its description of the Church as the people of God.

The Pastoral then goes on to add, however, that:

> The hierarchical ministry in the Church is ordained entirely to the service . . . of God. Thus the Second Vatican Council teaches that Bishops, as successors of the apostles, have received from the Lord the mission of teaching authoritatively to all peoples so that all may attain salvation . . . For Bishops are "authentic teachers, that is, teachers endowed with the authority of Christ, who preach the faith to the people assigned to them, the faith which is designed to inform their thinking and direct their conduct". . . . The particular process of consultation which culminated in the proposals of the Call to Action conference was helpful and important. However, it cannot be the sole factor in determining the pastoral agenda of the Church. It is our task to assess those proposals in the context of God's plans revealed in and through Christ.[74]

In many respects, the Bishops responded to the Bicentennial Program in much the same way they responded to Vatican II. Both responses can be characterized by a "structured ambiguity". Such an ambiguity allows the Church hierarchy to retain a privileged place in the overall Church schema while at the same time allowing for a controlled dispersion of authority throughout a Church defined as "the people of God". The Church hierarchy thus attempts to keep an increasing number of disparate, at one time "peripheral", groups under one roof.

Newsweek reporters Margaret Mantagno and Sylvester Monroe who attended the May meeting summed up the Bishops' general response as follows:

> The National Conference of Catholic Bishops wound up praising the impulse for reform, approving purely political and social proposals such as promoting racial justice and working toward nuclear disarmament and flatly rejecting most of the controversial doctrinal changes. . . . Although few expected the Bishops to move far from the Vatican line on matters of faith and morals, the prelates promised to continue the process of consultation. "Shared responsibility is in", insisted Phoenix Bishop James Rausch. That, in the end, may be the legacy of Call to Action.[75]

Kenneth A. Briggs, analyzing the conference for the New York Times, follows with his general assessment:

> The Bishops . . . insured that the vast majority of recommendations made by the Call to Action conference last fall would be carefully weighed with the goal of formulating a five-year "plan of justice". . . . A few proposals were clearly in opposition to Vatican teaching and were at once rejected by most Bishops. But others in areas such as racial justice, international peace and family life were acceptable . . . the hierarchy approved an initial response to the Detroit proposals that was seen as basically positive.[76]

David J. O'Brien, while agreeing with both the Newsweek and Times reporting of the event, nonetheless differed somewhat is his interpretation. For O'Brien:

> . . . Observers were confident that resolutions on social justice and

74

family ministry would receive prompt attention and speedy action. Yet none of this can change the explicit rejection of controversial and important resolutions and the almost total ignoring of resolutions on financial accountability, lay participation in the selection of pastors and Bishops and other matters of internal Church reform.[77]

The Bishops' Pastoral responded, most generally, as follows:

In most cases the recommendations on domestic and international issues are consistent with our own publicly stated positions and provide a welcome impetus for continued effort. A few, however, involve matter with which we have not dealt up to now; in some cases, the issues appear more complex than the recommendations would suggest. We strongly encourage our committees to continue to study these questions and develop policy recommendations for our consideration.[78]

However, the Bishops' Pastoral noted that:

some (proposals) pertain to the teaching or discipline of the universal Church; in regard to them we recall our duty, as members of the College of Bishops united with the Holy Father, to respect the principles of collegiality and universality and, in particular, our fundamental obligation of fidelity to the teaching of Christ entrusted to the Church.[79]

Alfred P. Klausler follows with his assessment:

While approving statements affirming human rights and justice for American Indians and Eastern Europeans and applauding the television film Jesus of Nazareth, the Bishops opposed married priests, freedom of choice in contraception, and the removal of Church strictures against active homosexuals. Thus many of the Detroit Call to Action recommendations were either jettisoned or referred to committees for further study. Nonetheless, despite the heavy authoritarian approach by the bishops to problems plaguing their Church, this observer had the rather indefinable feeling that the Bishops, thanks to sometimes not-so-gentle prodding by impatient clergy and laity, were getting ready for some remarkable changes in Church policy and action in American Catholicism.[80]

It is interesting to point out that the pre-meeting maneuvers of the Bishops carried over into the May meeting itself. Kenneth Briggs informs us that the "Bishops' Pastoral Reply was the seventh draft document in a six month effort to reach a compromise".[81] As Mr. Briggs follows:

> On the one hand, some Bishops led by John Cardinal Dearden of Detroit . . . sought to emphasize the value of consultation with and sympathetic approaches to Catholics who feel alienated from the Church. Other Bishops, notably John Cardinal Krol of Philadelphia and John Cardinal Carberry of St. Louis, stressed the binding nature of Church law. . . . Thus, while the one group welcomed the Call to Action as a further development in the consultative, democratic process, the other was concerned that such initiative could dilute the power or hierarchical teaching authority.[82]

David J. O'Brien captures for us some of the more specific reactions according to the respective justice sub-themes:

> Many of the leading figures in the hierarchy attended the group on Church, where they exchanged views on the resolutions without seeking any formal expression of opinion. In general the tone was favorable save of those issues expected to meet a negative response:

women's ordination and clerical celibacy.
The discussion of Personhood, the other
section dealing with controversial resolutions, was more negative. Most Bishops
felt that the Church teaching on sexuality
was very firm, reflected the demands of
the Gospel and was unchangeable. A
hesitant auxiliary Bishop's suggestion
that perhaps the position on birth
control might be changed was met with
a stony silence. Dealing with the more
pastoral sections, the Bishops present
seemed satisfied that they met the needs
expressed in their Pastoral Letter on
Moral Values published in the preceeding
fall. In all six of the other groups,
discussion was far more positive. Bishops
found the recommendations fully in accord
with Church teaching; they expressed their
hope that their committees could act quickly,
and on some issues, like those of family
life, they were confident that this would
happen. Even in Humankind, there was no
expression of dissent from the disarmament
resolution but only serious discussion of
how the conference could more effectively
met the objectives which had been set,
objectives the Bishops felt were almost the
same as those they had already set for
themselves in their programs and statements
on world peace and justice.[83]

     As Kenneth Briggs makes clear, the Bishops'
results were far from disastrous from the liberal
point of view. While the Bishops did turn down many
controversial proposals including one proposing the
granting of a greater role to conscience in the use
of contraception, Briggs notes that "even those
issues were technically referred to committees for
possible study, over the objection of some Bishops
who considered these matters closed".[84] Archbishop
Borders of Baltimore also saw his amendment to the
women's ordination statement ratified. The amendment
read, "we invite theologians to join us in a serious
study of the issues to which this document addresses
itself. Further study of these issues may allay some
of the anguish felt by many whose love for the Church
is unquestioned". In addition, on the second day of
the meeting, the Bishops voted to ask Rome for

permission to lift the law of automatic excommunication of divorced Catholics who, as the Third Baltimore Council of 1884 put it, "dare to remarry". While the removal of the penalty still does not admit this group of an estimated 3 million Catholics to the sacraments of communion and penance, the doors are open for them to now participate in all other aspects of Church worship. In presenting this decision, the Bishops emphasized the need for strong pastoral outreach to divorced Catholics. The Bishops also expressed strong sentiments in favor of retaining the simplified tribunals that have been used experimentally in this country in recent years. In addition, the grounds for granting annulments were widened to include many forms of "psychological" causes.

Perhaps most importantly for the liberal wing was the decision to establish an Ad Hoc Committee to push ahead with the implementation of the accepted recommendations. Some Bishops opposed the establishment of a separate committee, arguing that the task belonged to the 60 member Advisory Council which serves as the sounding board for the Bishops on a variety of matters. This was the proposal of the Bernardin Task Force. The task force's proposal to assign a simple overview to the Advisory Council was challenged by an amendment from twenty Bishops led by Archbishop Gerety. Gerety's amendment provided for the formation of a Bishops committee with far more authority than the Advisory Council has. The Gerety amendment passed by a standing vote, with about 60% of the Bishops voting in favor. Archbishop Gerety, who had reportedly lobbied for days to see his amendment pass, responded with a "I'm delighted . . . this establishes a clear means of handling all which has to be done".[85]

The Bishops' Pastoral Reply to the Call to Action put it as follows:

> Conscious of the fact that the hearings and the Detroit conference aimed at providing us the material for a five year "Plan of Action", we direct the president of the N.C.C.B. to appoint, as soon as possible, an Ad Hoc Committee to be chaired by a Bishop, and to be drawn from the Advisory Council. The committee will have as its charge to

develop the five-year plan of action in consultation with our N.C.C.B. and U.S.C.C. committees. It will establish appropriate deadlines for its work, and once the Plan of Action had been accepted by the N.C.C.B., it will have responsibility for oversight of its implementation. Finally this committee will submit a written public report on the implementation process at each of our general meetings in November. We believe these steps will insure effective implementation and responsible accountability, to us and to all others, on the part of our national structures.[86]

A few weeks after the May meeting, Archbishop Bernardin appointed a mostly sympathetic Call to Action committee, with Bishop John Roach of Minnesota appointed to the Chair. Archbishop Thomas Donnellan of Atlanta, Archbishop Gerety, Bishop McNicholas, Bishop Joseph Howze of Biloxi, and Bishop Manuel Moreno of Los Angeles were also named. Four lay members of the Advisory Council were appointed as was Father Thomas Kelley, soon to be Bishop Kelley and General Secretary of the N.C.C.B./U.S.C.C. And very significant was the fact that Dr. Frank Butler, consciously snubbed by Bernardin's Task Force between December and May, was given the task of directing the daily operations of the committee.

Kenneth Briggs, describing the overall deliberations of the Bishops in evaluating the Call to Action, noted that they "showed a tendency to express diverse, often contrary opinions on many issues. This trend in style toward debate and compromise was seen by many observers as the key element enabling the response to the Call to Action to take its final form".[87]

The Following May, 1978 Bishops' Meeting

The Bishops' Pastoral Reply on the Call to Action ended by reminding the reader that "the present preliminary and partial response is not intended as a total response to the bicentennial celebration. Such a response must come in carefully planned actions, carried out over a period of years".[88] One of those "carefully planned actions" turned out to be the National Conference of Catholic Bishops' Call to

79

Action Plan, later entitled To Do The Work of Justice, published on May 4th, 1978, during the 1978 May meeting of the Bishops. As the Call to Action Plan put it:

> Convinced that (the Call to Action) program could bear much fruit today, we undertook a detailed evaluation of all the recommendations through the committees of the N.C.C.B./U.S.S.C. In addition, we directed the President of the N.C.C.B. to appoint an Ad Hoc Committee to coordinate the evaluation process and develop a five year pastoral plan of action based on its results. We are now prepared to set forth this plan and we invite the cooperation of the entire Catholic community in its implementation.[89]

An America editorial briefly summarized the plan as follows:

> The new plan cannot be called radical, and it certainly is not propaganda. It covers six areas with varied thoroughness: human rights; economic justice, the Church as people, parish and community; education for justice; family life; and world hunger. Among other things, it calls for national offices or commissions for justice education, economic justice and research, and mandates pastoral letters on racism and on the handicapped. The plan schedules a meeting of representatives from each diocese on human rights in 1979, and a national conference on economic justice in 1981. Unsatisfied merely to mandate, the plan calls for a review in 1983 of national accomplishments and shortfalls.[90]

A mostly disappointed David J. O'Brien in a National Catholic Reporter article, "Lifeboat Ethics", had this to say of the plan:

> Of course the plan has some good points. It incorporates initiatives already undertaken to develop an organized program of family ministry in dioceses and parishes. It assigns to the (newly formed) "Ad Hoc Committee on the Parish" the task of identifying and sharing

models of parish based social action.[91]

O'Brien, however, sadly notes that while the Bishops "promised to do some unspecified good things for women and the handicapped, they specifically rejected the establishment of national offices to deal with these subjects".[92] Furthermore, for O'Brien:

> Most of the proposals regarding justice in the Church, revision of Church teaching or shared responsibility have disappeared, either into the custody of existing N.C.C.B./U.S.C.C. committees or into the deepest recesses of the episcopal files. . . . While the plan is something more than a mouse, it is far less than the "new way of doing the work of the Church" that the delegates to the Call to Action conference were asked to begin by Cardinal John Dearden of Detroit in October of 1976. Instead, the plan follows procedures characteristic of the episcopal conference, exhorts everyone to work for justice, initiates a few programs and respectfully asks for dioceses to participate, and solemnly promises to be serious.[93]

On the one hand, it is obvious that the Bishops' Plan did fall far short of the envisioned by the more zealous advocates of the Bicentennial movement in that the Bishops suppressed initiatives to allow the generation of doctrine to fall into the hands of anyone but themselves and in their ignoring of the sensitive matters of internal Church reform. Nonetheless, on the other hand, it is not hard to disagree with O'Brien's evaluation that the plan "reflects the broader errosion of what used to be called 'liberal Catholicism'".

The truth of the matter is that "liberal Catholicism in America" has never been stronger, more vital, nor more widely accepted among the mass of modern day American Catholics. In 1919, when Reverend John A. Ryan wrote his manifest, On Social Reconstruction, it was generally greeted by American society, Catholic or otherwise, as "radical, socialistic propaganda". The substance of all but one ("labor

81

participation in management") of the eleven proposals Father Ryan made are now facts of life. These include his calls for social security, public housing, and the minimum wage. Unlike Father Ryan's proposals, though, the content of the plan as it was approved by the Bishops in Chicago in May of 1978 enjoys widespread support among most Americans and American Catholics. As Andrew Greeley has indicated in his works that stretch from The Catholic Experience to Why Can't They Be Like Us? to The American Catholic[94] most "average" American Catholics love their Church, respect (if not venerate) its leaders, and share a sense of responsibility for its future. These "communal" Catholics, as Greeley calls them, may not take everything the Church hierarchy has to say "literally", in a "fundamentalist" interpretation, but nonetheless they are probably more concerned with the broad, religio-humanitarian concerns of liberal Catholicism than the "average" American Catholic was during the "mythical" hay-days of liberal Catholicism in the last half of the 19th century. Using the nomenclature of Alfred Shutz, one can say that the liberal Catholicism of the last half of the 19th century operated against the matrix of an American society that took an unmitigated capitalism as a "taken-for-granted" reality; contemporary American Catholic liberalism operates in a society that "takes it for granted" that the existence of the "welfare state" is both a "given" of life and, moreover, to a great degree, desirable. When gauged against what Peter Berger has coined the "socialist myth"[95] prevalent among many American intellectuals, O'Brien is correct: the Bicentennial results are disappointing. When gauged against the facts of American and world history, the Bicentennial Program represents a decided advance, although certainly not an unqualified victory, for the cause of liberal Catholicism in America. Furthermore, the state of American Catholicism was, until recently, at a perpetual "ad hoc", unorganized state. Using Weber's nomenclature, there was little evidence of a "rationalized approach" to questions of social justice. On the contrary, the N.C.C.B. May 1978 reply is a rational, five year plan, systematically laid out in stages, bureaucratically implemented, with activities and objectives identified, time schedules established and a review called for. And one final point must be clearly stated: despite the present day reality of an American "states rights"

Church, the fact remains that it is presently less of a states rights Church than ever before. Simply put, the Bishops have come to depend, perhaps more practically than either theoretically or doctrinally, on a centralized and well-organized national episcopal conference, the N.C.C.B./U.S.C.C. As a matter of fact, and indicative of this increased activity, the Ad Hoc Committee on the Call to Action Plan noted that:

> After the publication of To Do the Work of Justice, several further statements and letters were issued by the N.C.C.B. or U.S.C.C. to support and to strengthen the call of the initial document. These included various publications of the N.C.C.B. Ad Hoc Committee on the Parish; The Family Farm: A Statement of the Committee on Social Development and World Peace; the Pastoral Letter on Racism, Brothers and Sisters to Us; the N.C.C.B./U.S.C.C. Affirmative Action Plan; Pastoral Statement of the U.S. Bishops on Handicapped People; and U.S.C.C. materials dealing with the 1980 programs on family life.[96]

The 1979 "Mini-Call to Action" Conference

The next chapter in the biography of the American Catholic Bicentennial Program is that of a three day meeting held in Washington, D.C. from March 18-20 in the year 1979. The convention consisted of over 300 official delegates and included representatives from the United States Catholic Conference, national level Catholic research and policy making institutes like the Center for Concern, national level catholic social activist organizations like the Catholic Committee on Urban Ministry, with the majority consisting of "diocesan bicentennial coordinators". The latter are those individuals asked to come to the follow-up workshops by their Bishops because they are playing, or are expected to play, important roles in devising ways to carry out the 1978 Bishops' Call to Action Plan, To Do The Work of Justice, in their home dioceses and parishes. The convention was termed a "mini-Call to Action" by the influential liberal social activist Monsignor John Egan. The convention was chaired by a liberal prelate, Archbishop John Roach, chairman of the N.C.C.B. Call to Action Committee. As Roach put it

83

during his opening convention address:

> We are gathered here today to continue a process which is now almost six years old. Yes, it was that long ago that the N.C.C.B. initiated its bicentennial celebration on the theme of justice in the world. This, in turn, led to the national consultation, "Liberty and Justice for All", and culminated in the "Call to Action" conference in October, 1976. As that program developed, the Bishops promised to receive the recommendations of the Catholic community and reflecting upon them develop a plan of action for justice for implementation within the American Church. That plan has finally been formulated, principally through the document, <u>To Do The Work of Justice</u>, adopted by the Bishops last May. We are now here to discuss how we can help one another implement aspects of that plan in dioceses and parishes across the country.[97]

The meeting's agenda was as follows. On Sunday and Monday, the 18th and 19th of March, a series of workshops were held. Some of the workshops were led by the U.S.C.C. personnel on the subject of what the N.C.C.B./U.S.C.C. is doing to carry forward the twenty or so projects listed in the plan and about what N.C.C.B./U.S.C.C. resources are available to assist the diocesan bicentennial coordinators with the local implementation process. Other workshops were led by Bishops, clergy, or laity on Call to Action inspired developments within their home dioceses. Still others were chaired by representatives from the various national organizations for the purpose of explaining their work in social ministry and in outlining the various forms of assistance that they could offer the local Church in connection with <u>To Do The Work of Justice</u>. Tuesday's agenda focused on the more global dimensions of the work for justice, and upon the Church's evolving theological legitimation for such as well as the developing structures within the Church whose task it is to address such issues. Both the theological and formal organizational concerns stressed the movement towards "internationalization". Archbishop Roach stated succintly the manifest purpose of this three day agenda when he stated that "central to all of this, of course, will be you, the diocesan participants. We want to get you to share your information, ideas and thought on how to get moving on the plan locally. We hope to have a diologue here with emphasis on ideas, models, resources, and plans of action".[98]

One very important vehicle for the sharing of information was that of a questionnaire distributed to the diocesan bicentennial coordinators at the very end of the conference. This questionnaire was devised to determine just what programming had been instituted at the diocesan level as a response to To Do The Work of Justice. The Bishops' Call to Action Plan, again, laid out six areas of appropriate response. They are (1) education for justice; (2) family life; (3) people, parishes, and communities; (4) economic rights; (5) human rights; and (6) world hunger. This information was collected and distributed to all participants by Dr. Frank Butler and the U.S.C.C. staff. A total of 33 dioceses reported some form of Bicentennial activity. In addition, as Dr. Butler pointed out in letter dated May 4th, 1979 and sent to all convention delegates, "I would also point out that an additional twenty-six dioceses, through their representatives at the U.S.C.C. workshop in March, indicated that they would meet with diocesan leadership when they returned to institute some form of follow-up activity on the plan, To Do The Work of Justice". Of the thirty-three dioceses that filled out a questionnaire, however,

(1) five have held some diocesan level equivalent to a "mini-Call to Action" assembly

(2) twenty-two have published materials on the Call to Action throughout their diocese

(3) twenty-one have established some new structure (e.g., a committee, commission, pastoral council, etc.) to both study/ implement proposals

(4) twenty-six have utilized existing diocesan structures (e.g., priests' senates, pastoral councils, justice and peace centers, social action departments, etc.) to both study/implement proposals.[99]

Of the six sections of To Do The Work of Justice,

 (1) eighteen dioceses have responded, in some way, to "Education for Justice"

 (2) twenty-four dioceses have responded, in some way, to "Family Life"

 (3) twenty-six dioceses have responded, in some way, to "People, Parishes, and Communities"

 (4) nine dioceses have responded, in some way, to "Economic Rights"

 (5) thirteen dioceses have responded, in some way, to "Human Rights"

 (6) eight dioceses have responded, in some way, to "World Hunger".[100]

 Caveats are immediately in order regarding the questionnaire study. First of all it is important to point out that it is impossible, given the very general one page questionnaire, to determine just how effective and vital are the commissions/programs, other structures being instituted at any one diocese. Second of all, only less than half the nation's dioceses were represented at the March meeting. One cannot simply assume that all dioceses not represented at the March meeting are not active in any way in the implementation of proposals emanating from Detroit. And third of all, the questionnaire results only monitor the diocesan activity started in less than a year from the issuing of the Bishops' Plan for the Call to Action.

The July, 1980 Survey on Diocesan Implementation

 To ascertain in a more thorough and systematic fashion the progress of the five year (1978-83) plan To Do The Work of Justice at midpoint, the Ad Hoc Committee on the Call to Action Plan, now under the chairmanship of the liberal Bishop Joseph Francis, carried out a diocesan-based national survey. The survey was sent to the diocesan Bishops in mid April of 1980. Analysis of the data began on July 15, 1980, at which time 106 completed surveys had been returned, representing 62.3% of the nation's dioceses. The results of the survey, from the viewpoint of the proponents of the Bicentennial Program, were mixed. According to the report, The Diocesan Implementation of "To Do The Work Of Justice: A Plan of Action For the Catholic Community in the United States":

> The survey results have many encouraging aspects. Work is being done, for example, to improve textbooks and courses in social justice in Catholic schools, seminaries, and cathechetical programs. Nearly two-thirds of the nation's dioceses now have a specific agency for justice education and advocacy. Almost all dioceses now have family life offices. Fifty percent of the dioceses report work on behalf of human rights, and most have undertaken major anti-hunger campaigns. These and other findings are a promising sign of commitment to social ministry by the Church nationwide.[101]

On the other hand, however, the report states that "the N.C.C.B. survey contains less than reassuring data. Most bishops, for example, feel strongly that white, middle-class Catholics and their parishes do not see social justice as a priority for themselves. The Ordinaries feel that the N.C.C.B. program, To Do The Work of Justice, has not been well received locally by the laity and that its overall impact will be quite small when it is brought to a conclusion in 1983". More specifically, the survey disclosed that:

> --only slightly more than one-third of the Bishops have appointed individuals, committees, or other advisory bodies in their dioceses to guide implementation of the plan of action;

> --where programming occurred, it most often centered on family life, with an emphasis on programs for the pre-married;

> --Justice education and economic justice, major focal points of the 1978 N.C.C.B. proposal, received the least attention among the major categories comprising the overall program;

--national pastoral statements receiving their impetus in the adoption of the N.C.C.B. plan, such as the Bishops' letters on Racism and the Handicapped, both published in November of 1979, have also had a modest impact on the activities of the dioceses;

--only one-fourth of the dioceses had undertaken a needs assessment of rural pastoral and social needs as requested in the 1978 plan;

--among dioceses reporting that they had social advocacy agencies, nearly three-fourths reported no increase in funding or personnel for these bodies since 1978.[102]

The report also noted that total activities related to To Do The Work of Justice were (1) greater in larger dioceses, (2) greater where there are more priests, and (3) greater where the Ordinary has a more positive perception of the Call to Action Program. The report ended on an up-beat where it stated:

> Sobering as the results of the survey are, the Ad Hoc Committee believes that present obstacles to local implementation are not insurmountable. At the very least, there is much which can be done to improve the quality of communication on the various aspects of the program . . . . As a start, the N.C.C.B. along with these survey findings will be distributed to such bodies as priests' senates, pastoral councils, diocesan administrative offices, pastors, and others.[103]

The July 1980 survey monitored diocesan implementation of the directives of To Do The Work of Justice in the two years that had elapsed since the latter's publication on May 4th, 1978. The degree of diocesan implementation during this short period can be interpreted in radically different fashions, according to the expectations that one has for the Church's role as "servant". From the perspective of Catholics like David O'Brien, the results of the program would be considered more of a failure than of a success. From the perspective of those advocates of pluralism who feel that the Church has many other roles to play simultaneously in conjunction with its concern for the social apostolate, the results of program can be viewed very satisfactorily. Three points, however, should be made here. First of all, an overall assessment of the impact of the program must wait until the next survey is conducted sometime after the 1983 completion date of the program. Second of all, it is clear that the program has generated concern for social justice at the diocesan level as of the date of the survey. And finally one must bear in mind that, while the program officially ends in 1983, the actors involved in the Bicentennial movement will continue to fight, if "unofficially", in the decades ahead for the further establishment of the liberal perspective in America.

One final observation, of a social-psychological nature, is in order regarding the diocesan implementation. It is that the momentum and enthusiasm reported by so many during the Call to Action conference in October of 1976 was replaced by a mood of cynicism and disappointment by many of the March 1979 delegates. Frank Butler offered an explanation for this change.[104] For Butler it involved the misplaced hopes of many liberal social activists on the N.C.C.B./U.S.C.C. as an agent for forcing change at the local level. As a matter of fact, Archbishop Roach himself noted that:

> While the program was conducted under the auspices of the episcopal conference, many participants were understandably unclear as to how the episcopal conference fitted into the life of the Church at the local level and just how specific the five year program was to be. Participants wanted action in their parish, their neighborhood and their diocese and in many cases they seemed to want the Conference to issue directives or to legislate to this effect in its proposed plan of action. Yet, as most of you know, the Conference itself is, to a great extent a cooperative agency; each Bishop remains responsible for the work of his local Church. This decentralization the Church poses many difficulties, to be sure, but few of us would seriously desire to expand the role of the episcopal conference so that it could

> dictate policy and programs to local
> Churches . . . . Thus, in this case, while
> many people clearly wanted action at the
> local level, our episcopal conference can
> do no more than recommend a framework for
> such action and suggest programs which could
> assist local dioceses choosing to participate
> within that framework.[105]

On one hand, it may be true that among the American Catholic population-at-large "few of us would seriously desire to expand the role of the episcopal conference so that it could dictate policy and programs to local Churches". Unfortunately, however, the "few of us" represent precisely the more ideological and bureaucratic elements of a liberal social activist wing with a national/international outlook that was heavily overrepresented throughout the Bicentennial Program.

Another compatible explanation for the waning of the enthusiasm generated by the Call to Action can be found in the social-psychological analogue to what Max Weber has referred to as "the routinization of charisma". Very simply put, the very institutionalization--indeed the very success-- of significant parts of the Bicentennial Program "deadened", in a sense, the unrealistically high expectations aroused at Detroit. The bureaucratization of the program, with all that such entails, brought the program "down to earth", thus exposing the inevitable discrepancy between the ideal and utopian, on the one hand, and the real and practical, on the other.

Both the "utopian" hope in the transforming power of the national level bureaucracy and the routinizing effects of the charismatic ideals through that very bureaucracy reinforce, once again, our previous point: the inability of the more ideologically prone of the American Catholic Church to recognize and appreciate substantial, albeit less than complete, gains in its overall program. The truth of the matter is that the "progressive" programs and policy statements of the N.C.C.B/U.S.C.C. have provided the legitimation needed for "progressive" dioceses to move ahead rapidly on their own. In the cases in which an unsympathetic Bishop/clergy/laity form the majority force at the diocesan level, the N.C.C.B./U.S.C.C. provides the liberal, social activist minority with a solid ground for contention. What will be eventually argued is that the Bicentennial Program represents only one of several alternative forms of a democratization away from an ecclesiastically/ hierarchically defined and controlled Catholic Church. Concomitant with this multidimensional dispersion in authority, the Church hierarchy is increasingly becoming sensitive to the desires of the various local Catholic communities as the latter are shaped by their surrounding socio-cultural matrix. Crudely put, the Church hierarchy is allowing the Bicentennial movement (or for that matter the Catholic charismatic movement) to be institutionalized in those dioceses/ parishes that are strongly motivated, for whatever combination of reasons, to push for it (so long as the demands do not represent a serious threat to the existence of the hierarchy herself). It is in light of this increased display of "civility", then, that one can interpret the significance of the Bishops' May 1977 statement. As the Bishops then declared, "The different recommendations of the bicentennial consultation must be approached in several different ways, some recommendations pertain specifically to dioceses and parishes, and other structures and the final response must come at these levels".[106] As Pope John Paul II put it similarly to the Bishops of Brazil during the summer of 1980, "The Church's social action ought to be the accomplishment of all who bear significant shares of the Church's mission on their shoulders, <u>each in accordance with specific functions and responsibility</u>."[107]

FOOTNOTES

[1] Pope Paul VI, A Call to Action, Washington: U.S.C.C., May 14, 1971.

[2] David J. O'Brien, A Call to Action: The Church Prepares for the Third Century, unpublished manuscript, July 1978.

[3] "Report of The Bicentennial Committee on The Call to Action", unpublished report, December, 1976.

[4] Detroit and Beyond: The Continuing Quest for Social Justice, Washington: Center of Concern, 1977.

[5] Ibid.

[6] "Report of The Bicentennial Committee on The Call to Action", unpublished report, December, 1976.

[7] O'Brien, op. cit., July 1978 and Detroit and Beyond, 1977.

[8] O'Brien, op. cit., July, 1978.

[9] Detroit and Beyond, 1977.

[10] Ibid.

[11] John Cardinal Dearden, "Humankind" Washington Justice Hearing, Washington: N.C.C.B. Committee for the Bicentennial, 1975.

[12] C.W. Mills, The Sociological Imagination (N.Y.: Oxford University Press, 1959).

[13] The following quotations are from the testifiers at the Washington Justice Hearing, "Humankind", Washington: N.C.C.B. Committee for the Bicentennial, 1975.

[14] The following quotations are from the testifiers at the San Antonio Justice Hearing, "Nationhood" Washington: N.C.C.B Committee for the Bicentennial, 1975.

[15] The following quotations are from the testifiers at the St. Paul-Minneapolis Justice Hearing, "The Land", Washington: N.C.C.B. Committee for the Bicentennial, 1975.

[16] The following quotations are from the testifiers at the Atlanta Justice Hearing, "The Family", Washington: N.C.C.B. Committee for the Bicentennial, 1975.

[17] The following quotations are from the testifiers at the Sacramento Justice Hearing, "Work", Washington: N.C.C.B. Committee for the Bicentennial, 1975.

[18] The following quotations are from the testifiers at the Newark Justice Hearing, "Ethnicity and Race", Washington: N.C.C.B. Committee for the Bicentennial, 1975.

[19] The following quotations are from the testifiers at the Maryknoll Justice Hearing, "Bicentennial Convocation on Global Justice", Washington: N.C.C.B. Committee for the Bicentennial, 1975.

[20] "Report of the Bicentennial Committee on the Call to Action", unpublished report, December, 1976.

[21] Undated Bicentennial memo found in the files of Bicentennial Committee member, James Finn.

[22] Ibid.

[23] Ibid.

[24] John Cardinal Dearden, "Report on the Justice Conference" in Handbook: A Call to Action, Notre Dame: Catholic Committee on Urban Ministry, November 9, 1976.

[25] O'Brien, op. cit., July, 1978.

[26] Thomas Stahel, "More Action Than They Called For", America, November 6, 1976.

[27] Thomas Fox, "Made in Detroit", Commonweal, November 19, 1976.

[28] James Finn, "Catholics Called to Action", Worldview, March, 1977.

[29] Sister Margaret Cafferty quoted in O'Brien, op. cit., July, 1978.

[30] John Cardinal Dearden, "Opening Address", October 21, 1976 quoted in Stahel, November 6, 1976.

[31] Thomas Stahel, op. cit., November 6, 1976.

[32] Thomas Stahel, op. cit., November 6, 1976.

[33] James Finn, op. cit., March, 1977.

[34] Thomas Fox, op. cit., November 19, 1976.

[35] Frank V. Manning, Call to Action: A Review and Assessment, unpublished manuscript, 1977.

[36] "Report of the Bicentennial Committee on the Call to Action", unpublished report, December, 1976.

[37] Russell Kirk, "The Mice That Roared", The National Review, December 10, 1976.

[38] Ibid.

[39] Frank Manning, op. cit., 1977.

[40] Ibid.

[41] Fox, op. cit., Nov. 19, 1976.

[42] Vilfredo Pareto, The Mind and The Society, (N.Y.: Dover, 1963).

[43] "Editorial", Christian Century, November 17, 1976.

[44] O'Brien op. cit., July 1978.

[45] Manning, op. cit., 1977.

[46] Manning, ibid.

[47] John Cardinal Dearden, op. cit., November 9, 1976.

[48] Ibid.

[49] Mark Winiarski, "Cardinal Fights to Save Call to Action Process: Infighting Follows Task Force Recommendations", The National Catholic Reporter, April 22, 1977.

[50] Ibid.

[51] Reported in O'Brien, op. cit., July 1978.

[52] Winiarski, op. cit., April 22, 1977.

[53] "Editorial", "No Need For The Great Wait", America, March 19, 1977.

[54] As reported in O'Brien, op. cit. July 1978.

[55] "Editorial", "Bishops Pastoral", America, November 27, 1976.

[56] James Finn "Second Call to Action", Commonweal, April 29, 1977.

[57] Finn, ibid.

[58] Bishop Joseph McNicholas, Origins: National Catholic Documentary Service, May 19, 1977.

[59] As indicated in the "N.C.C.B. Call to Action Reference Document" in A Call to Action: An Agenda for the Catholic Community, Washington: N.C.C.B./U.S.C.C.

[60] For a complete list of the Call to Action proposals and their respective assigned categories, see appendix A.

[61] Finn, op. cit., April 29, 1977.

[62] "Report of the Bicentennial Committee on the Call to Action", op. cit., December, 1976.

[63] O'Brien, op. cit., July, 1978.

[64] Ibid.

[65] Ibid.

[66] Bishops Pastoral Reply to the Call to Action, Origins: National Catholic Documentary Service,

[67] O'Brien, "Lifeboat Ethics", The National Catholic Reporter, op. cit., July 14, 1978.

[68] Ibid.

[69] James Finn, op. cit., April 29, 1977.

[70] Archbishop Joseph Bernardin, quoted in O'Brien, op. cit., 1978.

[71] Bishop Romeo Blancette, Origins, op. cit., May 19, 1977.

[72] Edward Shils, Center and Pheriphery (Chicago: University of Chicago Press, 1975).

[73] Andrew Greeley, The Communal Catholic (N.Y.: Seabury, 1976).

[74] Bishops Pastoral Reply to The Call to Action, op. cit., May 19, 1977.

[75] Margaret Mantagno and Sylvester Monroe, Newsweek, May, 1977.

[76] Kenneth A. Briggs "Catholic Bishops Give Positive Reply to Call to Action", The New York Times, May 5, 1977.

[77] O'Brien, "Lifeboat Ethics", op. cit., July 14, 1978.

[78] Bishops' Pastoral Reply to the Call to Action, op. cit., May 19, 1977.

[79] Ibid.

[80] Alfred P. Klausler, "Editorial Correspondence", The Christian Century, May 25, 1977.

[81] Briggs, op. cit., May 5, 1977.

[82] Ibid.

[83] O'Brien, op. cit., July, 1978.

[84] Briggs, op. cit., May 5, 1977.

[85] Archbishop Peter L. Gerety quoted in Briggs, op. cit., May 5, 1977.

[86] Bishops Pastoral Reply to The Call to Action, op. cit., May 19, 1977.

[87] Briggs, op. cit., May 5, 1977.

[88] Bishops Pastoral Reply to The Call to Action, op. cit., May 19, 1977.

[89] To Do The Work of Justice, Washington: U.S.C.C., 1978.

[90] "Editorial", America, May 20, 1978.

[91] O'Brien, "Lifeboat Ethics", op. cit., July 14, 1978.

[92] Ibid.

[93] Ibid.

[94] Andrew Greeley, The Catholic Experience (N.Y.: Doubleday 1969); Why Can't They Be Like Us? (N.Y.: E.P. Dutton, 1975); The American Catholic (N.Y.: Basic Books, 1977).

[95] Peter L. Berger, "The Socialist Myth" in Facing Up to Modernity (N.Y.: Basic Books, 1977).

[96] The Diocesan Implementation of "To Do The Work of Justice: A Plan of Action For The Catholic Community in the United States, Ad Hoc Committee on the Call to Action Plan, Sept. 15, 1980.

[97] Archbishop John Roach, "Doing Justice: Some Reflections on The Call to Action Plan" unpublished manuscript, March, 1979.

[98] Ibid.

[99] Personal statistical compilation of material mailed to me by Dr. Frank Butler.

[100] Ibid.

[101] The Diocesan Implementation of "To Do The Work of Justice: A Plan of Action For the Catholic Community in the United States, Ad Hoc Committee on

the Call to Action Plan, September 15, 1980.

[102] Ibid.

[103] Ibid.

[104] Personal interview with Dr. Frank Butler.

[105] Archbishop John Roach, op. cit., March, 1979.

[106] Bishops Pastoral Reply to the Call to Action, op. cit., May 19, 1977.

[107] Address of John Paul II to the Bishops of Brazil, Fortaleza, Brazil, July 10, 1980.

CHAPTER FIVE

CRITICISMS OF THE BICENTENNIAL
PROGRAM AND MOVEMENT

The spectrum and types of criticism levied at and during the Bicentennial Program was extraordinary in its breadth and intensity. The program was attacked by conservative factions, both clerical and lay, for its unrepresentativeness of American Catholic opinion on certain issues, its supposedly unthinkingly critical posture toward existing institutional arrangements, and for its implicit and allegedly heretical theological underpinnings. It was also the subject of ridicule from the viewpoint of the more radical fringe of the Catholic Church; a fringe convinced that nothing possibly good could result from a process operating from within the Church "defined as hierarchy". From the latter perspective, the whole program represented a clever strategy of lay containment on the part of the Bishops. The authors of the statement, "A Declaration of Christian Concern", claimed that the Call to Action represented a "revived clericalism--of the left". And finally, and perhaps most significantly for the future of American Catholicism, the Bicentennial movement gave evidence of a potentially divisive split within the American Catholic liberal camp itself; between what Andrew Greeley has termed the "old" form of Catholic social activism characterized by its practicality, pragmatism and issue-orientation and an emerging "new" form of Catholic social activism characterized by its more systematic and comprehensive critique of the existing social order, a critique calling for the "rational reconstruction of society" along presumably socialist lines. Within perhaps this ongoing and, at times, bitter "priestly-prophetic" exchange lies the elements of a creative synthesis indicative of the future of American Catholicism, or at least, of the future of liberal Catholicism in America. Conversely, a failure to compromise on the part of those two liberal factions might very well lead to the alienation from the Church of large numbers of individuals. During the Bicentennial Program the figures of Andrew Greeley and David J. O'Brien emerged as the symbolic and rather eloquent spokesmen of the "old" and "new" forms of Catholic social-theological activism.

The conservative theological criticism of the Call to Action involved the "heresy" of claiming a right to generate doctrine on the part of those not imbued with the teaching authority of the Church as passed down through the ages through the concept of "apostolic succession". This was expressed both concisely and lucidly by John Cardinal Krol of Philadelphia when he charged in Detroit that "the overwhelming thrust of the conference was to tell the institutional Church what to do rather than to remind the people of God what they have to do to realize the goals of 'Liberty and Justice for All'".[1] This point was reaffirmed by the then President of the N.C.C.B., Archbishop Joseph Bernardin, in his opening address at the May, 1977 Bishops' meeting. As Bernardin argued, "amidst the controversy of the Call to Action people have forgotten that the role of the Bishops as guardians of the faith is to lead and guide the rest of the Church".[2] The early reaction of the Vatican to the assembly was equally as unenthusiastic. One "high-ranking prelate in Rome", according to a story in Time magazine, said, "I'll take the event for what it was: an opportunity for anyone who had something to say to stand up and say it. The last word necessarily belongs to the hierarchy".[3] Pat Spencer, a lay delegate also reflected on the potentially diluting effect of the program on the teaching authority of Magisterium when she wrote of "liberal delegates ridiculing conservatives and laughing at wording taken from major Vatican documents".[4] Mrs. Spencer then declared that:

> the conference was a major victory for the advocates of a "new Christianity" which holds that "man is the center of the universe" and for those who make no distinction between Church and world, and hold that the Church is fraternal, with all members equal and with no need for hierarchy. Only the still solid working authority of the ordinary Magisterium, Pope and Bishops, stood against these ideas. Detroit was a mistake, a production of zealots.[5]

The conservative Catholic newspaper, The Wanderer, had criticized the unrepresentativeness of a part of an earlier stage of the Bicentennial Program. Speaking about the Washington Justice Hearing,

William H. Marshner declared:

> Had you been there, you could have witnessed Marxist-socialist Gary MacEoin denouncing Rerum Novarum and Quadragesimo Anno as self-contradictory; Brazilian Church activist Marina Vandeira vilifying the Church's history and that of her own country as a tale of oppression from the year 1600 to the present day; an employee of the U.N. International Year for Women, Ms. Irma De Mazelis, rejecting Western civilization outright; Sister Marie Augusta Neale, a professor of sociology, denouncing the family, no less, as presented in both the Old and the New Testaments, and rejecting every form of social or ecclesiastical hierarchy--and these people were not received as kooks. Every one of them had been formally invited by the Bicentennial Committee. Then the Bishops sat with stony faces, as their "guests" abused them, their country, and above all, their Christ. But the audience was not so impassive. Composed of Justice and Peace types from neighboring dioceses, Maryknollers on furlough from Peru, hard-faced nuns in pantsuits, and a scattering of bureaucrats from the U.S.C.C., it joyfully applauded the worst excesses.[6]

The article then went on to advise its readers that in order to improve one's chances of appearing before any of the remaining hearings one:

> . . . will do well to disguise yourself as a radical-chic researcher from the Center of Concern. Another good cover would be as a theologian of liberation from the Mexican-American Cultural Center, or failing that, here's one for the ladies that's money-back guaranteed: represent yourself as a former I.H.M. who has escaped sex-role stereotypes by becoming a full-feathered Comanche warrior.[7]

The article then closed by imploring conservative Catholics to make their presence known throughout the remainder of the Bicentennial Program.

101

"Then, at least, if the final record of the American Catholic Bicentennial program is an unrelieved shriek of hatred against the Faith and the Catholic people, the cause will be Cardinal Dearden's manipulation and not our fault".

Russell Kirk called the assembly "the monstrous baby of Cardinal Dearden of Detroit",[9] and portrayed the delegate population as follows:

> This (the conference) is a convention of Church Mice. By Church Mice I mean members, paid or volunteer, of the spreading bureaucracy of the Catholic Church in America . . . . Catholic Charities functionaries . . . malcontent newbreed nuns who would prefer anything to fasting and prayer; activist new breed priests of the sort who find lettuce boycotts far more lively than visiting the sick; members of parish committees and auxiliary organizations, parochial or provincial (at best) in their outlook; folk who have small knowledge of the real world beyond the shadow of the Church.[10]

Andrew Greeley, a leading figure of a populist American Catholic liberalism, characterized the constituency of the Detroit assembly as follows:

> . . . a ragtag assembly of kooks, crazies, flakes, militants, lesbians, homosexuals, ex-priests, incompetents, castrating witches, would-be messiahs, sickies, and other assorted malcontents.[11]

Furthermore, for Greeley,

> The Bishops should reject the entire proceedings and initiate a process of convening a truly representative, democratically elected, assembly and commission some regular, systematic high quality research . . . . (The Bishops ought to) reassert their control over what goes on in the Church . . . and replace the self-anointed messianic cults for the rest of us.[12]

102

as t...   · Greeley, however, offered no advice
"conve...   ...merican Catholic Church could
assembly   ...entative, democratically elected
lack of su...   ...haracterized by a complete
given the "o...   ...cal level. Furthermore,
"bread and but... ...y" of most ethnic,
as difficult to ... ...t seems almost equally
choice of liberal ... ...Bishops for their
backgrounds. David ... with social activist
"the most serious prob... ...a, while admitting that
...m of representation was the
apparent absence of significant numbers of working
class, European ethnic Catholics at Detroit", then
goes on to say that:

> While the complaints of the Polish community
> regarding representation were justified,
> their absence from diocesan delegations
> could not be blamed on the Bicentennial
> staff. Instead it appears that few ethnic
> Catholics are deeply involved in diocesan
> wide activities, or in major Church move-
> ments. Whether because of chancery dis-
> crimination or their own preoccupation
> with parochial or ethnic concerns, Polish,
> Slavic, and one suspects, Italian pastors,
> sisters, and lay people are invisible at
> the diocesan level. As a result, persons
> from these groups were less apt to show
> up when dioceses selected their delegations.
> In addition, it might be speculated that,
> Church professionals in specialized ministries,
> educated middle-class Catholics and poor
> people who look to the Church for support,
> all have reason to be interested in Church
> affairs beyond the parish level. Working
> class Catholics, Catholics in parishes they
> find satisfactory, and Catholics with no
> particular interest in Church policy may
> have neither the time nor inclination to
> join actively in Church programs beyond the
> parish. This too may help account for the
> relative lack of working class and European
> ethnic Catholics at the Call to Action
> Conference.[13]

Following a vote in a section meeting on the "ordination of women" Cardinal John Krol charged that "the conference had fallen into the clutches of

103

rebels".[14] For Krol, the Call to Action Conference was "manipulated by a few people who received the support of a naive group of little ladies".[15] But, added the Cardinal, "they won't make it. This isn't a legislative body".[16] Thomas Stahel reported that while at the conference "a Bishop friend walking down the hall calls me over to say that, before another one of these meetings, all the delegates should have to attend a . . . symposium on ecclesiology".[17] Stahel also reported "overhearing a prominent theologian commenting on the theological sophistication of the delegates by exclaiming, 'it's like asking a group of children to rewrite the constitution'".[18] James Finn reported that Father Charles Curran, a leading Catholic theologian, called the conference "a disaster".[19]

Thomas Fox also noted the theological reservations on the part of the underrepresented conservative Call to Action laity. "One delegate in a working section argued to other members that "Catholics in the pews back home will not understand and will be offended by the conference's recommendations".[20] Thomas Stahel reports that one woman, at a sub-section on "Women the Church", exclaimed in disbelief, "How can Roman Catholics even discuss the question of the ordination of women when the Holy Father has said there will be no women priests?"[21] And finally, (and reminiscent of the charge levied during the 1972 Democratic Presidential Convention by party regulars) Thomas Stahel recounts "one distraught woman approaching a Bishop and saying "Oh, Bishop, who are these delegates? They're all Indians, and blacks and Hispanics. Where are the regular people".[22]

It wasn't only conservatives who found fault with the Call to Action. A prominent group far to the left of many of even the staunchest advocates of the thrust of the Bicentennial charged that the program was guilty of a "clericalism of the left". The argument is that clergy and religious, since Vatican II, have tended to impose "from the top down" their agendas on the layman. Lay activity for the promotion of the Gospel's call for liberty and justice for all is, as such, hindered. The layman's concern for ordering the everyday realm of temporal affairs, "according to God's plan", his true calling, is neglected as such a clerical "top-down" approach encourages lay activity primarily within the realm of "internal Church matters". The Call to Action conference, due to an over-emphasis on "internal Church matters", is viewed, according to "A Chicago Declaration of Christian Concern", as something less than an unambiguous step forward for the laity. The document states:

> Our own reaction to the Detroit Call to Action conference reflects (an) ambivalence. Without a doubt it was historic, precedent setting in its conception, in its consultative process, in helping all levels of the Church listen to each other and in facing challenges to growth affecting the inner life of the Church. But devoting, as it did, so much of its time to the internal affairs of the Church, the conference did not sufficiently illuminate the broader mission of the Church to the world and the indispensible role of lay Christians in carrying out that mission.
>
> During the last decade, especially, many priests . . . and religious have sought to impose their own agendas for the world upon the laity. Indeed, if in the past the Church has suffered from a tendency to clericalism from the right, it may now face the threat of a revised clericalism--on the left.[23]

"A Declaration of Christian Concern", furthermore, makes a crucial claim regarding the role of the laity within most of the social programs that emanate from the church hierarchy:

> Although concerns for justice and peace are now built into Church bureaucracy more so than (ever before), there is no evidence that such bureaucratization has led to further involvement of lay Christians . . . We are deeply concerned that so little energy is devoted to encouraging and arousing lay responsibility for the world. The Church must constantly be reformed, but we fear that the most obsessive preoccupation with the Church's structures and pro-

cesses has diverted attention from the essential question: reform for what purpose? It would be one of the great ironies of history if the era of Vatican II which opened the windows of the Church to the world, were to close with a Church turned in upon herself.[24]

Sociologist John Coleman criticized the Chicago Declaration's claim of a new "clericalism of the left". Invoking Max Weber, Coleman claims that the main threat to the layman in his attempt to fulfill his proper religious role "called there by God" is <u>not</u> clericalism, but "Weber's prime bogeyman, the professional bureaucracy".[25] Coleman lucidly summarizes his position:

> The Declaration is wrong in . . . its allegation which draws a line mainly between clergy and laity instead of one between the new religious professional class (ordained or lay) and the laity in a worldly calling. Nor is the major threat to the Church in America that of a new clericalism of the left. The main danger is Weber's prime bogeyman, the professional bureaucracy. Because the professional bureaucracy predominated in the final convocation of Detroit's Call to Action, its preoccupation, like all bureaucracies, was with internal affairs. Bureaucracies-- even religious ones--are prone to the temptation of what Ivan Illich calls "professional monopoly". Despite a rhetoric of "service orientation" they tend to substitute self-interest, expert's control and mystification by certification for genuine service. Professionals have a penchant for turning coparticipant peers into clients. When they do so they lose touch--as the Declaration alleges--with their constituency.[26]

Coleman's insightful commentary highlights two very important points. The first is that both "conservatives" and "radicals" have a strong distaste for the reality of the bureaucratization of the American Catholic Church, although for totally different reasons. And second of all, Coleman's analysis makes clear that the voice of the layman heard in the American Catholic Church today, for better or worse, is the voice of the professional Catholic bureaucrat or specialist.

The Bicentennial Program and movement, finally, gave evidence of a potentially dangerous split within the liberal Catholic camp itself. Andrew Greeley[27] contends that there is a line of demarcation between the "old" and "new" Catholic social action; between a "pre-Berrigan" and a "post-Berrigan" approach to influencing people and facilitating social change. As Greeley, a strong advocate of the "old" Catholic social action, put it:

> preparation by the N.C.C.B. for the Bicentennial of the Republic may lead to a great debate about Catholic social action . . . I think it worthwhile to set down what seems to me some distinctions between the "old" Catholic social action and the "new" Catholic social action.[28]

The fundamental distinctions between these two approaches are as follows:

> 1. The old Catholic social action was practical and project oriented. It dealt with short-range problems, short-range goals. It was pragmatic partly by choice and partly because the personalities and training of the people involved did not predispose them to any other style.
>
> The new social action is systematic, principled and ideological. It has a mystique that inclines it to system-wide criticism and system-wide programs for reform.
>
> 2. The old Catholic social action was flexible, prone to compromise, ready--perhaps even eager--to tolerate the imperfections of the world. It is fundamentally accepting of the American social and economic system.
>
> The new Catholic social action is concerned with moral ideals and moral vision. It dreams of a neat and perfect world in which justice

reigns supreme. It wants no part of compromise, seriously raises the question as to whether socialism might just be a preferable alternative in American society to capitalism.

3. The old Catholic social actionists by and large respect American society and the American way of doing things. They are not unaware of the imperfections of American society but they look inward for the principles, the traditions, the methods by which American society can be both criticized and transformed.

The new Catholic activists are rigidly anti-American. They look outside American theology to Marxism, socialism and third world liberation theology for their principles and methods. They feel ashamed of the American people and seek to "raise their consciousnesses" preparatory to conversion.

4. The old social actionists are largely men of action: doers, not talkers.

The new social actionists are intellectuals . . . They are masters at manipulating words and sometimes ideas . . . They are fervant crusaders. Winning strikes, forming unions, organizing communities are not their "things", they are much more concerned about creating world economic justice.

5. The old social actionists are listeners, soaking up, absorbing everything they hear.

New social actionists tend not to be listeners; they are rather preachers intent on converting you or raising your consciousness. Dialogue with them is extremely difficult, if not impossible.

6. Finally, the old social action was self-consciously Catholic. It drew its principles from the Catholic social encyclicals and from the Catholic social teachings shaped in the early decades of this country in the United States.

The new social action is relatively little concerned with Catholic tradition, though it may occasionally quote a papal encyclical. Its positions, its programs, even its rhetoric are drawn from the currently fashionable liberal or "radical chic".[29]

For Andrew Greeley, the old social action is in the tradition of labor schools, labor priests, community organizations and Catholic interracial councils that have "mastered the politics of coalition building within the system". Leading figures in such a tradition include men like John Ryan, George Higgins, John Egan, Gene Baroni, and Henry J. Browne. The new Catholic social action, on the other hand, comes out of the Berrigan experience, and the peace movement and it is heavily involved in "confrontation" and "protest". As Greeley put it, the "new" Catholic action "exists to some extent in the Catholic Committee on Urban Ministry, to a greater extent in the Division of Justice and Peace of the U.S.C.C., and in totality in the Jesuit-sponsored Center for Concern".[30]

Greeley"s set of distinctions are terribly important given the liberal constituency of the Bicentennial movement. On one hand, there was no doubt whatsoever that educated conservative or working-class-ethnic Catholics were underrepresented at Detroit and throughout the program. This was, understandably enough, also the same case for these Catholics who feared that the Bicentennial Program represented a new emerging form of clericalism. On the other hand, however, the Bicentennial Movement attracted both the "old" and "new" social actionists as discussed by Greeley. In analyzing Greeley's distinction one must allow for the realities that:

(1) the alleged distinctions are not as sharp empirically as they are analytically,

(2) that great numbers of liberals have not thought through their own positions on Greeley's set of distinctions and, appear, willy-nilly, on both sides of the argument and

(3) that many liberals are reluctant to define the differences between themselves because of the close personal relationships

engendered by a "liberal wing" that has been, more or less, suppressed since "The Heresy of Americanism" episode around the turn of the century.

After making such allowances, one can still argue that Greeley's distinctions are intimately tied into an analysis of the ultimate state of the Bicentennial movement. Very simply, a victory for the former camp, advocates of what Max Weber has aptly termed the "ethics of responsibility",[31] especially in light of supportive theological legitimation, might guarantee that American Catholic liberalism will emerge as an important position in the American Church for many years to come. A victory for the more utopian advocates of what Weber has called the "ethics of absolute ends"[32] might very well lead to a total rejection of the movement by both conservative, and more importantly, moderate wings. The final result in such a case might very well be a move back into the direction of the conservative right in reaction and the loss, for the institutional Church, of large numbers of splinter groups of socialist-oriented leftists.

[1] John Cardinal Krol, quoted A Call to Action: The Church Prep Century, unpublished manuscript, J

[2] Archbishop Joseph Bernardin, quc above.

[3] "Report on the Call to Action", Time, November 8, 1978.

[4] Patricia Spencer, as reported in O'Brien, op. cit., July, 1978.

[5] Ibid.

[6] William H. Marshner "Bicentennial Alert", The Wanderer, February 20, 1975.

[7] Ibid.

[8] Ibid.

[9] Russell Kirk, "The Mice That Roared", National Review, December 10, 1976.

[10] Ibid.

[11] Greeley, quoted in O'Brien, op. cit., July 1978.

[12] Ibid.

[13] O'Brien, op. cit., July 1978.

[14] John Cardinal Krol quoted in Thomas Fox "Made in Detroit", Commonweal, Nov. 19, 1977.

[15] Ibid.

[16] Ibid.

[17] Thomas Stahel, "More Action Than They Called For", America, November 6, 1976.

[18] Ibid.

[19] Reported in James Finn, "Catholics Called to Action", *Worldview*, March 1977.

[20] Thomas Fox, op. cit., November 19, 1977.

[21] Stahel, op. cit., Nov. 6, 1977.

[22] Ibid.

[23] "A Chicago Declaration of Concern" in *Commonweal*, December, 1977.

[24] "A Chicago Declaration of Concern", op. cit., December, 1977.

[25] John Coleman, "The Worldly Calling", *Commonweal*, February 17, 1978.

[26] Ibid.

[27] Andrew Greeley, "Catholic Social Activism: Real or Rad/Chic?", *The National Catholic Reporter*, February 7, 1975.

[28] Ibid.

[29] Ibid.

[30] Ibid.

[31] Max Weber, "Politics as a Vocation" in *From Max Weber* (editors H.H. Gerth and C.W. Mills) (N.Y.: Oxford University Press, 1956).

[32] Ibid.

PART III

THE PRESUPPOSITIONS OF THE
BICENTENNIAL PROGRAM AND MOVEMENT

CHAPTER SIX

THE CULTURAL PRESUPPOSITION:
THE AMERICAN CIVIL RELIGION
AND THE
THEOLOGY OF VATICAN II

In this chapter the "cultural" presupposition for the American Catholic Bicentennial movement will be analyzed. Such an analysis will argue that, in the minds of the movement's advocates, the promulgation of Vatican II theology marked a legitimation for the religious dimension most historically meaningful for American Catholic liberalism, that of the American Civil Religion. The American Civil Religion will be defined as the public or central religious dimension of a United States that is politically democratic, pluralistic in terms of denomination centered religiosity, structurally differentiated, concerned with humanistically oriented issues and possessing a belief in the One God common throughout the Biblical Orbit. The empirical evidence that is illustrative of this assertion lies in both the form and content of the overwhelming percentage of the Call to Action proposals. These proposals are consonant, in varying degrees and of course with certain qualifications, with the historical vision of liberal Catholicism from the earliest period of its American existence. With the legitimation of the theology of the Second Vatican Council, they now take on prophetic meaning as sanctioned Catholic activity. Most generally, it will be pointed out that those Call to Action proposals which were oriented centripetally, i.e., toward "internal" Church questions of reform were consonant with both the American Civil Religion and with the spirit of Vatican II in that they stressed the need for the Church to evolve structures that fit the democratic, voluntaristic, pluralistic and fraternalistic culture of the United States. Those Call to Action proposals, on the other hand, which were directed more in a centrifugal direction, i.e., "toward the world", were also in line with both religious constructions in that they stressed a strong concern for social activism to bring about justice for all people regardless of religious, racial, ethnic, or sexual affiliation, in the name of God, and in conjunction with any/all religious, humanistic, or governmental associations willing to cooperate in such endeavors.

While the Bicentennial movement is being analyzed as inspired at the cultural level by the American Civil Religion as filtered through a selective reading of Vatican II theology, mention must be made of the role of the "theology of liberation" for a certain "lead" segment of the New Catholic Knowledge Class. The latter theological construction is both similar and dissimilar to the American Civil Religion. The basic similarity of the Marxist-Christian synthesis with the American Civil Religion lies in its concern for the institutionalization of this worldly justice in the name of the Biblical God. The basic dissimilarity lies in the acceptance of the former of socialism as the vehicle for such an institutionalization. The American Civil Religion, on the other hand, promises redemption through a covenant made between God and his new "chosen" nation, the United States. Given the historical failure of socialism--until relatively recently--to capture the hearts and minds of even a significant minority of either the American or American Catholic populations, it is clear that liberal social activist movements associated with religious denominations--whether Catholic or not--were for the most part not inspired by socialism but rather by the promises inherent in an American nation defined as the latest in a series of "new Israels". In the Catholic case, the recent introduction of the theology of liberation has made strong in-roads among the more radical segment of the contemporary liberal Catholic social activist camp-- among what will later be termed the "ideological-intellectual" camp of the New Catholic Knowledge Class. Like the American Civil Religion, the theology of liberation is strengthened, in the minds of its advocates at least, by a selective reading of Vatican II theology. Even today, however, the case remains that the more general, and by far and away, more historically relevant cultural support system for the liberal wing of the American Catholic Church is that of the American Civil Religion. It is this religious dimension as filtered through a selective reading of Vatican II theology that constitutes our immediate concern here. The role of the theology of liberation will be analyzed in greater detail at a later point.

Before analyzing the nature of the American Civil Religion and its relationship to American Catholicism and then to Vatican II theology, it is first important to discuss and define the nature of religion in general. Religion will be defined here as a view that everyday earthly reality is imbued by the supernatural, an explanation of human experience as permeated by a sense of what Rudolf Otto[1] has termed something "totally other" than human, through which, depending on social and psychological circumstance, either entire societies, groups, or individuals make sense of their lives. It is important to point out two things about the religious experience. The first is that it is being defined in such a way as to exclude explanations of reality that are distinctly and totally "humanistic", like for instance, the "scientific socialism" of Karl Marx or the "psychoanalytic" interpretations of Sigmund Freud. This, emphatically, does not rule out as "religious" those cases in which religious explanations are inextricably interwined with human, "earthly" interpretations. The second is that religion operates at different levels, or "frames of reference" through which the religious experience is mediated, i.e., is made "real" in everyday thought and activity.[2] The three different levels are those of the individual, the societal sub-group, and the society-at-large. These different levels constitute a "private-public" continuum of the forms of religious expression.[3]

In small and totally encapsulated pre-industrial communities religion permeates every sphere of social thought and activity. It provides, in and by itself, a truly comprehensive explanation of the daily round of events experienced by any one individual. Religion, in such settings, explains in a definitive fashion, "the meaning of life". It is a thoroughly "public" affair in the strictest Durkheimian sense,[4] in terms of both its scope and source. At the other extreme, and for a very few individuals regardless of social context and who are highly creative, charismatic, and individualistic to the borderline of psychosis, religion may very well be a truly "private" affair, in terms of both scope and source, a matter of "personal experience". Much more frequently, the "frame of reference" through which religion operates is through some primary group such as the extended family, village community, or city-state. Such a discussion follows an intellectual

117

tradition that stretches from Durkheim's teacher, Fustel de Coulanges The Ancient City[5] to one of his contemporary students, Will Herbert Protestant, Catholic, Jew.[6] "Earthly", "public", and more purely pragmatic concerns of the "everyday round of existence" are interwined with supernatural considerations on occasions like birth, death, marriage, and other special dates, both solemn and festive. Religion is, following the logic of the symbolic interactionist G.H. Mead's discussion of the "I" and "Me",[7] both private and public in nature as the individual's perceived contact with the forces of the divine is impinged upon, infused with, "made a reality through", the broader, public world of symbols. In a real sense, all religious apprehension is "symbolic"; it is symbolic in the sense that the internalization of the devine requires a culturally specific worldview.

Using as an example the case of first generation Italian Americans, Catholicism as a religion was made "real" in everyday thought and practice through the veil of southern Italian family and village customs and beliefs.[8] This was much to the chagrin of the Irish clergy who thought such customs and beliefs (a belief in the "evil eye", charms to protect oneself and one's house, praying to God for luck in gambling, making "deals" with one's patron saints, etc.) to be paganistic at worst and infused with magical elements at best. The frame of reference of many second through fourth generation Italian American Catholics, especially those residing in heterogeneous ethnic suburbs and away from the "national parishes" of the inner-city, is, much to the relief (at least historically) of the Catholic hierarchy, that of a "church-centered" Catholicism defined by Catholic theological experts as "official", "pure" and formally and legalistically correct. A belief in the existence of evil spirits is, for instance, replaced with an understanding of the role of the antichrist. Or perhaps, one's understanding of the place that Mary, Mother of God, holds in the Catholic universe is downplayed as the figure of Jesus is highlighted. Neighborhood religious festivals and other "particularistic" devotional forms are either eliminated or lose importance as the "universality" of the celebration of mass and the partaking of the sacraments are stressed. For some modern day Italian American Catholics, again to the chagrin of the hierarchy, the frame of reference in which Catholicism is mediated extends even more in a centrifugal direction, i.e., away from a "churchy" definition of what Catholicism is to a Catholicism that is more intimately involved with the broader symbol system of the American nation, or that of the international perspective of Marxism, or that of the world community. In the specific case of American Catholicism, one would put it sociologically by asserting that "Catholicism in the United States has progressively been institutionalized at higher levels of generality"[9] as a once immigrant population becomes ever more acculturated into a national or world cultural system. Conceptions of "particularity" and "universality" are constantly upgraded. To be a "liberal Catholic" at the turn of the century meant to be an "Americanizer" and against the concept of the national ethnic parish. To be a "liberal Catholic" today means (for many) to be aware of Catholic America's commitment to the broader world community. A total commitment to America, once the hallmark of liberal Catholicism, is now characteristic to many of the "conservative Catholic" position in America. For many modern American Catholics, one may very well "symbolically"--this time perhaps more consciously--interpret the meaning of the anti-christ, or that of the Real Presence of Christ in the Eucharist instead of accepting a more "fundamentalist" position. Perhaps one starts to take less seriously the basis in either Scripture or Church tradition upon which the authority of the Bishops' status in the Church rests. Such a Catholic defines--as all Catholics before him did--his Catholicism in a way that "fits" the ever new worlds of meaning that he encounters as his social and geographic locations constantly change. In all these cases it is the individual who "rearranges" both the components of his Catholicism and of non-Catholic culture to make his religion and overall worldview relevant to the immediate world that surrounds him. As the individual Catholic's moral vision extends, the strain towards consistency between thought and praxis, however imperfectly realized in most is maintained through the process of syncretization.

The point is to stress that religion is, for the overwhelming percentage of everyday individuals, "mediated", that is, made real in everyday thought and activity through many different symbolic constructions of reality, be it the family, one's ethnic group, one's neighborhood, one's local parish congregation, one's nation, one's political philosophy, or concept of world community. One can properly argue the case that all religious sentiment has a dual source of generation, that of religious experience in a "pure" form akin to Rudolph Otto's psychologically grounded conception of the "numinous"[10] and that same experience as articulated sociologically through humanly-created symbolic constructions of reality in line with Mircea Eliade's conception of "hierophanies".[11]

Of more immediate relevance is the assertion that for some modern day American Catholics it is partially through the nation and that of the world community that their Catholicism is imbued with a relevance, a realness in human consciousness. The conversation in thought and activity for these Catholics--Catholics whose "everyday round of existence" is intimately involved with "public sphere" considerations--is between the driving force of their reason and their inner divinity on the one hand, and, on the other, an interesting affinity between the national and world level symbolic constructions of the American Civil Religion and Vatican II theology. (Again, it must be pointed out that for the more radical segment of the Catholic left in America the internal dialogue is much more apt to include the Marxist inspired "theology of liberation".) In great part, it was such conversations that took place throughout the Bicentennial program and represent constitutive features of the sociological social-psychology of contemporary American Catholic liberalism.

The American Civil Religion has previously been defined as the public or central religious dimension of a United States that is democratic politically, pluralistic in terms of denomination centered religiosity, structurally differentiated, concerned with humanistically oriented issues, and possessing a belief in the One God common throughout the Biblical Orbit. As Robert Bellah in his "Civil Religion in America" put it:

> . . . few have realized that there actually exists alongside of and rather clearly differentiated from the churches an elaborate and well-institutionalized civil religion in America . . . I conceive of the central tradition of the American Civil Religion not as a form of national self-worship but as the subordination of the nation to

ethical principles that transcend it and
in terms of which it should be judged . . .
the civil religion was not . . . ever felt
to be a substitute for Christianity. Under
the doctrine of religious liberty, an
exceptionally wide sphere of personal piety
and voluntary social action was left to
the churches.[12]

It is Talcott Parsons who has written most incisively on this religious dimension. As Parsons writes:

The three dominant "faiths" of American
society have come to be integrated into a
single socio-religious system, a development that even in the late 19th century
seemed highly unlikely. This system has
evolved under the historical leadership
of American liberal Protestantism but has
very much involved and modified all three
faiths. For instance, the parish status
of the Jewish faith . . . has been modified,
not only through greater "toleration" of
Jews by Gentiles, but also by a new level
of Jewish acceptance of the legitimacy of
the outside order in which Jews come into
contact with Gentiles, especially in the
occupational system. For all Jews except
the most rigidly orthodox, a religiously
sanctioned life is no longer confined to
the internal life of the Jewish community.
The position of the Roman Catholic community
in the U.S. is undergoing similar modifications, of which visible indices can be found
in the broad acceptance of a Roman Catholic
president and the American Catholic hierarchy's failure to repudiate the president's
expressed position on the separation between
Church and State. These changes have
occurred by a developmental restructuring,
without a prophetic break with the established order. The basic value pattern common
to all three faiths has been at least partially
institutionalized at a higher level of generality.[13]

What, then, is the role of the traditionally-defined organized religions vis-a-vis the American

Civil Religion? Parsons answers that:

> from a religious point of view, this means the discrimination of two layers of religious commitment. One of these is the layer which defines the bases of denominational membership and differentiates one denomination from another. The other is a common matrix of value-commitment which is broadly shared between denominations, and which forms the basis of the sense in which the society as a whole forms a religiously based moral community. This has, in the American case, been extended to cover a very wide range. Its core certainly lies in the institutionalized Protestant denominations, but with certain strains and only partial institutionalization, it extends to three other groups of the first importance; the Catholic Church, to various branches of Judaism, and, not least important, those who prefer to remain aloof from any formal denominational affiliation. To deny that this underlying consensus exists would be to claim that American society stood in a state of latent religious war. Of the fact that there are considerable tensions every responsible student of the situation is aware. Institutionalization is incomplete, but the consensus is very much a reality.[14]

In an earlier essay, Parsons had this to say about the incomplete institutionalization of the American Civil Religion:

> The American system is far from being fully integrated. It must contend with important elements which are anchored in earlier patterns of religious organization, notably fundamentalist Protestantism and the Catholic Church, both of which make claims which are anomalous within the main American framework. It (also) must contend with the proliferation of exotic religious movements of dubious longer-

run religious soundness . . . . It must
finally contend with the various aspects
of secularism . . . . On balance, however,
I think that the main trend is toward
greater integration of these various
elements in a viable system which can be
a vital part of a larger society.[15]

Parsons elaborates on the specific "strain" and "partial institutionalization" of the pre-Vatican II American Catholic Church into the American Civil Religion:

> It is perhaps to be expected that in this setting the policies of the Catholic Church should exhibit a certain lag relative to the rest of American society. It has been, particularly in the last generation or two, taking advantage of the framework of American religious toleration, setting out to create a complete system of religious education whereby, in ideal, the Catholic child will from primary school through the university be educated exclusively in church-controlled organizations. This is only one the variety of respects in which the Catholic Church occupies a special position in American society, but it may be a question of how far it will be able to maintain this special policy in the face of powerful general forces pointing in another direction.[16]

Parsons revised somewhat his evaluation of the "special" or "anomalous" position that the American Catholic Church occupies within the greater American cultural matrix in light of the Second Vatican Council:

> Eventually, through many conflicts and struggles, Protestantism and Catholicism have come to constitute differentiated sectors of the same ecumenical religious community. The inclusion of Jews in such a community was, again, not a very long step . . . . The great steps of our time have, of course, been those taken by the Roman Church with the Papacy of John XXIII and Vatican Council II, which he called into being.[17]

123

Parsons sums up this development of a single "socio-religious system" up to and including recent elements of a "rationalistic secularism" that simultaneously allows for the continuation of an important, although somewhat more limited, role for the traditionally organized religions:

> The older patterns do not disappear, but continue to function, though in modified form, which often means in more restricted circumstances than before. Thus to go way back, Christianity did not extirpate Judaism, but the latter is now persisting ecumenically together with a wide variety of Christian churches and sects. Protestantism did not extirpate Catholicism, nor vice-versa and they not only coexist peacefully but have become integrated into a more general religious structure. Then, very recently, I suggest, rationalistic secularism has not only failed to extirpate church religion, but has gone far toward becoming included with it as a still broader religious framework, in which all the older religious groups-- with some qualifications--survive.[18]

Interestingly enough, Parsons only half-facetiously adds that:

> I look forward to the day when, in a Jewish, Catholic, or Protestant high ceremony like the Kennedy Memorial Mass, the Director of the Institute of Philosophy of the Soviet Academy of Sciences--a post which I interpret to be the equivalent of Dean of the Theology faculty of the religion of Marxism-Leninism--will march in the procession and sit in the sacristy as one of the assemblage of the clergy of all faiths.[19]

Just what, in some more detail, are some of the underlying assumptions about man and society that the conception of the American Civil Religion presupposes? How does the conception of the American Civil Religion fit in with our previous discussion of the nature of the religious experience? Of what relevance is such a conception for American Catholicism?

Regarding the former, it first of all presupposes the usefulness of positing the basic Durkheimian assumption that all societies are bound together by some overarching symbol-system that provides some minimal form and articulation to that society. Within these boundaries, "meaningful", "moral", "understandable" activity occurs. Outside of these boundaries, a meaningless void exists. To someone standing within the societal circle, thought and action occurring outside of those boundaries are "incomprehensible", much akin to what anthropologists call "culture shock". The claim here is that the American Civil Religion represents for contemporary America the actualization of the Durkheimian premise.

The conception of the American Civil Religion, furthermore, presupposes that, like any other symbol-system, it is always imperfectly and unevenly realized in society. There is always present, more or less depending on social circumstance, a differential distribution of attachment to any value system. In fact, in any society one can posit a continuum of individuals who range from being "in" society to those merely "of" society. Put another way, people unevenly partake of "the action" either psychologically, socially, materially, or physically in any society. In terms of something more relevant for American Catholicism, one can say that, with the exception of a few clerical and lay leaders, the history of American Catholicism until recently has been a history of various immigrant peoples more "of" American society than "in" it. Put another way, Catholic religious sensibilities have been "mediated", made "real" in thought and action far short of the society-wide symbol system, i.e., at the family, neighborhood, ethnic group or institutional Church level. One speaks here not so much of the alleged pre-Vatican II "Catholic ghetto", but of a seemingly infinite number of more or less segregated ghettoes along familial, ethnic, parish, and neighborhood lines. Using for the moment the distinction between the "public sphere" institutions of the State, economy, and educational system and the "private sphere" institutions of the family, ethnicity, neighborhood, and parish,[20] one can say that, historically speaking, Catholics have had a fragmentary and incomplete participation in "public sphere" activities. However, as Catholics become more middle-class, professionally-oriented and highly educated, as the "frame of reference" by which their Catholicism is actualized becomes wider, they simultaneously become more "in" society, more involved "publicly", and more included in the abstract, outwardly-looking considerations of the American Civil Religion.[21]

Several characteristics of the American Civil Religion should be pointed out. First of all, the American Civil Religion has the characteristic of a rather broad scope, serving as it does as a common denominator religious expression in a society that is denominationally pluralistic. This rather broad scope allows it to serve as the vehicle for conversation, compromise, and synthesis. More specifically, it is that religious expression that seeks out the commonalities of the Judeo-Christian (and perhaps, very soon, the Islamic) religious traditions with its central conception of an all-powerful and all-merciful God, utterly and majestically transcendent, active in the affairs of human history, demanding of justice, love and obedience, and judging morally responsible individuals for their earthly involvements. It is a religious belief system that is characterized by what Max Weber has termed "inner-worldly ascetism",[22] that the kingdom of God is to be constructed, as far as humanly possible, here on earth, by human beings who embrace the world, not for the world, but against the world and in the name of God. John Kennedy's phrase, uttered in his Presidential Inaugural address, that "God's work must truly be our own" marks clearly the orientation of a certain segment of American Catholics to this ecumenically-oriented religious dimension. Furthermore, the ecumenical nature of the American Civil Religion extends itself "to all men of good will", most definitely including individuals from outside the Biblical orbit, both religious and secular. Following the previous discussion of Parsons, it is the case that the common religious symbols of the Biblical orbit are inextricably interwoven with various humanistic threads that are Enlightenment in origin, man-centered, shorn of any supernatural referent but that, nonetheless, blend in at certain points due to the ethical, prophetic, partially world-affirming nature of the Biblical orbit, especially with its liberal Protestant vanguard.

The development of the American Civil Religion is concomitant with a society that is "structurally differentiated".[23] By this is meant that institutions once directly influenced by religious organizations now take on a partial autonomy. The classical example of a direct religious influence is that of the European Middle Ages and the role that Catholicism played in defining political, economic, educational and family life. Historical events and social forces such as the Enlightenment, the Renaissance, the Reformation, urbanization, and industrialization are seen here not so much as destroying organizational religion, but making organizational religious influence on these disparate institutions much more indirect and voluntary. This indirect and voluntary contribution of religion to other spheres of life is embodied in the United States in the first amendment of the Constitution. The import of the "separation of church and state" is that no organizational religion is to be established in this country and that organizational religious and civic spheres are to be separated, at least in a formal sense. No religious body in this country has, for instance, the right to impose itself directly in matters of economic and political exchange, marriage, divorce, or educational instruction. The various "denominations", of course, are still capable of influencing these spheres, but only indirectly as "interest groups" through the democratic political process and to the degree that they successfully "socialize" those individuals involved in such activities. The key term to note here is the word "voluntary". Simply put, both attachment to organizational religion either in and by itself or the promoting of organizationally defined religious themes in non-religious symbolic spheres is a matter of choice and personal commitment.

Several qualifications must be quickly noted. First, the American Civil Religion is not granted a "realness", a "facticity", by a significant part of the American population. For many Americans, it is (reversing W.I. Thomas's famous dictum) a social construction not defined as real and hence of no consequence in either daily thought and action. For many individuals, religious sensibilities are usually met within smaller, less inclusive frames of reference. The non-reality of the American Civil Religion has, for far fewer, like Peter Berger[24] and Thomas Luckmann[25] a self-conscious intellectual rejection. Such scholars deny, through their discussion of the "privatization" of religion in modern life, the possibility that religion can be an effective "public" force in society. Secondly, there are those who agree to the publicness of the phenomenon, but deplore its existence. These types run the gambit from orthodox believers, like Will Herberg[26] (who consider the existence of the American Civil Religion to constitute a threat to the continued existence of the traditional faiths), to those avowed humanistic atheists like Edward Shils[27] or Sigmund Freud[28] (who feel that the existence of a belief in the supernatural to be hindering the development of a true humanism).

Thirdly, the American Civil Religion has been criticized by those who feel that it represents a symbol system in some sort of idolatrous support of the American nation. This is a position that runs the gambit from orthodox theologians like Will Herberg to socialist-leaning leftists like David J. O'Brien.

Fourthly, the American Civil Religion is a vague, and at least vis-a-vis the more established religions, "contentless" phenomenon. It is far from being crystallized clearly in even the minds of its strongest proponents. It has no definite dogma or unambiguous prophetic figures. The indeterminacy of the phenomenon, however, does not deny either its existence or its usefulness. The existence of the American Civil Religion allows for dialogue, respect and possible synthesis among disparate positions. And finally, at least given the present amorphous state of the American Civil Religion, it does not serve to radically preempt the commitment and loyalty of individuals to their traditionally defined religious attachments. Those individuals whose "frame of reference" is broad enough to include the numerous disparate intellectual and religious traditions of the American Civil Religion, have, in all likelihood, this religious dimension refracted through their own denominational attachment. This type of attachment, however, would hardly be considered as theologically "adequate" by the more traditionally orthodox or as politically "adequate" by advocates of the theology of liberation.

That the American Civil Religion, or something analogous to it, held the devotion of at least a significant segment of the Catholic intellectual leadership in the 19th century is suggested by Andrew Greeley:

> . . . it is true that many of the themes
> and practices of American Catholic life
> at the turn of the century, particularly
> in those dioceses where liberal leadership
> such as Gibbons, Ireland, Keane, and
> Spalding were in power, were profoundly
> threatening to Rome. Ironically, most
> of these emphases--openness to non-
> Catholics, strong social concern, con-
> sultation with clergy and laity in
> decision making, optimism about the
> modern world, willingness to conduct
> a dialogue with anyone, endorsement of
> scientific and technical progress--
> became Church policy after the Second
> Vatican Council.[29]

It is also quite plausible to speculate that the religious dimension most meaningful to pre-Vatican II liberal social activists was not that of existing Catholic theology but some sort of inarticulately perceived and half-understood American Civil Religion. That perhaps this is more than just mere speculation is made clear by Robert Cross's description of The Faith of Our Fathers, the magnum opus of the turn of the century advocate of liberal Catholicism, James Cardinal Gibbons:

> The Faith of Our Fathers sought to answer
> (Protestant) objections by finding analogies
> to American ideals; papal infallibility was
> compared to the power of the supreme court,
> the adoration of the Virgin to American's
> traditional respect for womanhood. Over
> and over, Gibbons denied that any grounds
> existed for doubting Catholic's reverence
> and loyalty to American political and social
> institutions. He was a master apologist, and
> his book became one of the best sellers of
> American religious history.[30]

The argument to be presented subsequently is that Vatican II theology bears a certain affinity to the American Civil Religion that has allowed the liberal Catholic position in America to assert itself publicly and with far less fear of reprisal from the conservative element of the Church hierarchy. The claim is not that Vatican II theology is equivalent to, or endorses the reality of the American Civil

Religion. The claim is that the "spirit", if not the "law", of Vatican II theology approximates the American Civil Religion enough for certain liberal Catholics to blur any meaningful distinction between these two theological constructions. Practically, if not theoretically, the Bicentennial movement was, for some, a call to merge American Catholicism into the more inclusive religious dimension of American society. Theoretically, if not necessarily practically, the aim is to "Catholicize" hitherto non-Catholic culture. Here, as always, one must be aware of the social-psychological realities of an imperfect internalization of Vatican II theology or that of any ideational system and that of the "selective perception"--both unselfconsciously and consciously--of components of an ideational system. The phrase "one sees what one wants to see, or what one was brought up to see" makes the social-psychological point. Prior to Vatican II, the liberal wing of American Catholicism, with the exception of a few great "social encyclicals", namely, Leo XIII's Rerum Novarum and Pope Pius XI's Quadragesimo Anno, had no theological support for Catholic sponsored programs making a demand for "liberty and justice for all". And even these encyclicals provided far from sufficient legitimation for a strong, viable American Catholic liberal wing to emerge.

In order to make this latter point more forcibly, the theology of Vatican I can be contrasted to that of Vatican II. The point to be made is that the "inwardly-looking", "authoritarian", "Roman", posture of a Vatican I theology is far less sympathetic to the spirit of the American Civil Religion than the more "outwardly-looking", "democratic", "western", posture of the theology of Vatican II.[31] Vatican I is "conservative" in that it stresses that the leadership of the Church properly and exclusively belonged to the Pope and, more practically, given a limited communications network, to the individual Bishop in his diocese. Furthermore, the view was that salvation was to found only through the Church and that, as such, Catholic participation in non-Catholic affairs was dangerous, if not sinful. The latter, conversely, is "liberal" in that it stressed the concept of "collegiality" implying shared authority among all baptized Catholics in a Church defined as "the people of God" and that, furthermore, salvation could be found outside the Church. Catholic participation with "all men of good will", a central tenet of the American

Civil Religion, was to be encouraged. These theological constructions which emanate from Rome have a strong, if unevenly distributed, impact on the nature of the American Church both "internally" and in terms of its relationship to non-Catholic culture.

In 1864, Pope Pius IX issued the Syllabus of Errors, containing the "Eighty Principal Errors of our Time". A few of the condemnations, striking in both their theological intransigence and in their stark opposition to the spirit of the American Civil Religion, Vatican II theology and the American Bicentennial movement, are as follows:

5. Divine revelation is imperfect and therefore subject to continual and indefinite progress, corresponding with the progress of human reason.

15. Every man is free to embrace and profess that religion, which guided by the light of reason, he shall consider true.

16. Man may, in the observance of any religion whatever, find the way of eternal salvation, and arrive at eternal salvation.

17. Good hope, at least, is to be entertained of the eternal salvation of all those who are not at all in the true Church of Christ.

18. Protestantism is nothing more than another form of the same true Christian religion, in which form it is given to please God equally as in the Catholic Church.

21. The Church has not the power of defining dogmatically that the religion of the Catholic Church is the only true religion.

37. National Churches, withdrawn from the authority of the Roman Pontiff and altogether separated, can be established.

38. The State, as being the origin and source of all rights, is endowed with a certain right not circumscribed by any limits.

55. The Church ought to be separated from the State, and the State from the Church.

56. Moral laws do not stand in need of the divine sanction, and it is not at all necessary that human laws should be made conformable to the laws of nature and receive their power of binding from God.

57. The science of philosophical things and morals and also civil laws may and ought be kept aloof from divine and ecclesiastical authority.

77. In the present day it is no longer expedient that the Catholic religion should be held as the only Religion of the State, to the exclusion of all other forms of worship.

80. The Roman Pontiff can, and ought to, reconcile himself and come to terms with progress, liberalism, and modern civilization as lately introduced.[32]

It is clear that "modern civilization as lately introduced" is to be fought where possible, and where not, at least ignored. The Syllabus of Errors expresses, in quintessential form, the "conservative" Catholic opinion that the outside world is, at worst, evil, and, at very best, neutral. To embrace such a world, even if but in dialogue, or to allow any but those who stand in succession to Peter to guide the Church through such murky waters, would eventually mean the self-destruction of the Catholic religion.

In 1870, during the Vatican I Council Pope Pius IX issued the Dogma of Papal Infallibility, thus strengthening the "centralizing" power of the Papacy, and, matter-of-factly, that of the Papal bureaucracy, the Curia. As Pius IX declares in the encyclical:

Therefore faithfully adhering to the tradition received from the beginning of the Christian faith, for the glory of God our Savior, the exaltation of the Catholic religion, and the salvation of Christian people, the Sacred Council approving, we teach and define that it is a dogma divinely revealed: that the Roman Pontiff, when he speaks ex cathedra, that is, when in discharge of the office of pastor and doctor of all Christians, by virtue of his supreme Apostolic authority, he defines a doctrine regarding faith or morals to be held by the universal Church, by the divine assistance promised him by Peter, is possessed of that infallibility with which the divine redeemer willed that his Church should be endowed for defining doctrine regarding faith or morals; and therefore such definitions of the Roman Pontiff are irreformable of themselves, and not from the consent of the Church. But if any one--which may God avert--presume to contradict this our definition: let him be anathema.[33]

While the political intransigence of the Church crumbled in light of the acknowledgment of the irreversable development of autonomous nation-states, its theological intransigence continued, more or less, until the startling turn of events ushured in during Vatican II. This continued intransigence can be best expressed through the Encyclical Letter of Pope Pius X, Pascendi: Dominici Gregis "On the Doctrine of the Modernists",[34] and the Syllabus of his Inquisition, Lamentabili Sane,"Syllabus Condemning the Errors of the Modernists",[35] both published in 1907, which served to suppress the so-called "modernist movement"--"the synthesis of all heresies"--within the Church at the turn of the twentieth century.

Modernism can most generally be described as a religious interpretation of Catholicism that downplays the acknowledgement of divinely inspired revelation as mediated by the authority of the Church hierarchy and through Church tradition and highlights religious explanations that proceed from within man and through human experience. It is a religion of "immanence" and not of transcendence. If one defines "objective" as "that defined by the Church hierarchy", then modernism is clearly a "subjective" religious interpretation. It is predicated on the belief that one can find God internally by personal experience and private inspiration and not primarily through the teaching of the Church and by external signs. As such, according to conservative orthodox critics, the uniqueness of Catholicism is replaced by the perceived "realness" in human consciousness of any "religious" experience. "Modernism" can be viewed as the natural prelude to the emergence of the so-called "secular theologies" of contemporary liberal Protestantism and of the "theology of liberation", the attempted marriage of Christianity and Marxism. Both are consistent with "modernism" in that "experience", "praxis", and "personal interpretation", gain ascendency over "divinely inspired" revelation as mediated through the Magisterium and the worship of the transcendent God.[36]

As Pope Pius X, quite in line with Vatican I logic, put it in Pascendi Dominci Gregis:

> From this, Venerable Bretheren, springs that most absurd tenet of the Modernists, that every religion, according to the different aspect under which it is viewed, must be considered both natural and supernatural. It is thus that they make consciousness and relevation synonymous. From this they derive the law laid down as the universal standard, according to which religious consciousness is to be put on an equal footing with revelation, and to it all must submit, even the supreme authority of The Church, whether in the capacity of teacher, or in that of legislature in the province of sacred liturgy or discipline.[37]

The propositions of Lamentabili Sane may help illustrate more clearly the Church's Vatican I inspired negative mentality toward religious individualism, toward a dynamic view of the relationship between Catholicism and history, and toward forms of non-Catholic culture. A few of the "condemned and proscribed" propositions are as follows:

> 2. The Church's interpretation of the Sacred Books is by no means to be rejected; nevertheless, it is subject to the more accurate judgement and correction

of the exegetes.

5. Since the deposit of Faith contains only revealed truths, the Church has no right to pass judgement on the assertions of the human sciences.

7. In proscribing errors, the Church cannot demand any internal assent from the faithful by which judgements she issues are to be embraced.

12. If he wishes to apply himself usefully to Biblical studies, the exegete must first put aside all preconceived opinions about the supernatural origin of Sacred Scripture and interpret it the same way as any other merely human document.

21. Revelation, constituting the object of the Catholic faith, was not completed with the Apostles.

22. The dogmas the Church holds out as revealed are not truths which have fallen from Heaven. They are an interpretation of religious facts which the human mind has acquired by laborious effort.

53. The organic constitution of the Church is not immutable. Like human society, Christian society is subject to a perpetual evolution.

58. Truth is no more immutable than man himself, since it evolved with him, in him and through him.

64. Scientific progress demands that the concepts of Chrisitan doctrine concerning God, creation, revelation, the Person of the Incarnate Word, and Redemption be re-adjusted.

65. Modern Catholicism can be reconciled with true science only if it is transformed into a non-dogmatic Christianity; that is to say, into a broad and liberal Protestantism.[38]

Only once in American Catholic history has its official orthodoxy of doctrine been called into question by the Papacy. The "Heresy of Americanism" at the turn of the century involved, very broadly, a series of differences within the American Catholic hierarchy on such questions as to the proper relationship of American Catholics to non-Catholic organizations like labor unions, the teachings of socialist oriented American political figures like Henry George, and Catholic participation in ecumenical religious gatherings like the World's Parliament of Religions which was held in Chicago in 1893. In general, liberals or "Americanizers" were tolerant of such activities, philosophies and events while conservatives or "anti-Americanizers" were not. These series of disagreements came to a head over the question of the orthodoxy of certain of the ideas of the distinctly "liberal" Father Hecker, a Protestant convert, who stressed the importance of the relationship of the Holy Spirit to the individual Catholic, at the expense, as claimed by the conservatives, of the "external guidance" of the Church. "Americanism", the conservatives declared, smacked, among other things of an undue "subjectivism", inevitably leading to the placing of "natural" virtues over those "supernatural".

In 1899, Pope Leo XIII intervened in the dispute, both in a general and specific way, by issuing his Encyclical, <u>Testem Benevolentiae</u> "On Americanism", which was quite in line with Vatican I inspired theology and marked a decisive victory for the conservative wing in Catholic America, a victory that dampered considerably the vision of the American liberal wing until the occurrence of Vatican II. In the words of Pope Leo XIII, regarding the general "liberalizing" tendency to embrace outside, non-Catholic culture:

> The principles on which the new opinion
> We have mentioned are based may be reduced
> to this: that, in order the more easily
> to bring over to Catholic doctrine to
> those who dissent from it, the Church ought
> to adapt herself somewhat to our advanced
> civilization, and, relaxing her ancient
> vigor, show some indulgence to modern popular
> theories and methods. Many think that this
> is to be understood not only with regard to
> the rule of life, but also to the doctrines
> in which the deposit of faith is contained

. . . Now, Beloved Son, few words are needed to show how reprehensible is the plan that is thus conceived.[39]

Pope Leo XIII follows, more specifically lambasting the very "Heckerism", "modernism", "subjectivism" that characterizes so well much of contemporary American Catholicism:

> For one who examines the matter thoroughly, it is hard to see, if we do away with all external guidance as these innovators propose, what purpose the more abundant influence of the Holy Ghost, which they make so much of, is to serve. In point of fact, it is especially in the cultivation of virtue that the assistance of the Holy Spirit is indispensible; but those who affect these novelties extol beyond measure the natural virtues as more in accordance with the ways and requirements of the present day, and consider it an advantage to be richly endowed with them, because they make a man more ready and more strenuous in action. It is hard to understand how those who are imbued with Christian principles can place the natural ahead of the supernatural virtues, and attribute to them greater power and fecundity . . . If we do not wish to <u>run in vain</u>, if we do wish to loose sight of the eternal blessedness to which God in His goodness has destined us, of what use are the natural virtues unless the gift and strength of divine grace be added?[40]

One important qualification is in order. In some respects the "Liberty and Justice for All" program did have a pre-Vatican theological precedent. It was, admittedly, a rather meagre precedent. The precedent is to be found in the "social encyclicals" of Leo XIII, <u>Rerum Novarum</u> "On the Condition of the Working Classes" (1891) and Pope Pius XI's <u>Quadragesimo Anno</u> "Forty Years Later: On Social Reconstruction".

These encyclicals can be termed "social" in that they stress that the mission of the Church is not solely to bring a sense of the transcendent and of eternal salvation in the next life to earth's inhabitants but also to be active for the enactment of justice in this world. Rerum Novarum concerned itself directly with the "scandal" of the worker's condition in Europe. As Pope Leo XIII put it, "We approach the subject with confidence and in the exercise of the rights that belong to us. For no satisfactory solution to this question will ever be found without the assistance of the religion of the Church".[41] Furthermore, he stated the main message of his pronouncement as follows: "the poor must be speedily and fillingly cared for, since the great majority of them live undeservedly in miserable and wretched conditions".[42] In the letter, Pope Leo XIII set forth a clear set of obligations for both the employer and employee, treading as it does between the unbridled individualism of the economic philosophy of liberalism and the equally unrestrained totalism of a transcendentless Socialism. On the fortieth anniversary of Pope Leo's encyclical, Pope Pius XI promulgated Quadregesimo Anno which reiterated and supported Pope Leo XIII's various positions. Most generally, the basic Catholic position that all economic undertakings must be governed by justice and charity was reaffirmed.

As Archbishop Peter Gerety made clear through the Maryknoll Justice Hearing testimony:

> I wish to make clear what we are using as the theological and ethical basis for our discussion of Liberty and Justice. Simply put, it is the tradition of Catholic social teaching articulated in the Church from Leo XIII through Paul VI, including the contributions of Vatican II and the Roman Synod of Bishops in 1971 and 1974.[43]

But in at least three important respects these two impressive documents are at variance with the spirit of Vatican II and its American child, the Bicentennial movement. The qualifications have to do with the lack in the early social encyclicals of any consideration of questions of "internal" justice or reform within the Church, the severely limited nature of Catholic cooperation with other groups seeking to enact justice in the world, and, finally, with the means and degree of commitment for such an enactment.

First of all, there is a complete lack in either document of questions concerning "internal" matters of justice and reform within the Church. In contrast, the Second Vatican Council established a principle of trust among all those who constitute the "people of God". In the principle document of Vatican II, Lumen Gentium ("Dogmatic Constitution on the Church"), the concept of "collegiality" is spelled out. It is in essence a principle whereby the Pope extends greater trust and confidence to the consensus of the Bishops of the Church. Although collegial rule was expressedly affirmed by Vatican II only for the Bishops, the internal logic of that affirmation can be argued to imply a collegial relationship between each Bishop and his priests, and between each pastor and the laity he serves. The former point is brought home in Presbyterorum Ordinis ("Decree on the Ministry and Life of Priests"); the latter in Apostolicam Actuositatem ("Decree on the Apostolate of the Laity"). In Presbyterorum Ordinis the call is for a senate of priests in the administration of the diocese. Apostolicam Actuositatem calls for a council in every diocese in which lay people will participate with the priests in advising the Bishop on policy matters. This emphasis on a decentralized approach to authority can be found also in Christus Dominus ("Decree on the Bishops Pastoral Office in the Church") which gave legal Church expression for the creation of national or regional conferences of Bishops where they did not exist and an enlargement of the powers of existing conferences such as the one founded in the United States immediately after World War I. The same document also called for the creation of councils, which "will render especially helpful assistance to the Supreme Pastor of the Church . . to be known by the proper name of Synod of Bishops".[44] Such internal reforms along "democratic" lines have encouraged an attenuation of the enormous influence of both the Pope and the international Church bureaucracy, the Curia, and aided in the development of the autonomy of national communities and their social programs. Such a dispersion of authority, and of the charisma latent within such authority, along centrifugal lines, again, must be viewed as a necessary presupposition for the American Bicentennial Program and movement.

Douglass J. Roche summarizes the importance of internal reform within the Church as a result of Vatican II:

Following the inspired initiatives of Pope John XXIII, the Second Vatican Council had laid the groundwork for the Catholic revolution between 1962 and 1965 by formulating a concept of Church membership, organization, and function very different from that which had prevailed since the proclamation of Papal Infallibility in 1870 and before. Incorporation into Christ by baptism was exalted as the identifying mark of the Christian giving him an active part in building up the Kingdom of God, a rejection of the former two-class society that in practice gave rights to the clergy and duties to the laity.[45]

The second respect in which the great "social encyclicals" are somewhat incongruent with the Vatican II position on "justice in the world" lies in the heavily qualified nature of Catholic involvement in social programs designed to enact justice. The basic incongruence lies in the Vatican I Catholic position that all truth lies within the confines of the Church, and as such, even tactical alliances with non-Catholic organizations and ideologies are, in principle, unthinkable and anathema. Speaking to "certain Catholic quarters" who hope that the Church and a "moderated and attenuated form of Socialism" might find some "middle ground", Pius XI in *Quadragesimo Anno* replies:

But such hopes are in vain. Those who wish to be apostles amongst the socialist should preach the Christian truth whole and entire, openly and sincerely, without any connivance with error. If they wish in truth to be heralds of the Gospel, let their endeavor be to convince Socialists that their demands, in so far as they are just, are defended much more congently be the principles of the Christian faith, and are promoted much more efficaciously by the power of Christian charity.[46]

And a little latter on, Pope Pius XI continues:

If, like all errors, Socialism contains a certain element of truth (and this the Sovereign Pontiffs have never denied), it is nevertheless founded upon a doctrine

of human society peculiarly its own, which
is opposed to true Christianity. "Religious
Socialism", "Christian Socialism" are expressions implying a contradition in terms.
No one can be at the same time a sincere
Catholic and a true socialist.[47]

Such an attitude was not the majority one
during the Bicentennial Program. Indeed, the movement
was overrepresented by those "new social activists"
advocating, or at least somewhat sympathetic to, some
variation of the "theology of liberation" and to those
more moderate liberals or "old social actionists" who
have felt quite comfortable in dialogue and joint
action with "all men of good will".

A final qualification lies in the pre-Vatican
II position that a concern for the enactment of justice
is "derivative" and not "constitutive" of the call of
the Gospel. Such a "derivative" status places less
emphasis on the attempt to "institutionalize" justice
in the world in a systematic, rational and large-
scale manner than does Vatican II statements. While
Vatican II theology clearly affirms the utter transcendence of God, it is still much more of a "horizontal"
religious dimension than pre-Vatican II theology. Avery
Dulles comments of the difference between the two great
"post-Vatican II" social encyclicals, Pope Paul's
Populorum Progressio ("On the Development of Peoples")
(1967) and the Synod of Bishops (1971) statement
Justice in the World with the earlier social encyclicals
as follows:

> These two documents coming from the last
> few years take full advantage of the development of the Second Vatican Council and do, I
> think, show a much more intimate involvement
> of the Church and of the concerns of the
> Gospel with the present situation of world
> development than one perhaps finds in the
> earlier social encyclicals which accent,
> rather, the eternal principles of social
> justice on a rather abstract level more to
> the natural law than to a social analysis
> of the present situation of the world.[48]

Avery Dulles continues, this time summarizing
his interpretation of Pope Paul's message in Populorum
Progressio. Dulles makes clear that the new social

encyclical, like the American Catholic Bicentennial which it partially inspired, calls for a systematic and rational approach to the question of social justice. As he put it:

> The Development of Peoples seeks to show that the demand to contribute to the benefit of the poorer nations is a simple consequence of the Gospel read in the context of today's world. There are many allusions to Gospel parables such as Lazarus and quotations from the epistle of James and other New Testament loci in which the obligation of charity or mercy toward the poor and needy is brought out in the Gospel. The Pope draws the conclusion that now this duty exists on a global scale. It is not just individuals who are poor and lying at the gate, but there are whole continents that are ravished with hunger where people are literally starving to death.
>
> Although private charities and relief activities may be of some help, they cannot provide a true and lasting remedy. What is needed, rather, is preventive action on an organized scale. And thus, the encyclical insists that there is an evangelical basis in revelation for the program to establish a kind of world fund for the development of life and industry and whatever may be needed in these starving areas of the world.[49]

Dulles encapsulates the central thesis of the Synod of Bishops Justice in the World, a thesis close enough to the tenets of the "theology of liberation" to give great encouragement to this particular segment of American liberal Catholicism. As Dulles puts it:

> The central thesis is perhaps strikingly expressed in a single sentence that is often quoted and, I think, cannot be too often quoted. Let me quote it myself: "Action on behalf of justice and participation in the transformation of the world fully appear to us as a constitutive dimension of the preaching of the Gospel or, in other words, of the Church's mission

for the redemption of the human race and
its liberation from every oppressive situation".
This sentence, as I understand it,
says in effect that Christ has promised a
total redemption that includes freedom from
all forms of want and oppression. The Church
cannot sincerely preach the message of Christ
unless it takes an active role in seeking to
eliminate these evils as they exist in the
present world.[50]

It is, perhaps, unfair to draw too sharp a
contrast between Vatican I and Vatican II theology.
Using the phenomenological concepts of "foreground"
and "background"[51] one can honestly point out that
the continuities between the Councils remained in
the "background" of most people's consciousnesses
while the discontinuities and changes were highlighted
and brought to the "foreground" of human consciousness
by most commentators. This social-psychological
insight is grounded in the fact that it is only
"problematic" and not "taken-for-granted" aspects of
social reality (theological documents most obviously
included) that "stand out for attention". Is it that
theological novices have a tendency to exaggerate
the discontinuities while "experts" are perhaps more
aware of the underlying regularities?

There are two relevant points here. The first
is that while Vatican II theology "may never bind"
the so-called "immobilist" Catholic wing, the fact
remains that it was almost always the "spirit" and not
the "law" that was utilized by the majority of the
moderately educated Catholic population that participated
in the Bicentennial movement. The second point
is that just what the "clear intention of the Council
was"--even to the "expert"--is perhaps unclear. The
two great social encyclicals of Pope John XXIII make
this second point. In 1961, John XXIII promulgated
Mater et Magistra ("Mother and Teacher: On Recent
Developments of the Social Question in the Light of
Christian Teaching"). In this document Pope John
does (to the obvious delight of Catholic liberals)
seemingly modify Pope Pius XI's attitude toward all
non-Catholic moral systems by declaring that Catholics:

in their conduct should weigh the opinions
of others with fitting courtesy and not
measure everything in the light of their

own interests. They should be prepared to
join sincerely in doing whatever is naturally
good or conducive to good.[52]

On the other hand, Pope John immediately
followed:

> If, indeed, it happens that in these matters
> sacred authorities have prescribed or decreed
> anything, it is evident that his judgement is
> to be obeyed promptly by Catholics. For it is
> the Church's right and duty not only to safe-
> guard principles relating to the integrity of
> religion and morals, but also to pronounce
> authoritatively when it is a matter of putting
> these principles into effect.[53]

Less than two years later, during the Vatican
II process, in Pacem in Terris "Peace on Earth:
Address to All Mankind", Pope John XXIII declared that
"Catholics, if for the sake of promoting the temporal
welfare cooperate with men who either do not believe
in Christ or whose belief is faulty because they are
involved in error, can provide them either the
occasion or the inducement to turn to truth".[54] Nonetheless, in the same paragraph the Pope asserts the
right of the Church to "intervene authoritatively with
her children in the temporal sphere".[55]

Indeed, such ambiguities and "cross-messages"
can be found throughout all the Vatican II documents,
including the principal document, Lumen Gentium,
especially on the subject of leadership in the Church
as expressed through the concept of collegiality.
Indeed, in the "commentary" that follows Lumen Gentium
in Walter Abbott's The Documents of Vatican II, Albert
C. Outler, an "official observer" during the Council,
noted:

> . . . the . . . tragic danger is that
> (Lumen Gentium) may be interpreted and
> implemented piecemeal: that the pro-
> gressives will stress only its pro-
> gressive ideas, even as immobilists
> attend only to its traditional residues;
> that the Bishops may be more preoccupied
> with the implications of collegiability at
> the level of their dioceses than at the level
> of parish life and work; that the laity mis-
> take Lumen Gentium as a warrant for self-

assertion without fully assuming their
commission to an apostolate of Christian
witness in the world; that members of
religious orders may become too intent
upon their life apart; that the studied
ambiguities . . . may be over-simplified
in one direction or another.[56]

Douglass J. Roche also indicates the various
modes of response to the disruption of Catholic routine
brought about by Vatican II as follows:

The progressives found themselves into
two schools, the first willing to let
the reform be paced by the institution's
leaders, the second veering around an
institutional roadblock to launch their
own kind of non-institutional Christianity.
The traditionalists varied from those who
gave only a grudging submission to the
updating process. The great majority of
Catholics, who were not intellectually
prepared for the dynamic of Vatican II and
did not understand it, felt themselves
hardly touched by it.[57]

Roche might just as well have been commenting
on the various stances taken toward the American
Catholic Bicentennial program. The majority of
"ethnic" Catholics--those Catholics for whom religion
is primarily mediated through the symbols of the
family, friendship networks, neighborhood, and, on
Sunday, the parish, were overwhelmingly indifferent
and apathetic toward the program. "Parish" or
"Church" centered types, including the Bishops, were
most probably split evenly between the "institutionally
progressive" and "grudgingly conservative" responses.
A very small percentage--similar in orientation to,
and sympathetic with, the Traditional Catholic Move-
ment--represent the "immobilist" or "in-group" adapta-
tion. The Bicentennial participants and Call to Action
delegates--Catholics themselves open to the world and
the symbols that actualize such attention--were split
between, and perhaps combined in certain respects,
the "institutionally progressive" option and the
"creative" response of allegiance to some kind of
"non-institutionalized Christianity" such as the
American Civil Religion or theology of liberation.

145

How, then, do the advocates--in an "ideal-typical" reconstruction--of the Bicentennial movement "imperfectly internalize" or "selectively interpret" the calling of Vatican II? It is an interpretation that "highlights" or brings "to the foreground of consciousness" the figure of Pope John XXIII who, in his opening speech before the Council, rebuked "those prophets of doom, who are always forecasting disaster, as though the end of the world were at hand" . . . and of those (like Pope Pius IX and Pope Pius X) who "in these modern times . . . can see nothing but prevarication and ruin. They say that our era, in comparison with past eras, is getting worse, and they behave as though they had learned nothing from history, which is, none-the-less, the teacher of life. They behave as though at the time of former Councils everything was a full triumph for the Christian idea and life and for proper religious liberty".[58] It is an interpretation that, following Pope John XIII in his Humanae Salustis, envisions a dynamic, historical Church "always living and always young, which feels the rhythm of the times and which in every century beautifies herself with new splendor, radiates new light and achieves new conquests."[59] Vatican II was a call, for the supporters of the Bicentennial, as Pope John XIII put it in his Message to Humanity "not only upon our brothers whom we serve as shepherds, but also upon our brother Christians, and the rest of men of good will . . . for this is the divine plan, that through love God's kingdom may already shine out on earth in some fashion as a preview of God's eternal kingdom."[60]

Commenting on Pope John's Message to Humanity, Walter Abbott offers his interpretation as follows:

> These opening words of the Council look to the renewal of the Catholic Church, to compassionate dialogue with modern men, to peace, to social justice, to whatever concerns the dignity of man and the unity of mankind. The message shows awareness of the world's problems and a keen desire to help. It emphasizes the quest for a community of peoples, the motivation that comes from Christ's love, the need for cooperation with all men of good will.[61]

Speaking on the principal document of Vatican II, Lumen Gentium, Avery Dulles informs the reader that it:

> envisages the Church as continuing the work of the Good Shepherd, who came to serve and not to be served, and who did not hesitate to lay down His life for the sheep. But the Church is represented very realistically as a "little flock" made up of frail and sinful men. Weak and humble, it stands in constant need of purification and renewal. At the same time, however, it feels confident of God's loving help which guides it step. The tone of the document is, moreover, strongly ecumenical. Every effort is made to speak in language which will be readily understood by other Christians and by all men of good will, and to explain Catholic teaching in a way that avoids giving unnecessary offense to persons accustomed to other modes of thought and speech . . . It wished to propose its teaching without anathemas and condemnations . . . (While) attention is given to the clergy and religious, (it is) always within the general picture of the Church's total mission. Authority is therefore viewed in terms of service rather than domination. In many respects the constitution strikes a "democratic" note.[62]

This "democratic note" was turned into an impressive symphony by Pope Paul VI in his Apostolic Letter, A Call to Action (1971). This Apostolic Letter provides a great deal of the legitimation required for (a) the emergence of the American Catholic Bicentennial Program, (b) the merging of at least the spirit of post-Vatican II with the American Civil Religion and (c) the recognition of the democratization impulse as a fundamentally religious one; that "charisma", or as Rudolph Sohm defines it, "God's gift of grace", is increasingly being dispersed to hitherto peripheral human groupings in the modern world. As Pope Paul follows:

> The passing to the political dimension also expresses a demand made by the man of today: a greater sharing in responsibility and in decision-making. This legitimate aspiration becomes more evident as the cultural level rises, as the sense of freedom develops and

as man becomes more aware of how, in a
world facing an uncertain future, the
choices of today already condition the
life of tomorrow. In Mater et Magistra
Pope John stressed how much the admittance
to responsibility is a basic demand of
man's nature, a concrete exercise of his
freedom and a path to his development,
and he showed how, in economic life and
particularly in enterprise, this sharing
of responsibilities should be ensured.
Today the field is wider, and extends to
the social and political sphere in which
a reasonable sharing in responsibility and
in decisions must be established and
strengthened. Admittedly, it is true that
the choices proposed for a decision are
more and more complex; the considerations
that must be borne in mind are numerous
and the foreseeing of the consequences
involves risk . . . However, although
limits are sometimes called for, these
obstacles must not slow down the giving
of wider participation in working out
decisions, making choices and putting them
into practice. In order to counter balance
increasing technocracy, modern forms of
democracy must be devised, and to express
himself, but also by involving him in a
shared responsibility.[63]

    The following passages give dramatic testimony
to the, for practical purposes, interchangeability of
a Vatican II Catholicism with that of the American Civil
Religion, at least for those American Catholics whose
religious sensibilities are mediated at the level of
national and international symbol systems. The social-
psychological jump between the two religious expressions
is a short one. In Nostra Aetate the following is
propounded:

The Church rejects nothing of what is
true and holy in these religions. She
has a high regard for the manner of life
and conduct, the precepts and doctrines
which, although differing in many ways
from her own teaching, nevertheless
often reflect a ray of that Truth which
enlightens all men . . . The Church,

therefore, urges her sons to enter with prudence and charity into discussion and collaboration with members of other religions. Let Christians, while witnessing to their own faith and way of life, acknowledge, preserve, and encourage the spiritual and moral truths found among non-Christians, also their social life and culture.[64]

Similarly, in Gaudium et Spes, the strain, lag, and partial inclusion between Catholicism and the American Civil Religion is reduced, theologically at least, as follows:

> Those also have a claim on our respect and charity who think and act differently from us in social, political, and religious matters. In fact the more deeply we come to understand their ways of thinking through good will and love, the more easily will we be able to undertake dialogue with them.[65]

In this same document, Parsons' previously mentioned and only half-facetious remark regarding comradeship between religious and atheistic elites is given credibility as "respect and charity" is extended even to the non-believer:

> (The Church) tries . . . to seek out the secret motives which lead the atheistic mind to deny God. Well knowing how important are the problems raised by atheism, and urged by her love for all men, she considers that these motives deserve an earnest and more thorough scrutiny.[66]

In Dignitatis Humanae "Declaration on Religious Freedom", the Church finally made formal its positive acknowledgement of the principle of religious freedom, thus explicitly reversing its stated position in the Syllabus of Errors (1864). In doing so, it vindicated one of the historically "constitutive" and suppressed positions of American Catholicism liberalism and supported the followers of Father John Courtney Murray, author of We Hold These Truths. As Dignitatus Humanae put it:

149

> Furthermore the private and public acts of religion by which men direct themselves to God according to their convictions transcend of their very nature the earthly and temporal order of things. Therefore the civil authority, the purpose of which is the care of the common good in the temporal order, must recognize and look with favour on the religious life of the citizens. But if it presumes to control or restrict religious activity it must be said to have acted in excess of its power.[67]

In *Apostolicam Actuositatem* "Decree on the Apostolate of the Laity", yet another "constitutive" element of hitherto suppressed American Catholic liberal or "Americanizer" position was affirmed: the promotion of active involvement in the American society public sphere. In *Apostolicam Actuositatem* it is urged that:

> In their patriotism and their fidelity to their civic duties Catholics should feel themselves bound to promote the true common good; they will make the weight of their convictions so influential that as a result civil authority will be justly exercised and laws will accord with moral precepts and the common good.

And, finally, in *Populorum Progressio*, Pope Paul VI, after noting that the "social question is now world-wide", acknowledges the need for institutions like that of the United Nations. This is a distinctly American Catholic liberal position in that it not only pushes the "frame of reference" of Catholicism past that of one "Church-centered", but also one past that of the nation and into an international perspective. The focal point of the Civil Religion moves from, or perhaps, alternates between Washington, D.C., and the United Nations Headquarters in New York City. In *On the Development of Peoples*, Paul VI observes that:

> This international cooperation which embraces the whole world demands institutions which prepare the way for it, coordinate, and direct it until a new juridicial order is established which

all recognize as fixed and firm.[69]

Peter Steinfels, writing in Commonweal and just prior to the May 1977 Bishops' meeting, summarized the overriding theme of the Bicentennial Program as follows:

> Whether in the remarks of scholars like David O'Brien, John Coleman and Richard McBrien, or in the comments of the Bishops, clergy and lay activists present, the theme that stood out was the democratic, voluntaristic character of American culture and religion, and the need for the Church to evolve structures that fit it.[70]

In doing so, Mr. Steinfels illustrates nicely the merging of a once distinctly Catholic theological system to the surrounding American social structure. Mr. Steinfels observes that, at least among many of the more "conservative" Bishops, the dynamic of the Bicentennial Program was perceived as one heading toward the self-liquidation of Catholic influence in America. As he puts it:

> A good number of Bishops are afraid that with the Bicentennial consultation they went for a ride on a tiger. They want to dismount. There is a large element of truth in the perception; but the tiger they are astride is not the "Call to Action" but America itself.[71]

Translating Mr. Steinfels' acute observations into our previous discussion of the relationship of a Vatican II inspired American Catholicism to the American Civil Religion, one can assert that the former has, in a sense "legitimated" the more "American" religious dimension of American liberal Catholicism. Vatican II allowed and encouraged American Catholics--particularly of liberal stripe--to enter into theological dialogue with, and, for practical purposes, to join the American Civil Religion. What to John Cardinal Dearden represents a "necessary risk", is from the perspective of the conservative wing, a foolhardy and disastrous flirtation with the central religious dimension of American society.

151

The Call to Action proposals illustrate the close-to-isomorphic relationship between our previously discussed symbolic constructions of Vatican II and the American Civil Religion. A _completely_ symmetrical relationship is _not_ the case given the exception of a bare handful of proposals, like that of the reaffirmation of the Catholic commitment to the indissolubility of marriage and that of the protection of human life from the moment of conception. The Call to Action proposals that follow will be divided into two groups, those centripetally or inwardly oriented to matters of Church structure and process and those centrifugally or outwardly oriented to the world community. Centripetal proposals are consonant with the American Civil Religion and Vatican II in that they stress the need for the Church to evolve structures and processes that fit its democratic, voluntaristic, fraternal and pluralistic character. Centrifugal proposals are consistent with both in that they stress a strong concern for social activism to bring about justice for people regardless of religious, racial, ethnic or sexual affiliation, in the name of God, and in conjunction with any/all religious, humanistic, or governmental associations willing to cooperate in such endeavors.

The major "centripetal" proposals are as follows:

--that the Church affirm, in a Catholic Bill of Rights, the fundamental rights and consequent responsibilities of Church members, including among others, the right to freedom of conscience, freedom of speech, freedom of assembly and freedom to participate in the life and ministry of the Christian community on a non-discriminatory basis

--protection for free speech within the Church and for the reputation of scholars in theology

--involvement of local Church in the selection of pastors and Bishops

--creation of a National Review Board to guarantee procedures of due process

--the formation of small eucharistic communities recognizing diversity

--a proportional representation of racial, ethnic and cultural groups in the formation and implementation of Church policy

--a proportional representation in the Church hierarchy along racial, ethnic, and cultural groups

--institutionalization of an equal employment opportunity program in the U.S.C.C.

--promotion and incorporation of multilingual and multicultural values in all Church educational policy and programs

--that all vocations, if fostered by a proper Catholic environment, are to be recognized as equal in dignity whether those called are married, single, religious or ordained clergy

--that women, unordained men, married couples, laicized priests should be allowed to preach

--that there should be an option to permit reception of Holy Communion in the hand as a sign of adult Christian commitment and human dignity

--affirmation of the right and responsibility of married people to form their own consciences regarding contraception in the light of Church teaching, contemporary theological reflection, and biological and social scientific research

--pastoral efforts encouraged to help the Church and its homosexual brothers and sisters in reconciliation

--pastoral programs which encourage formation of family groups for prayer, worship, sacramental preparation, marriage enrichment, family life education and mutual support

--that committees for political responsibility composed primarily of lay people be designated at all levels of the Church to establish priorities for public policy

--that the Church standardize the procedures for the handling of marriage annulments, thus ending the reality of a "geographic" morality

--that there be established local structures to enable people to participate in decision-making processes so that trust can grow between the Bishop and the people, the pastor and the people, and the powerful and the powerless

--recognition by the Church of the special competency of permanent deacons and lay people in family ministry by seeking them out and assuring them roles of leadership and authority

--that the Church and Church-related institutions, recognizing sincerely the pluralism that exists among us, work to eliminate every form of discrimination on the basis of race, language, sex, sexual orientation, culture, nationality, and mere physical considerations

--that the Church recognize the right of collective bargaining for Church employees

--that the Church recognize the right for girls to serve at the altar

--that American Bishops should request the Pope to allow the ordination of women and married men

--that the Church move to achieve racial integration in the faculties, student bodies and curriculum in Catholic schools

--decisions to close parishes and Catholic schools ought to involve neighborhood and community individuals

--that every diocese should undertake an affirmative action program

--that the Church establish an American Indian secretariat in the U.S.C.C.

154

--that each diocese establish a black,
Hispanic, Indian, and ethnic secretariat
to keep the Bishops informed of the needs
and feeling of these racial and ethnic
groups

--that the Bishops ought to repeal the
penalty of automatic excommunication
decreed for Catholics "who dare to remarry
after divorce"

--that the N.C.C.B. and Catholic publishers
should expunge all sexist language and
immagery from official Church publications

--that Church authorities should be financially
accountable to "the people of God".

The major "centrifugal" proposals that are quite consonant with both the American Civil Religion and Vatican II theology are as follows:

--that the whole Church, through the example
of the lives of its members and through
action undertaken in cooperation with other
religious and civil groups, pledges itself
to combat those contemporary social, economic,
and cultural forces which threaten the family

--that the Church in the U.S. actively support
and work with all established organizations
engaged in the effort to end all forms of
racism and discrimination

--that the U.S.C.C. should stimulate, either
through new or existing organizations, dialogue
with groups such as labor unions, professional
societies, business organizations, cooperative
movements and citizen's groups to translate
the implication of justice into practical norms
of action

--that the U.S.C.C. collaborate with other
national ecclesial communities, the National
Council of Churches, the Jewish community
with other world religions on the issues of
justice and peace

--that the N.C.C.B should invite all scholars to participate in the ministry of justice and peace by collaborative research into questions of global justice, including the relation of Catholic and other (e.g. socialist, Gandhian) traditions to contemporary situations

--that the Catholic community of the U.S. advocate before their government a foreign policy that is in keeping with the defense of human rights as stipulated in the U.N. Universal Declaration of Human Rights

--that the Church commit itself to the concept of "open neighborhoods", whereby new residents of any race, ethnic group, cultural background or religious faith would be welcomed as brothers and sisters in Christ

--that the Church should develop cooperative relations among parishes and with other religions, social, civic, governmental, and health service organizations

--that the Church support the Equal Rights Amendment

--that the Catholic Bill of Rights include sections indicating the Church's commitment to defend and promote human rights and human dignity, to include the assertion that all human beings are entitled minimally to food, clothing, shelter, health care and fulfilling economic opportunity

--that the Catholic social action agencies and offices take steps to change the conditions which dehumanize oppressed groups like Blacks, Hispanics, Indians, and Asian-Americans

--that the Church increase its support for the Campaign for Human Development, for Catholic Charities, Operation Rice Bowl, Bread for the World and Catholic Relief. Services

--that the Office of International Justice and Peace of the U.S.C.C. be encouraged and supported in its work

--that the Church ought to invite
indigenous representatives of the Third
World to raise the "critical consciousness" of the U.S. population

--that the N.C.C.B./U.S.C.C. ought to
mobilize the international conscience
on behalf of all political prisoners
under repressive governments

--that the Church ought to challenge U.S.
and corporate involvement in Third and
Fourth Worlds

--that the Church ought to promote a
public policy consisting of comprehensive
health care, liberal immigration laws,
tax reform, housing guarantees, quality
education, and student rights

--use Church investments to influence
social justice in the Third World

--the Church ought to do everything in
its power to expose U.S. multinational
interests in Latin America

--the Church ought to encourage and assist
unemployed and unorganized workers, regardless of immigrant status, to join or form
unions

--unconditional amnesty should be extended
to all Vietnam war resisters

--that the Church establish an office in
laison with the United Nations so that
the U.S. community will have close contact
with international and national organizations
concerned with global issues.[73]

  This chapter has tried, among other things,
to make the point that ideas, even when expressed in
slogans like the cry for "liberty and justice for
all", are an important ingredient for social change
within the American Catholic Church. Yet no idea
exists in a vacuum; it is only influential in the

157

context of other social forces and personality orientations. Those forces and orientations that are interdependent with each other are the respective foci of the next several chapters.

FOOTNOTES

[1] Rudolph Otto, The Idea of the Holy (N.Y.: Oxford University Press 1950).

[2] I am combining quite compatible insights from the reference group theory as developed by Robert Merton and the sociology of knowledge perspective as developed by Peter Berger and Thomas Luckmann.

[3] I go into greater detail on this point in the last chapter.

[4] Emile Durkheim, The Elementary Forms of the Religious Life (N.Y.: Free Press, 1947).

[5] Fustel de Coulanges, The Ancient City (N.Y.: Doubleday, 1955).

[6] Will Herberg, Protestant, Catholic, Jew (N.Y.: Doubleday, 1955).

[7] Gorge Herbert Mead, On Social Psychology (Chicago: University of Chicago Press, 1964).

[8] Richard Gambino, Blood of My Blood (N.Y.: Harcourt, Brace and World, 1959).

[9] I am following here the general analysis of Talcott Parsons which will be elaborated on in later parts of this chapter.

[10] Otto, op. cit., 1950.

[11] Mircea Eliade, The Sacred and The Profane (N.Y.: Harcourt, Brace and World, 1959).

[12] Robert Bellah "Civil Religion in America" in Daedalus 96 Winter, 1967.

[13] Talcott Parsons "Introduction" in Max Weber The Sociology of Religion (Boston: Beacon Press, 1963).

[14] Talcott Parsons "Christianity and Modern Industrial Society" in Sociological Theory, Values and Sociocultural Change (Editor, Edward A. Tiryakian) (New York: Free Press, 1963, pp. 33-70).

[15] Talcott Parsons "Religious Organization in the United States" in *Structure and Process in Modern Societies* (N.Y.: Free Press, 1960).

[16] *Ibid.*

[17] Talcott Parsons "Belief, Unbelief, and Disbelief" in *The Culture of Unbelief* (editors, Rocco Caporale and Antonio Grumelli) (Berkeley: University of California Press, 1971).

[18] *Ibid.*

[19] *Ibid.*

[20] I am here following Berger and Luckmann's usage of the work of Arnold Gehlen as posited in *The Social Construction of Reality* (N.Y.: Doubleday, 1966).

[21] As Georg Simmel might put it, the "social circles" through which Catholic thought and activity take place expand.

[22] Max Weber, *The Protestant Ethic and the Spirit of Capitalism* (N.Y.: Scribner, 1958).

[23] I am here following basic Parsonsian thought.

[24] Peter Berger, *The Sacred Canopy* (N.Y.: Doubleday, 1967).

[25] Thomas Luckman, *The Invisible Religion* (N.Y.: MacMillian, 1963).

[26] Will Herberg, op. cit. 1955.

[27] Edward Shils, "The Sanctity of Life" in *Center and Pheriphery* (Chicago: University of Chicago Press, 1975).

[28] Sigmund Freud, *The Future of an Illusion* (N.Y.: Anchor Books, 1964.

[29] Andrew Greeley, *The American Catholic* (N.Y.: Basic Books, 1977, p. 337).

[30] Quoted in Robert Cross, *The Emergence of Liberal Catholicism in American* (Chicago: Quadrangle

Books, 1958.

[31] Edward Wakin and Father Joseph F. Scheuer, The De-Romanization of the American Catholic Church (N.Y.: MacMillian, 1966).

[32] The Syllabus of Errors in Walter Kaufman (editor) op. cit., 1964.

[33] Dogma of Papal Infallibility in Walter Kaufman (editor) op. cit., 1964.

[34] Pope Pius X Pascendi Dominici Gregis September 8, 1907, Boston: St. Paul's Edition.

[35] Pope Piux X Lamentabili Sane July 3, 1907, Boston: St. Paul's Edition.

[36] And while Vatican II stopped considerably short of affirming the "modernist" position, the movement was clearly in this direction. Indeed, a great deal of the energy of His Holiness Pope Paul VI's reign was spent admonishing "theology of liberation" types for their notion that "urbi Lenin, ibi Jerusalem". Conservative Catholics could only sadly acknowledge the problem of this social-psychological self-escalation; "that's what one gets for opening up a pandora's box was the orthodox reply to Pope Paul's plight.

[37] Pope Pius X, op. cit., September 8, 1907.

[38] Pope Piux X, op. cit., July 3, 1907.

[39] Pope Leo XIII Testem Benevolentiae in John Tracy Ellis, The Documents of American History (Milwaukee: Bruce, 1956).

[40] Ibid.

[41] Pope Leo XIII, op. cit., Testem Benevolentiae, 1956.

[42] Ibid.

[43] Archbishop Peter L. Gerety quoted in "Bicentennial Convocation on Global Justice", Washington: N.C.C.B. Committee for the Bicentennial, 1976.

[44] Christus Dominus in (Abbott editor) The Documents of Vatican II (Washington: America Press, 1966).

[45] Douglass J. Roche, The Catholic Revolution (N.Y.: McKay, 1968, p. 8).

[46] Pius XI, Quadragesimo Anno, 1891 Boston: St. Paul's Edition.

[47] Ibid.

[48] Avery Dulles quoted in "Humankind", "Washington: N.C.C.B. Committee for the Bicentennial, 1975.

[49] Ibid.

[50] Ibid.

[51] This point is consistent with the analysis of Arnold Gehlen as presented in Berger and Luckmann's The Social Construction of Reality.

[52] Pope John XXIII Mater et Magistra 1961 Washington: National Catholic Welfare Conference.

[53] Ibid.

[54] Pope John XXIII Pacem in Terris 1963 Boston: St. Paul's Edition.

[55] Ibid.

[56] Dr. Albert C. Outler quoted in Abbott, 1966.

[57] Douglass J. Roche, op. cit., 1968.

[58] Pope John XXIII "Opening Speech" in Abbott, 1966.

[59] Pope John XXIII Humanae Salustis in Abbott, 1966.

[60] Pope John XXIII "Message to Humanity" in Abbott, 1966.

[61] Walter Abbott, "Commentary" in Abbott, 1966.

[62] Avery Dulles "Commentary" in Abbott, 1966.

[63] Pope Paul VI, A Call to Action, 1971, Washington: United States Catholic Conference.

[64] Nostra Aetate in Abbott, 1966.

[65] Gaudium et Spes in Abbott, 1966.

[66] Ibid.

[67] Dignitatus Humanae in Abbott, 1966.

[68] Apostolicam Actousitatem in Abbott, 1966.

[69] Pope Paul VI, Popularum Progressio, 1967, Washington, U.S.C.C.

[70] Peter Steinfels, "New Chance for The Bishops" in Commonweal, April 1, 1977.

[71] Ibid.

[72] All 182 Call to Action proposals can be found in Origins: National Catholic Documentary Service Vol. 6, Number 20, Nov. 4, 1976 and Vol. 6, Number 21, November 21, 1976.

CHAPTER SEVEN

THE FORMAL ORGANIZATIONAL PRESUPPOSITION:
THE MACHINERY OF THE AMERICAN CATHOLIC CHURCH

This chapter will attempt to apply a sociological understanding of how the formal organizational structures of the American Catholic Church "channel" the democratizing impulse of the Bicentennial Program. The points here are twofold, the first dealing with the formal organizational presupposition of the Bicentennial Program, the second with its formal organizational constraints. The first point entails an understanding that "power", i.e., as Weber defines it, "the ability to get things done in the face of opposition", is, in the modern world, embedded within organizational structures, whether they be churches, government, political parties, business firms, schools, or protest movements. Of more specific relevance is the point that the democratizing ideals of both Vatican II and the Bicentennial Program, in order to be made a reality, involve highly patterned processes which are shaped and molded by the formal organizational context. The second point represents, in a sense, the reverse side of the coin. Just as formal organizational structures make possible the implementation process, they limit implementation. Put another way, the routinization of the charismatic ideals of the Bicentennial movement are to be found in their embodiment in the everyday round of institutional existence. The "routinization of charisma" represents the basic dilemma of institutional religion, to wit: religion's accomodation to society. And such an accomodation, in the specific case under study, involves the analysis of organizational constraints that thwart the ideals of democracy. The "debunking" nature of sociological inquiry leads one to ask the question "liberty and justice for whom?" In order to answer this question one must link the development of the New Catholic Knowledge Class to an understanding that in a modern American society one can talk of significant social change only through the system and not against it. And to talk of power through the system means to talk of power through bureaucracy and formal organization.

A good deal of the argument of this chapter can be found *in nuce* in the following intellectual exchange between James Hitchcock, an important conservative Catholic intellectual, and Bishop Raymond Lucker, an equally important representative of liberal American Catholicism. Such an exchange goes far in exposing the underlying taken-for-granted assumptions of the conservative and liberal camp regarding the import of post-Vatican II changes for the American Catholic Church. The place is the St. Paul-Minneapolis Justice Hearing (June 14, 1975). The discussion centers on recent Vatican II inspired changes in both formal and social organization that have, among other things, resulted in the spread of the Church bureaucracy with an, unintentional or not, increased dependency on the "specialist" and "professional". The "typical" liberal response is a favorable one, stressing the newly created "organs of representation" within the Church that bring the lay Catholic into closer contact with the Bishops. On the other hand, the taken-for-granted "conservative" response is a "mixed" one, acknowledging the emergence of these "democratic structures", but also asking the question, "democracy for whom?" As Hitchcock put it in the exchange:

> any time you get specialization and professionalization . . . it tends to become more difficult for the lay person, i.e., the non-expert, to make his or her desires known . . . I see it (the recent social reorganization of the Church, as at best) a double-movement.

The remainder of the exchange proceeded as follows:

> Bishop Lucker: I'm convinced that in the last decade or so, there has been increased involvement of parents in educational decisions, particularly in regard to parish and diocesan educational boards and involvement of parents in the teaching of their children for the sacraments . . . There is much other involvement on the part of the parents with a great encouragement on the part of Bishops and priests and other leaders in educational circles.
>
> Dr. Hitchcock: I recognize what you're saying about the emergence in the last ten years of school boards and other things of

166

this kind, which I think are important. However, there's been a parallel process which has, perhaps, not been noticed. Not just in education but in every other area of the Church in the last ten years, there has been a tremendous increase in professionalization. We are much more professional than we were fifteen years ago. We have much larger bureaucracies, we have more specialists in all kinds of things . . . . And any time you get specialization and professionalization of that kind, it tends to become more difficult for the lay person, that is to say the non-expert, to make his or her desires known . . . . So I see it as perhaps a double movement. We do now have organs or representation which we didn't previously have, but perhaps there are still built-in difficulties (in representation).[1]

    This "double-movement" involves forces operating at cross purposes. On one hand, the movement does entail the leveling or democratizing impulse as discussed by Max Weber's analysis of bureaucracy. On the other hand, the movement simultaneously involves the continual reassertion towards elitism as discussed by Marx through his class analysis, by Vilfredo Pareto through his discussion of the "circulation of elites", and by Roberto Michels through his discussion of the "iron law of oligarchy".

    The call for the analysis of ideals as they are embodied in the routines of institutional life raises the central question of this chapter: what are the existing formal organizational structures that serve as the vehicle and, conversely, as the roadblock for the democratizing ideals of the Bicentennial movement? As Abigail McCarthy has acutely observed:

> The achievement of an ideal is more often frustrated by the failure to develop what we Americans have so usefully packaged in the indispensible word "know how" than it is frustrated by bad faith. Understanding the reality of existing structures, method, practice, technique, instrumentality . . . these are all parts of know how.[2]

Charles Perrow analyzes some of the more generally accepted foibles and pitfalls of bureaucracy:

> it is crucial to understand not only how (bureaucracy) mobilizes social resources for desirable ends, but also how it inevitably concentrates those forces in the hands of a few who are prone to use them for ends we do not approve of, for ends we are generally not aware of, and more frightening still, for ends we are led to accept because we are not in a position to conceive of alternative ones.[3]

Ms. McCarthy herself notes the difficulty of the American Catholic Church in institutionalizing the directive of <u>Apostolicam Actuositatem</u> that "the laity must take on the renewal of the temporal order as their own special obligation" through the Bicentennial Program. She follows:

> A committee, a secretariat, brief and selective consultations are frail instruments for the heavy burden of communicating the needs and concerns of 99.7 percent of the Church. The difficulty is complicated by the fact that, juridically, the Church is governed by dioceses; in theory the normal avenue of recourse for the laity is through diocesan structures. In reality, . . . however, the Bishops, have depended on a large Church bureaucracy which has been the natural outgrowth of the National Catholic Welfare Conference and the more recent reorganization of the N.C.C.B./U.S.C.C. The N.C.C.B./U.S.C.C. is staffed by Church professionals and theirs has been the lay voice actually heard . . . . Initiatives in the temporal order have increasingly come from this source in the Church--witness the "Call to Action". This is neither good nor bad, but a fact to be considered, when embarking on a dialogue with the laity living in the world, "called there by God" (<u>Lumen Gentium</u>).[4]

Ms. McCarthy's comments concerning the "frail" instruments of communicating the needs and concerns of 99.7 percent of the Church was echoed by the Archbishop of Newark, Peter Gerety, at the San Antonio National Justice Hearing. For Gerety:

> . . . someday, perhaps, we will have such a strong sense of common purpose in the Church in the U.S. that we will be able to consult one another instantly . . . . While we have made great progress in developing diocesan, regional, and national structures for consultation among Bishops, priests, religious and lay people, we do not yet have a fully developed network of national communication. So we must do what we can by such open invitations (i.e., the Justice Hearings), using the structure of the diocese where possible, adding consultation with independent national networks of all kinds, and urging those not touched by either to communicate with us directly.[5]

A large part of the "great progress" made in the consultative process (as limited as it still may be) involved the strengthening of the same national level structure of the American Catholic Church that, as Ms. McCarthy pointed out, initiated the Bicentennial Program, that of the N.C.C.B./U.S.C.C. Writing as late as 1958, Robert Cross could talk of the very limited success of, and strong resistance met by, the pre-Vatican II liberal-oriented national level structure and with its proposed national level programs. As Robert Cross put it:

> The liberals of the 1890's were eager to limit diocesian autonomies in order to obtain effective national action. Dominated in the early years by liberally-minded prelates, the national bureaucracy brought such results as the "Bishops' Program of Social Reconstruction", special plans to speed the "Americanizing" of Catholic immigrants, and a "standard apologetic" to guide the clergy in making compromises with public school authorities. Roman fears of a new Gallicanism were augmented by protests from particularistic and usually conservative American prelates so that the episcopal attendance was (made) purely voluntary. The National

Catholic Welfare Conference has proved its worth as a focus, but the American Church has continued to be plagued with local resistance to the intelligent national action Spalding and Ireland so much desired.[6]

Vatican II theology, however, strengthened the hands of the liberal faction and of those advocating national level programs like the American Catholic Bicentennial Program. As Christus Dominus ("Decree on the Bishops' Pastoral Office in the Church") put it:

> Nowadays especially, Bishops are frequently unable to fulfill their office suitably and fruitfully unless they work more harmoniously and closely every day with other Bishops. Episcopal conferences, already established in many nations, have furnished outstanding proofs of a more fruitful apostolate. Therefore this most sacred Synod considers it supremely opportune everywhere that Bishops belonging to the same nation or region form an association and meet together at fixed times.[7]

Of extreme importance to the liberal cause is that Christus Dominus provides for more than just a coordinating agency for the American Church. The purpose, rather, was to strike a balance between the proper authority of the local Bishop and the common good of an entire region. Christus Dominus provides for this balance as follows:

> Decisions of the episcopal conference, provided they have been made lawfully and by choice of at least two-thirds of the prelates who have a deliberate vote in the conference, and have been reviewed by the Apostolic See, are to have juristically binding force in those cases and in those only which are prescribed by common law or determined by special mandate of the Apostolic See, given spontaneously or in response to a petition from the conference itself.[8]

The American Catholic Bicentennial Program, to the chagrin of the liberal wing and to the relief of the conservative segment, was not mandated directly out of conciliar legislation or by Papal directive; rather it was conceived out of the busom of the N.C.C.B./U.S.C.C. Advisory Council as a response to Pope Paul's A Call to Action and the Synod of Bishops' Justice in the World. Put very simply, the Call to Action was not "ordered" to proceed by either Papal or Synodal legislation but rather is seen as an "interpretative" response to a Papal and Synodal call. Nonetheless, the point still holds that the "ordinary" power of the Bishop is practically, if not theoretically, no longer unquestioned and unchecked. As a matter of fact, the N.C.C.B. statutes state that when passed by a two-thirds vote, decisions, although not juridically binding, "should be observed by all members as an expression of collegial responsibility and in the spirit of unity and charity". All of this takes on added significance when one understands the "liberal" and "social" nature of much recent Catholic theology.

Several points should be made here regarding the very possibility of initiating something like the American Catholic Bicentennial Celebration. The first is that in light of Christus Dominus the national level structure of the American Church has been considerably strengthened, although still tied to the "structured ambiguity" historically consistent with much Church legislation. The Bicentennial Program (and the enduring movement it supported) was simply inconceivable without the legitimacy afforded to the N.C.C.B./U.S.C.C. by Christus Dominus.

The second point involves a discussion of Paul Harrison's[9] concept of "rational-pragmatic" authority. Simply put, many times large-scale decisions, like that of launching the Bicentennial Program, are made by individuals whose "authority" is "practical" and "matter-of-factly" rather than "theoretical" and "proper". Put another way, many of the decisions involving a myriad number of important issues of the Catholic Church are made at the national level. As Abigail McCarthy has previously acknowledged, these decision-makers occupy positions in the N.C.C.B./ U.S.C.C. and other national level organizations. Crudely put and flying in the face of a theoretical blueprint that has the Church run at the diocesan level, the fact remains that certain "coordinating" and directing functions are, by their very nature, "national" in scope (aided no doubt by recent centrifugally oriented theology) and must be carried out by various "knowledge" experts. This is so whether or not there is the required authority to make such decisions. In place of the existing void of "authority" that ensues from the disjunction between theory and praxis, a matter-of-fact "power" results. This type of ad hoc authority Harrison terms "rational-pragmatic". Speaking of the professionals and bureaucrats of the national level American Baptist Convention, Harrison follows:

> . . . the leaders of the Convention have obtained an "expediential authority", not fully legal, not based on ecclesiastical tradition, but an authority which arises out of the immediate needs of the denominational organizations . . . it is found that the executives, even though their official position is tenuous, exercise a tremendous control over the policies of the denomination and the activities of the local churches . . . (with) . . . their inclination to place the needs of their (national-level) agencies before the original goals for which they were created.[10]

Indeed, for those "in the know", the Bicentennial Committee was able to bypass the system of formal rules (at least to a certain degree) through the tremendous prestige and influence of Monsignor John Egan of C.C.U.M., and by such powerful U.S.C.C. officials and staunch Bicentennial advocates as Monsignor Francis Lally and Monsignor George Higgins. This is the case despite the far more "visible" presence of people like Frank J. Butler, Sister Margaret Cafferty, and David J. O'Brien.

Moreover, the nature of "rational-pragmatic" authority is that it operates in an unquestioned fashion until it openly and obviously trespasses some clear-cut rule that is undergirded and supported by clearly recognized authority. Harrison's discussion is relevant for our analysis of the American Catholic Bicentennial Program. Very simply put, national level types, in and around the U.S.C.C., devised and implemented a program that ran very smoothly until the Bishops realized that the very authority upon which their and the Pope's authority rests, that of "apostolic succession", was being challenged by the radically democratic ideals and proposals of the program. It was at this time that the Bishops asserted their authority and "put their foot down". The post-Detroit maneuvers of the Bernardin Task Force which, among other moves, conveniently "silenced" Butler, shipped off Cafferty, and "retired" O'Brien, has previously been chronicled.[11]

Of course, the analogy with Harrison's work is far from perfect. In the Catholic case, not only was a change in theology required, i.e., (Vatican II) but the program was acknowledged and--in a very loose sense--legitimated from the very start by the Bishops. The Bicentennial Justice Committee, again, was a Bishop's Committee. Put another way, the Catholic intellectual-bureaucrat, as compared to his Baptist bretheren, was forced to operate right under the very noses of the Bishops from start to finish. The difficulty of pulling off this undeniably marvelous accomplishment of a national consultation (at least from the liberal perspective) was, no doubt, aided by the general indifference of most conservative Bishops, clergy and laity toward the program, at least in the beginning when it was perceived by most to be quite harmless. Conversely, it was aided by the fact that many "liberal" Bishops, clergy and laity, while a minority, nonetheless are oriented to a national/international perspective and, as such, congregate in and around the U.S.C.C. and other national and international Catholic organizations. Again, while conservatives disperse themselves among more local and isolated enclaves, the saying that "birds of a feather flock together" holds true at least for the liberal wing of American Catholicism. Put another way, a "sect-like" group of liberals can accomplish a great deal more through concerted organization than can a mass of unorganized conservative Bishops, lower-echelon clergy, and lay Catholics.

This leads naturally to an important third point, first brought to attention by Jeffrey Hadden.[12] Hadden, in his study of the Protestant denominations, does demonstrate clearly that "liberal social activist" types congregate within and around the national level. In his study, the national organization was that of the National Council of Churches. Hadden's argument is also relevant for this study. The "gathering storm" entails the gulf between the younger clergy who take

to heart the radical message of the Gospel to hold a
strong and fundamental concern for the poor and the
disenfranchised on the one hand, and, on the other,
many of the laity who frown on such social activism.
This gulf was highlighted during the 1960's with
the "Civil Rights" movement in which many younger
clergy allied themselves with the movement much to
the chagrin of the "average" layman who viewed the
primary role of the minister as that of preaching (as
compared to implementing politically) the Word of the
Gospel. Given the fundamentally conservative nature
of the parish ministry, Hadden notes that the more
socially-active and liberal clergy migrate towards
non-parish ministry. Those social activists who
find themselves located at the parish level either
find themselves in potential and actual conflict
with the parishioners, or silence their opinions
and actions or, find themselves constantly attempting
to relocate to a more "congenial" national level
setting. Philip Hammond in an important study[13] makes
the complimentary point that liberal types see their
way to campus ministries where they can simultaneously
avoid the presence of a "conservative" parish group
and bask in the presence of college students supposedly
"more open to ideas" and to the more idealistic concern for the disenfranchised.

While hard empirical evidence is lacking in
the Catholic case, both my impressions and interviewing, on the one hand, and a study of those individuals
most visibly responsible for the creation, coordination,
and attempted implementation of the Bicentennial Program, on the other, strongly indicate the applicability
of Harrison's, Hadden's, and Hammond's insights for
the formal organization of contemporary Catholic
America. Qualifications are, again, in order. Based
on the various attitudinal studies of Andrew Greeley
stretching from his Why Can't They Be Like Us? to his
The American Catholic, it is clear that the majority
of American Catholics are, today at least, far more
"liberal" on social issues than their separated
Protestant bretheren, especially among the more
fundamentalist groupings. Following a basically
Franklin D. Roosevelt "New Deal" tradition, Catholics
are "private sphere" conservatives (i.e., on issues
involving family, neighborhood, ethnicity, morals
and ethics) but are very liberal on issues of economic
and social justice that are operant within the public
realm of American society.

Referring to Greeley's distinction between the "old" and "new" types of social action, it is fair to say that the "old" concept of social action is far more consistent with the tenor of mainstream Catholic life than is the latter group. The overwhelming generosity of Catholic institutions to the non-Catholic poor is indicative of the support that "average", "ethnic", "marginal" Catholic parishioners have for the poor, perhaps indicating the fact that American Catholics have not, at least as of yet, forgotten the plight of their recent and impoverished immigrant past. On the other hand, there is little evidence to support any ideological or systematic commitment, along quasi-socialist lines, to the "rational" elimination of poverty and injustice. Put another way, and Justice in the World notwithstanding, the claim here is that the average Catholic is concerned with the question of justice, but as it is "derived" and not "constitutive" of the message of the Gospel (as vaguely as that message is perceived by most of the Catholic population). Simply put, the "gathering storm" in the Catholic case is as much, if not more, between the elite exponents of the "old" and "new" forms of Catholic social action than it is between the vast group of moderately "liberal" and fast shrinking "fundamentalist" factions.

Given the still limited, although recently expanded, activity and scope of the N.C.C.B./U.S.S.C., the Bicentennial Program and movement relied heavily on other organizations for both member recruitment, advertising, and program implementation. Perhaps the most important of these is the Catholic Committee on Urban Ministry (C.C.U.M.) which operates out of Notre Dame. C.C.U.M. was founded by the "unofficial Bishop of the U.S." and an old-line social-activist, Monsignor John Egan, in the year 1967 with a charter membership of 16. Today, the Catholic Committee on Urban Ministry comprises a national network of over 5,000 priests, sisters, brothers and lay persons, all of whom are involved in one or another aspect of social ministry. As Monsignor John Egan and Sister Peggy Roach put it:

> C.C.U.M. and its constituents were deeply involved at every level of development of the "Call to Action"--in the planning and writing committees, in the diocesan hearings and in local parish discussions, as delegates

and observers. Most of the issues which
arose from the people to become part of
the process were issues in which C.C.U.M.
people had long been engaged and felt that
a response from the Church in its many
aspects was long overdue. Therefore,
C.C.U.M. people took a tremendous interest
in the process and in the call of the
Bishops, and along with other Catholic
organizations and groups, spearheaded
the development of interest and response
in a multitude of the dioceses . . . .
Many of the C.C.U.M. people who worked
long and hard in the development of the
research and organization of the Call to
Action are also pledged to work to
implement the recommendations which were
presented to the bishops at their annual
meeting in 1977. With the leadership
of Margaret Cafferty and Philip Murnion,
the C.C.U.M. network can make a significant contribution to the implementation
of the recommendations and keep alive the
listening-hearing process which was
developed in the . . . dioceses and
institutions across the U.S.[14]

    Another organization that represented an
important cog in the machinery of the Bicentennial
Program is called, aptly enough, "Network". Network
is a Washington based nun's lobby group, designating
itself as "a religious lobby for social justice".
Network, like C.C.U.M., publishes newsletters and a
quarterly journal (circulation over 3,000); it holds
workshops, intern programs, and it organizes a yearly
national assembly seminar and periodically conducts
telephone "alerts" on important legislation and,
finally, testifies before Congressional committees.
Network has "contacts" in over half of the 435
Congressional districts and has a full-time Washington
staff of 11 professionals. The organization was
founded by 47 sisters in the year 1971. As Sister
Carol Coston explains, it was no coincidence that
Network was founded in the year 1971. As Sister put
it:

    Two important Church documents issued in
    1971 influenced the sisters who began
    Network--the Synod Statement <u>Justice in</u>

the World and Paul VI's letter commemorating the 80th anniversary of Leo XIII's Rerum Novarum, A Call to Action. Both documents called for political action to change unjust structures that oppress peoples--especially the world's poor.[15]

In light of the Bicentennial Program in which large groups of laity exposed their interest in matters of social justice, Sister Coston follows:

> This year's goal is to broaden our image and made Network known as a religious lobby for social justice . . . (including) . . . lay people . . . Our experience of meeting so many concerned Catholic laity at the Detroit Call to Action Conference has further convinced us of the mutual benefit of working with the laity and with others who share our desire for a more just world order. Network has much to gain from the experience. Moreover, active participation by many concerned persons will enable Network to be more influential in effecting legislation for social justice.[16]

Robert L. Spaeth follows:

> Since its beginning in 1971 Network has been growing and developing both organizational values and criteria for judging social issues. The results of the reflection of Network's board, staff, and interns show concern for the structural causes of injustice, for self-determination of people, for conservation of the earth's resources, for Church teaching, for awareness of global interdependence. Network has attracted endorsements from prominent Catholics. Senator Edward Kennedy said "One of the rewards of public services is having the opportunity to meet with groups of concerned and articulate citizens, such as the Network delegates". Father Theodore Hesburg, President of Notre Dame University, has said that "Network offers Catholics an opportunity to assume responsibility for influencing legislation for justice" . . . Network continues the process of the politicization of the American Catholic

Church . . .[17]

Perhaps the post Vatican II organizational development that most characterizes "the politicization of American Catholic Church" and that was intimately involved in the Bicentennial is that of the Jesuit-sponsored research institute, the "Center of Concern", located in Washington, D.C. The Center of Concern was also founded in the year 1971 as a response to a meeting in which representatives of the N.C.C.B. met with leaders of the Society of Jesus in which the former asked for help in establishing an action/reflection center in North America. Its task would be, according to the Center of Concern's **Five-Year Report** (1971-6), to (1) evaluate global policy issues with a radically open interdisciplinary approach, readily moving back and forth between ethical, value-informed analysis, competent social science analysis and lived experience; (2) support the concerns of developing nations, particularly as voiced in the United Nations, in policy discussions in North America; (3) identify the single struggle for justice in both global and domestic issues-namely, who has the power and in whose interest is it exercised; and (4) integrate a commitment to social change with spiritual resources, that is, to link faith and justice.[18]

The **Five-Year Report** also noted the Center of Concern's specific involvement with the Bicentennial Program:

> Over the past year, the Center has worked with the Bishops' Bicentennial program, "Liberty and Justice for All" by serving on the Conference Justice Committee, contributing a background paper on "Humankind" for the widely circulated initial document of the program, by offering testimony on the issues of food and women, and by serving on the panel during the Washington, D.C. hearing. Several staff members had accepted invitations to the October meeting in Detroit as delegates. The program has had major significance for the future of the U.S. Church and the Center will be supporting and monitoring its progress in the months to come.[19]

The Center did show its support and did monitor the progress of the Call to Action through its detailed analysis entitled Detroit and Beyond: The Continuing Quest for Justice. In the introduction to Detroit and Beyond, the following is expressed:

> The more the Center of Concern staff has seen of the Liberty and Justice for All process, the more hopeful we have become. Over the many months of its unfolding, we have become involved along with many others in a variety of ways. Three staff members were delegates to the Call to Action conference. As a contribution toward that meeting, the Center prepared its own critique and offered reflections on the process and program. Following the conference, the Center newsletter told the Detroit story in brief. In addition, we have had numerous discussions with other delegates and informed persons and have assessed news stories and reports. In all that has happened, we feel the Bicentennial program of the U.S. Bishops has more than lived up to its promise . . . the Center offers (additionally) Detroit and Beyond, a tabloid which lays out for you the reasons for our hopefulness. It offers our analysis of the entire process including the recommendations made at the Detroit conference. We hope that this piece, like our first Quest for Justice prepared in response to the 1971 Synod statement, Justice in the World, and circulated to 200,000 readers, will continue to contribute to the ongoing search for justice.[20]

The Center for Concern was not the only recently-created Catholic research institute that was actively involved in the Bicentennial Program. The "Quixote Center" located in Mt. Ranier, Maryland, distributed well over 100,000 copies of the Call to Action proposals immediately after the Detroit Conference in an attempt to aid in the implementation process. At present the concerns of the Center are threefold: (1) equality for women and men in the Church; (2) food for the hungry; and (3) the Call to Action implementation. The Center's Agenda for

Justice: Basic Documents of the U.S. Church's Social Policy, 1978-83 includes a "committee index" and "committee assignment" which clearly indicates to the reader just which Bishops' committee is responsible for the overseeing of each and every Call to Action proposal. The hope, obviously, is that such a convenient summary will encourage the formation of organized interest group pressure on the Bishops to enact the respective proposals.[21]

There were approximately 100 other Catholic organizations that were involved in the program and that have become part of an informal (although increasingly formal) web of liberal, social activist group affiliations. A few would include the likes of the National Office of Black Catholics, the National Black Sisters' Conference, the Christian Family Movement, the National Center for Urban Ethnic Affairs, the Campaign for Human Development, the Catholic Relief Services, the National Catholic Rural Life Conference, the National Conference of Catholic Charities, the National Assembly of Women Religious, the National Federation of Priests' Councils, the Catholic Campus Ministry Association, the National Catholic Education Association, the International Justice and Peace Organization, the National Council of Catholic Laity, and last, the N.C.C.B. Advisory Council.

The Bicentennial Program, in addition to these national organizations, involved the cooperation of many Catholic universities and colleges that included, among others, Catholic University, The University of Notre Dame, Fordham, and Holy Cross. Many regional organizations and state Catholic conferences played their parts in the overall machinery of the Bicentennial. Perhaps most important to the post-Vatican II "formal organizational revolution" that made the Bicentennial Program a possibility was the creation of various diocesan advisory groups. Examples of such advisory groups are priests' senates, pastoral councils, sisters' councils, priests' councils, and lay councils. Indeed, a full 37% of the Call to Action delegates were recruited from within this diocesan level organizational matrix. The advisory councils, then, represent the "lower-echelon" formal organizational base of the attempted "democratic revolution" within the American Catholic Church.

Of particular importance are the first two, i.e., priests' senates and pastoral councils, because they are specifically mandated by the conciliar legislation of the Second Vatican Council. The conciliar mandate for the creation of priests' senates revived and reorganized a previous concept called the "cathedral chapters" while the call for the establishment of pastoral councils that include lay representation is something totally new. Christus Dominus makes this clear. Speaking of the reaffirmation and necessary reorganization of the "cathedral chapters", the document follows:

> Included among the collaborators of the Bishop in the government of the diocese are those priests who constitute his senate or council, such as the cathedral chapter, the board of consultators or other committees established according to the circumstances or nature of various localities. To the extent necessary, these institutions, especially the cathedral chapters, should be reorganized in keeping with present-day needs.[22]

Regarding the creation of the concept of the pastoral council, Christus Dominus follows:

> It is highly desirable that in each diocese a pastoral council be established over which the diocesan Bishop himself will preside and in which specifically chosen clergy, religious, and lay people will participate. The function of this council will be to investigate and to weigh matters which bear on pastoral activity and to formulate practical conclusions regarding them.[23]

While sisters' councils, priests' councils and lay councils can be considered important new structures of representation within the American Catholic Church, the fact remains that their existence as a "legitimate" advisory group is doubtful due to their lack of specific conciliar mandate. In a ground-breaking study by Richard A. Schoenherr and Eleanor P. Simpson, it was disclosed that by 1974 priests' senates have been created in 98% of the American Catholic dioceses, pastoral councils in 50%, sister councils in 87%, priests' councils in 32% and

181

lay councils in 20% of the American Catholic dioceses.[24]

Schoenherr and Simpson make two points that are relevant for the question of the Church's ability to institutionalize "liberty and justice for all" through the creation of these diocesan advisory councils. The first points to the general ineffectiveness of the councils as democratizing agents. They indicate the ability of a Bishop to coopt council members rather than transfer power to them. For Schoenherr and Simpson, the councils "seem to be content with their lot of sharing responsibility for authoritative decisions while not having any effective control over them".[25] Put simply, the advisory councils share responsibility for decisions that emanate "from the top" while having no control over them. The second relevant point regards the priorities among the advisory groups on a number of crucial subjects. Again, their findings point to the limitations of institutionalizing the thrust of the Call to Action. They note that "organized advisory groups in U.S. Catholic dioceses have notably weaker community or national concerns than Church personnel and administrative concerns". As an example, the number one priority of priests' senates involve retirement plans while a typical Call to Action concern like initiating or planning a program on prison reform ranks last. Schoenherr and Simpson's report, in this regard at least, provides some empirical evidence for the charges put forth previously by the authors of the "Christian Declaration of Concern". The latter statement points to the parochial, "inwardly-looking" self-serving nature of those who operate organizational structures.

Schoenherr and Simpson, however, conclude their report by noting that experiments with diocesan consultative groups should not be regarded as trivial or useless. As they put it:

> Given the centuries-long tradition of strict monocratic authority and the ambivalence of the council fathers manifested in the decree suggesting their establishment, advisory councils are, not surprisingly, fighting an up-hill battle. Apparently they will have to double their efforts if further gains are to be won.[26]

Schoenherr and Simpson's qualification ought to be expanded on somewhat. First of all, the advisory councils are so recent in origin as to demand at least a decade or more to pass before a more useful assessment of their "revolutionary" impact can be made. (This, of course, is also the case regarding the effective implementation of the Call to Action proposals through these very structures.) Secondly, Schoenherr and Simpson perhaps fail to fully realize that the supposedly "coopted" elements frequently exact a price, and it is not always clear that the gain is worth the cost, or, indeed, just who is coopting whom in the long run. Finally there is a point to be made of Schoenherr and Simpson's that is quite consistent with Jeffrey Hadden's argument in The Gathering Storm in The Churches. Simply put, whatever the case may be at the local level today, the fact remains that there is a constant pressure being placed on the local level by activist oriented groups of liberal Catholics located in national-level organizations. On one hand, Schoenherr and Simpson note that "not much of the councils' energies are directed outside of the diocese". On the other hand, they follow that:

> ongoing communication is maintained with relevant "roof" organizations. Senates and priests' councils have established links with the National Federation of Priests' Councils, pastoral councils with the national and state Catholic conferences, and sisters' councils with the National Assembly of Women Religious.[27]

This communication is a cause of hope for the advocates of the Bicentennial movement. The national level structures of the U.S.C.C., the National Assembly of Women Religious and the National Federation of Priests' Councils were all represented strongly among the planners of the Call to Action. Their constant pressure on their local diocesan level counterparts, coupled with the future likelihood of a more articulate and "rational" relationship between all levels of the Church, and an increasingly larger base of support among a larger "middle-class" Catholic population-at-large may very well lead to a Church in which a concern for the rational and systematic implementation of justice will be dispersed much more widely than is the case today. Schoenherr and Simpson note the following:

A recent urban pastoral released by the National Federation of Priests' Councils (National Catholic Reporter, April 14th, 1978) calls for a dramatic change in direction for priests' advisory groups. The federation feels that time and effort given to specifically ecclesiastical problems should be curtailed and involvement in problems of the urban poor and oppressed minorities should be increased. Perhaps the stance being taken by this umbrella organization is an attempt to shake its member councils from the lethargic position on social issues documented by these data.[28]

There is, of course, a very real danger of over-emphasizing just how politically involved regarding questions of social justice the American Church will ever become. First of all, as previously noted, many Catholics, while not opposed to the Church taking a stand on questions of social justice, do not have their lives focus, in any meaningful, central way, in and around the concern for the disenfranchised. This may very well hold true, the process of embourgeoisement notwithstanding. Secondly, there is the overwhelming fact that the Call to Action was a national call in a Church that is run by Bishops in their local dioceses. Again, and despite the recent strengthening--both morally and materially-- of the N.C.C.B./U.S.C.C., the national level structure is still only a "voluntary" organization holding no, with the exception of direct Papal or conciliar intervention, binding power over a local Bishop and his diocesan wide activities. Simply put, and despite the relentless "educating" materials/programs generated by the professional staffs of the U.S.C.C., many Bishops simply consciously ignore or are indifferent to the national pleas. An intransigent Bishop, obviously, can be an extremely difficult obstacle to overcome in attempting to implement programs in a diocese. Even in the event of a sympathetic Bishop, the successful implementation of the Call to Action proposals or other social justice concerns presupposes at least some support from the lower-echelon priests and women religious. Organizationally, this translates into the presuppositions of (1) existant and (2) effective advisory groups. Schoenherr and Simpson's study indicates the highly uneven development of advisory councils in the U.S. and of their effectiveness (or, better yet, ineffectiveness) in those dioceses where they do exist. The question as to the future role of the advisory councils as democratizing agents and as agents for social change in the Church is, at this time, a moot question.

Given the shaky legitimacy of the Church's contemporary authority structure, the "purposeful ambiguity" of Vatican II theology, the incomplete development of an elaborate formal organizational machinery, and the uneven reception of the Bicentennial Program by Bishop, priest, religious, and lay person alike, the Church hierarchy seems to be saying to the local Church, in effect, "make out of the Bicentennial Program what you want to make out of it". What a diocese wants may be genuine shared decision-making over the implementation of social justice issues or it may be the simple ignoring of the thrust of the whole program. In many cases the local Church may decide to focus selectively on a few of the Call to Action proposals. In all of this, however, lies a simple problem: just who is the local Church? Obviously, the degree of success or failure of the Call to Action at the local level involves an intricate series of possible alliances and conflicts between/among Bishop, priests, religious and laity, and their various organizations. One thing, however, can be safely claimed--at no time has the American Catholic Church made such a bold, systematic and rational attempt to implement firmly on the agenda of both the national and local level of the Church (the former, much more successfully and with comparative ease) a concern for social justice.

FOOTNOTES

[1] The Hitchcock-Lucker exchange can be found in "The Land" Washington: (N.C.C.B. Committee for the Bicentennial, 1975).

[2] Abigail McCarthy, "Laity and Church: II", Commonweal July 21, 1978.

[3] Perrow quoted in Jay Demerath and Gerald Marwell, Sociology (N.Y.: Harper and Row, 1976).

[4] McCarthy, op. cit., July 21, 1976.

[5] Archbishop Peter L. Gerety quoted in "Nationhood" (Washington: N.C.C.B. Committee for the Bicentennial, 1975).

[6] Robert Cross, The Emergence of Liberal Catholicism in America (Chicago: Quadrangle Books, 1958, pg. 214-5).

[7] Christus Dominus in Walter Abbott (editor), The Documents of Vatican II (Washington: America Press, 1966).

[8] Ibid.

[9] Paul Harrison, Authority and Power in the Free Church Tradition (Princeton: Princeton University Press, 1959).

[10] Harrison, op. cit.

[11] That the maneuvers, at least openly, did not affect the liberal triumvirate of Egan-Higgins-Lally or, even at a higher level, the Dearden-Gerety combination, is consistent with the insight that "only the footsoldiers get mud on their faces".

[12] Jeffrey Hadden, The Gathering Storm in the Churches (N.Y.: Doubleday, 1969).

[13] Phillip Hammond, The Campus Clergyman (N.Y.: Basic Books, 1966).

[14] Monsignor John Egan and Sister Peggy Roach "Catholic Committee on Urban Ministry: Ministry to

the Ministers" unpublished paper, September, 1977.

[15] Sister Carol Coston, Network Quarterly Vol. 6, Number 8, October, 1978.

[16] Ibid.

[17] Robert L. Spaeth, The St. Cloud Visitor Oct. 26, 1978.

[18] Five Year Report of the Center of Concern, 1971-6 (Washington: Center of Concern, 1976).

[19] Ibid.

[20] Detroit and Beyond: The Continuing Quest for Social Justice (Washington: Center of Concern, 1976).

[21] Quixote Center, Agenda for Justice: Basic Documents of the U.S. Church's Social Policy, 1973-83, 1979.

[22] Christus Dominus in Abbott (editor) op. cit., 1966.

[23] Ibid.

[24] Richard A. Schoenherr and Eleanor P. Simpson, The Political Economy of Diocesan Advisory Councils: A Report of the Comparative Religious Organization Studies, University of Wisconsin, Madison, 1978.

[25] Ibid.

[26] Ibid.

[27] Ibid.

[28] Ibid.

CHAPTER EIGHT

THE SOCIAL ORGANIZATIONAL PRESUPPOSITION:
THE DEVELOPMENT OF THE
"NEW CATHOLIC KNOWLEDGE CLASS"

The New Catholic Knowledge Class

The emergence of the New Catholic Knowledge Class involves, most generally, combining the crucial insights of Karl Marx on the subject of class struggle and of Max Weber on the subject of the changing basis of authority in the modern world and applying these to developments within the American Catholic Church. The emergence of this class might very well mark the beginning of a struggle between competing elites-- between the American Bishops and the New Catholic Knowledge Class or, perhaps, between the latter and the Pope--over the right to generate and control both the doctrine and the social policy of the Catholic Church in America.

From Marx is taken, in modified form, his economic class analysis. For Marx the chief criteria for the emergence of a class are twofold. The first is the sharing of the same objective relationship by a group to the prevailing modes of production. In the case of the new class, "production" refers not to material goods, but to the realm of knowledge, symbols, and ideas. A great deal of literature has recently been written by economists, historians, and sociologists on the importance of the "knowledge industry" in modern life, the role that ever expanding bureaucratic structures play in such a development and the groups of individuals that are the principle producers, distributors and benefactors of this phenomenon.

The second general criterion for Marx for the emergence of a distinctive class is the degree of subjective awareness of a group in sharing common interests with its attendant ability to organize politically to acquire those interests. A "class-for-itself" exists only when both criteria are fulfilled. The Bicentennial movement, in addition to encouraging the development of new cadres of liberal Catholics, brought together existing social activists who, while sharing similar orientations to the role of religion in society, had nonetheless, given certain theological and formal organizational realities, been hitherto in a fragmented and inarticulate relationship to each other. The eight year "consciousness-raising" (or, more literally, "creating") program, coordinated at the national level by the U.S.C.C. and the Bicentennial Committee, has been active in expediting the crucial change from a "class-in-itself" to one approximating a "class-for-itself". This latter development implies a common hostility to another group, i.e., the American Bishops or the Vatican Curia, and requires political organizations (i.e. "the machinery of the American Catholic Church") to fight for such interests. Furthermore a presupposition of successful revolutions is that the rising class is able to identify its own interests with those of the total society (and in this case with the total Church) or, if you will, with "liberty and justice for all".

From Max Weber is taken the perception that in modern society bureaucratic forms of administration proliferate in every major area of life. This development brings with it a change in the authority or charisma latent within every institution, from that of the Bishop or Pope whose authority is granted by virtue of the concept of "Apostolic succession" to the "professional expert" (or as they were called at the Second Vatican Council, the "pereti") whose authority emanates from his/her possession of knowledge and/other professional skills.

The starting point for our discussion of the New Knowledge Class in American Catholicism is through a general explication of the four fold division of the American Catholic population as developed by Andrew Greeley. Speaking of his first division, what he calls the "liberal elite", Greeley follows:

> This most important group would include many clergy, most of the younger clergy and religious, significant portions of the well-educated adult laity, and those youthful laity who are most concerned about the Church. Within the liberal elite there also to be found most Catholic intellectuals, journalists, social actionists, and ideological liberals.[1]

Speaking of the second category, that of the "conservative elite", Greeley asserts:

> Some of its members make a calm and carefully reasoned case against change, arguing that the Catholic Church has no business trying to adjust to the modern world but rather must await the eventual collapse of the modern world to build a new Christendom. Others would place the Church outside of culture and would permit it to sit in judgement on culture but not directly influence it.[2]

Regarding the third category, Greeley continues:

> By far the largest group within the American Church is what we could call the "liberal masses". These are people who are sympathetic with some or most or all the changes in the Church but take their position more out of instinct or convenience or prejudice without having fully understood or thought out the issues at stake.[3]

And completing the four fold categorization:

> The final group are the "conservative masses"--that body of Catholics which are deeply and profoundly upset by the modifications of the post-conciliar age and feel that the whole structure of the religion is crumbling about them as elements of Christianity thought to be essential are discarded with reckless speed.[4]

Regarding Greeley's categories, the "conservative mass" is least applicable to the concept of the New Catholic Knowledge Class while his discussion of the "liberal elite", while not synonymous, is most relevant. The "liberal masses" are relevant only to the degree that its existence provides justification for the activities of the New Catholic Knowledge Class and also to the degree that this new class requires a base of lower-echelon types to fill certain minor roles in the formal organizations and social programs devised by this new category of Catholic. The "conservative elite", or at least the most intellectual and articulate segment, shares an interesting and, in a sense, parasitical relationship to the liberal elite. This is the relationship of a "loyal opposition".

Peter Berger defines the development of the New Class in American society-at-large:

> The New Class emerges from a distinctive change in the production mechanisms of contemporary society. This change is precisely the one that has spawned the vast knowledge industry. The New Class consists of people whose social position rests on the manipulation of symbols rather than on the manipulation of things. This social position implies a specific relationship to the economy (the production of knowledge, of symbols and ideas is an economic activity no less than the production of material commodities). It also expresses itself politically in the furtherance of class interests, and last and not least, it generates ideological constructions that serve to legitimate the same class interests.[5]

The New Catholic Knowledge Class signals the end of a "brick and mortar" Church oriented solely to the practical day-to-day contingencies of educating and protecting a hitherto immigrant people. It marks the emergence of significant numbers of educated and professionally-oriented individuals within an increasingly more bureaucratic Church.

It is important to point out that Greeley's discussion of the "liberal elite", while overlapping considerably with Berger's, is not the same as that of the New Class. Greeley is basically referring to "intellectuals" or to the "cultured elite" of the American Church. Berger, on the other hand, is referring to those individuals whose occupations are inextricably intertwined with the changing mode by which contemporary society (or in this case, the contemporary Church) distributes its goods and services. Put ever so crudely, there have always been "intellectuals" within the American Catholic Church; on the other hand, there has only recently developed large-scale national, regional and local Catholic organizations, bureaucracies and institutes characterized by full-time professional staffs devoted to theory, research, planning, and the administration of social programs.

Of course, not all of the developing New Catholic Knowledge Class is directly concerned with the creation and manipulation of symbols and ideas. Simply put, this new class is stratified within itself; only its very top echelon members concern themselves with the purely theoretical and abstract. The social locales for such elites are to be found at prestigious Catholic and private universities and colleges; in the various departments of the N.C.C.B./U.S.C.C.; at the leadership level of archdiocesan and diocesan Administration; within research institutes like the Center of Concern and the Quixote Center; with professional lobby groups like Network, national social justice organizations like C.C.U.M., and with Catholic journals and publishing houses. Below this elite centre there is a much larger complex of New Catholic Knowledge Class types within the lower reaches of the massive Catholic religious, educational, and social service network. While these latter strata may not be actually creating or manipulating new imagery, they nonetheless provide the indispensible function of servicing and administering programs that are generated "at the top". The "Justice Hearing" testifiers read like a "who's who" of the various levels of this new class.

In order to discuss the nature and development of the New Catholic Knowledge Class from Berger's perspective, then, one must superimpose over Greeley's discussion of the Catholic "liberal elite" a crucial insight of Karl Marx. It is that all classes, by virtue of the fact that they share certain common social coordinates, including most importantly, one's relationship to the modes of production, have certain visions and concrete interests to push that are legitimated by ideological constructions.

The relevance of Marx's insight for the Bicentennial Program, both in terms of the "social location" of the delegates and in terms of their proposals, is nothing less than startling. One striking common coordinate among the delegates was the fact that over 90% of them were actively involved in various Church organizations. Even more telling is the disclosure that a full 65% of the delegates were directly employed by the Church. Holding constant the important "subjective" question of motivation, the "objective" set of concrete material interests of such a group is simple enough: more bureaucracy, more jobs, higher income and status, and an increased "say" in, if not immediately the "legal-rational" authority of a Church based on tradition, at least in day-to-day practical decision-making power that Paul Harrison has termed "rational-pragmatic" authority.[6]

The "objective" set of interests of those advocating the implementation of the Bicentennial can be seen through reanalyzing, only this time through a more economic lense, the Call to Action proposals. At the most general level, of course, all the proposals, if implemented, would serve to push the concrete interests of the New Catholic Knowledge Class. This is so for no other reason than to "implement" means to use or create the very organizations and structures that the knowledge elite either currently run, or given further expansion, would operate.

Many of the proposals, however, can be targeted more specifically at the various levels of the Church. As David O'Brien aptly pointed out, the Call to Action proposals ideally would have the concern for social justice systematically connected from and to the parish, diocesan, regional and national levels. Regarding those organizations either under the jurisdiction of, or intimately involved with the N.C.C.B./ U.S.C.C., there were calls for:

--the establishment of a U.N. Office through the Office of International Justice and Peace of the U.S.C.C.

--the establishment of a multiethnic office within the N.C.C.B.

--the expansion of the Spanish-speaking Secretariat and the establishment of a National Hispanic Research Center.

--the creation of an American Indian Secretariat within the U.S.C.C./N.C.C.B.

--the creation of a National Catholic
Women's Secretariat within the N.C.C.B./
U.S.C.C.

--the establishment of a National Catholic
Office for the Handicapped.

--the establishment of a "Marriage and
Family Life" standing committee within
the N.C.C.B. and the enlargement and
strengthening of the National Family
Life Office.

--the creation of a "Neighborhood Social
Concern" office within the U.S.C.C.

--the strengthening and systematizing of
the Campaign for Human Development,
Catholic Charities, and the National
Catholic Rural Life Conference.

--the creation of a National Catholic
Review Board.

--the establishment of a national
Catholic commission on "Economic Justice",
with representation from each diocese and
national organizations which will, in
addition, solicit the support of university
scholars.

--the creation of a National Catholic
Organization to "fight for tax funds to
parents to enable them to exercise their
religious freedom rights in the education
of their children in the schools of their
choice".

--the U.S.C.C. is "to stimulate, either
through new or existing organizations,
dialogue with other groups such as labor
unions, professional societies, business
organizations, cooperative movements,
and citizen's groups to translate the
implications of justice into practical
norms of action".

--the establishment of a Call to Action
Task Force through institutionalization

of the Bicentennial office to see through
to completion the implementation of the
proposals.

   At the state and diocesan level there were
calls for:

--the establishment of a "neighborhood
social concerns" office in each and
every Catholic State Conference.

--the creation of committees for "political
responsibility" at parish, diocesan, state
and national levels.

--the establishment within every diocese
of offices for "Justice and Peace", "multi-
cultural and interethnic curriculum", "adult
programs for education", "racism and discrimination", "black, Hispanic, Indian,
and ethnic concerns", "neighborhood social
concerns", "Catholic rural life", "economic
justice", "shared responsibility" and for
the monitoring of the implementation of the
Call to Action proposals.[7]

   The ideology of the New Catholic Knowledge
Class is derived from a "selective" reading of
Vatican II theology emphasizing a broad interpretation of the concept of "collegiality" that is reinforced by the democratizing ethos of the surrounding
American cultural matrix. In a very real sense the
ideology of the new class is consciously "carved out
of" Vatican II and post Vatican II statements. While
the pieces or the "content" of the supporting Catholic
theology/ideology for the new class is selectively
derived from Catholic documents, there is an important
observation to be made regarding its "formal" construction. Catholic theology/ideology has historically
claimed to be "explanatory" in that it derives most
of its wisdom and knowledge from the past and is
"handed down" from the hierarchy to a mostly passive,
inert mass. In contradistinction to this, more
modern Catholic theology is being increasingly
described in terms of "participation" and "process".
Simply put, in a social context that presupposes some
approximation of the democratic ideal, individuals
who hitherto were considered--and considered themselves-
beyond the pale of defining the theological universe are

expected to contribute to this enterprise in terms of what Avery Dulles has referred to as "exploratory" models and of what "theology of liberation" theologian Gutierrez describes as "critical reflection on praxis".[8]

This shift in the defining locus of the theological universe is concomitant with the development of the New Catholic Knowledge Class. That is, unlike the traditional clergy/laity who, for the most part, have historically concerned themselves with the "bread and butter" issues of a "brick and mortar" Church or with the more traditional theologians who interpret the Word strictly in light of a heavily circumscribed Church tradition, this new class deals in the creation (and subsequently, in the implementation) of new symbols and ideas. On the contrary, for most of Greeley"s "conservative mass", "conservative elite", and even a great deal of the "liberal mass", tradition is of primary importance. For the "liberal elite" or the new Catholic Knowledge Class, tradition is either easily modified or abandoned as "reason dictates". For the New Catholic Knowledge Class, tradition is interpreted in terms of "process", or more radically, subordinated to "praxis". The development of the New Catholic Knowledge Class essentially entails a struggle between competing elites, that is, on the one hand, between the Bishops or Pope who rule by virtue of a traditional authority, i.e., by virtue of the concept of "apostolic succession" and, on the other hand, the new class who claim a say in decision making by virtue of their belief in the reality of their own charisma, of their belief in the Bicentennial Program as a burgeoning "social movement" itself imbued with charisma, and of the idea that the social order can be made more "just" and "equitable" through the exercise of their professional "expertise".[9]

The relationship between these two classes is, in reality, not one of the unremitting conflict. The Bicentennial gave evidence of compromise, mutual cooperation, and perhaps, even the tacit beginnings of coalescence between some segments of the New Catholic Knowledge Class, that of Greeley's discussion of the "old social action", and the "liberal wing" of the American Catholic hierarchy. The segment of the new class most willing and able to cooperate with the Bishops represent the "moderate" and "pragmatically" oriented who have faith in the institutional Church's ability to adjust internally. As Andrew Greeley states, "some of the liberal elite are evolutionists who would be content with growth from the existing structures toward a substantially modified ecclesiastical organism".[10] Greeley then goes on to describe the more utopian segment of the new class as follows: "others, perhaps, a smaller number, are revolutionaries who expect nothing from the present structure and feel that it must either be destroyed or permitted to wither so that a fresh start can be made".[11]

One of the major unintended functions of the Bicentennial Program is that it serves nicely as a sort of experiment, to wit: to see whether or not cooperation between charisma-of-the-office and its dispersion is a viable proposition. A series of "ideal-typical" responses to this question can be identified. At one extreme lies the "radical" response of those who feel it totally futile to work within the existing Church structure: one must start anew totally ignoring and totally indifferent to the role of the Magisterium. The previous discussion of those advocating "A Christian Declaration of Concern" and an "institutionless Christianity" represent the "moderate" and "radical" viewpoint, respectively. At the other extreme lies the truly "conservative" response that demands that Catholic intellectuals and professionals submit completely to the authority of the Magesterium, thus absconding from a true participation in the outer, and to use Edward Shils' nomenclature, "civil" society. From the "conservative" viewpoint the Call to Action assembly and surrounding program represents a form of lay interference and abrogation of authority that, if either not suppressed or somehow contained, could lead to the radical transformation of the Catholic Church as it has historically presented itself to the world, at least since the third or fourth century.

There are two intermediate "liberal" ideal-typical responses that ought to be mentioned, one anchored more closely to the "conservative" endpoint, the other gravitating toward the "radical" solution. The "liberal-conservative" position would be that the Call to Action assembly and surrounding program represents precisely the cordial and sincere lay cooperation espoused by the Second Vatican Council, which, while leaving matters of doctrine ultimately in the hands of those who rule by "apostolic succession" would at the same time incorporate increasing numbers of Catholics in positions in the Church that are "advisory" in nature and that also function to actually increase the Church's ability to implement its social doctrine throughout the nation.

The response which gravitates toward, but stops short of, the radical solution may be termed that of the "liberal-radical" mode. It is given this label because, on the one hand, this solution makes unclear the questions of just how much ultimate authority the layman or lower-echelon clergy and religious will demand in the immediate future. On the other hand, this solution is one not necessarily at odds with the continuation of some sort of hierarchial authority. It is clear that the Bicentennial advocates can, in most cases, be fit into either the "liberal-conservative" or "liberal-radical" solutions to the question of authority in the contemporary Church.

The Bicentennial Program as an "experiment" in authority relationships takes even more urgent importance given the voluntary nature of the religious commitment in settings like that of the United States. As Peter Berger might put it, in a "market situation" of open competition between denominations and, just as important, other less institutionalized options like the American Civil Religion, the dissatisfied simply can leave and "go shopping" elsewhere.[12] The program then cannot be called "revolutionary" for yet another reason. As Crane Brinton informs us, the "anatomy" of a revolutionary movement presupposes a closed arena within which conflict ensues; the disenchanted Catholic, on the other hand, can just as readily leave the Church as fight within it.[13] Put another way, "open systems" breed as much indifference as conflict.[14]

There are several important additional points that must be brought up in our discussion of the New Catholic Knowledge Class. The first point involves the relationship of the new class to working-class, ethnic Catholics. On one hand, it was clear that ethnic Catholics were seriously underrepresented at Detroit and throughout the Bicentennial Program. What is terribly unclear is the question of whether it is the Pope, the Bishops as a group, or the new class that constitutes the "natural" ally of such Catholics. All make this claim. On the one hand, the New Catholic Knowledge Class points out that it is the avant-garde segment of the "democratic revolution" in the American Catholic Church. That the democratic spirit of the knowledge class may not necessarily extend down any further than its own enclave is an interesting question that must be pursued. Andrew Greeley does pursue this issue. Speaking of "urban ministry types (C.C.U.M.) at the University of Notre Dame" who feel "that we have to be ashamed of our own people", Greeley has this to say in defensive response:

> The precious elitists involved in urban ministry feel morally, intellectually, and religiously superior to the poor, simple Polack or Dago who lives in an ethnic parish and doesn't read the Commonweal or The New York Times. What in the world could we ever learn from the ethnic or ethnic parish that would have any pertinence at all to religious and social problems in American life?[15]

A leading conservative spokesman, James Hitchcock, also addressed this issue in an editorial entitled "Age of Renewal?" In this editorial Dr. Hitchcock exposes the false and overbearing elitism and arrogance of certain professionals (both clergy and lay) through an incident in the diocese of Richmond at Lynchburg. Hitchcock starts and ends his editorial as follows:

> In this age of "renewal", we often told, priests have come to regard themselves less as authority figures and more as servants of the people of God. This is supposedly the age of the laity, in which the voice of the people in the pews must be heard. But there is a sociological law which says that, in any community or institution, an elite group will always end up wielding power, no matter how democratic the formal structure may be. One of my favorite theses is that, in certain ways, we have more authoritarianism in the post-conciliar Church than we did twenty years ago . . . . The irony is that the Lynchburg parish is named for St. Thomas More. This is the same Thomas More who, in his debates with William Tyndale, defended the faith

of simple people against the pretensions of
the learned, and who remained loyal to the
Pope when so many religious professionals
were telling him that it was better to serve
the King.[16]

That the New Catholic Knowledge Class may be
out of step with the "faith of the simple people" is
again brought up by Andrew Greeley:

> I am . . . fed up with the self-hatred,
> the cryptonativism and assimilation of
> the Catholic elite--and more recently,
> with the official Church whose pro-
> nouncements are now strongly influenced
> by the currently fashionable left chic.
> Does the left warn of the dangers of
> pluralism? So must all the party-line
> Catholic journals like America or
> Commonweal. Does the left insist that
> we must turn to socialism in the post-
> Vietnam era? So do their pale Catholic
> imitators. Does the left decree that
> minority group spokesmen must have a veto
> on all public pronouncements? So does
> the committee that puts together the
> National Catechetical Directory. Does
> the left decide that the Bicentennial
> must be an orgy of recrimination over
> the nation's failures--unmitigated by
> even the thought that something might
> have gone right in the U.S.? The
> U.S.C.C. and its bureaucrats eagerly
> agree.[17]

Indeed, the present Pope or many of America's
conservative Bishops could point out that perhaps the
type and extent of "democratization" that the new
class has in mind is not only inapplicable given the
historic nature of the Church but, moreover, finds no
large base of support within the Catholic community,
Greeley's "liberal mass" included. Rather they might
argue that the "proper" emphasis of the Catholic
calling, one shared by both "liberal" and "conservative"
masses, is the other-worlding emphasis on the worship
of the One God as meditated by those who stand in
"apostolic succession" to Peter. As such, the heart
and minds of the very "people" that the new class claims
as their own actually are with the Bishops. Interestingly

enough, Avery Dulles has this to say about the vision of the Call to Action vis-a-vis the average layman:

> I doubt that people will come to the Church
> ... simply because of the Church's effective social ministry .... The Church, (if) it is to retain an enthusiastic constituency, must confer something distinctive that not even the best social system could confer. What draws people to the Church and keeps them united to it is, I suspect, a confidence that the Church is able to put them in Communion with God. They know that the world and its problems will be with them until they die, but they're desperate for a vivifying contact with the eternal spirit in Whom all things begin and end, the God who can bring life even to the dead.[18]

An equally important and interesting question is the relationship of this new class to the most recently defined group of "minorities", or as they were labeled throughout the Bicentennial Program, the "victims of injustice". Peter Berger is particularly lucid on this point:

> ... identification with the cause of the downtrodden is of particular importance in the moral legitimation of New Class interests. The "discovery" of every new group of deprived people in society legitimates the inauguration of programs that benefit the New Class-- no matter whether they also benefit those on whose behalf the programs are supposed to exist. Thus the poor probably did obtain gains from the redistribution of income inaugurated by the War Against Poverty--but there can be no doubt about the massive gains obtained by all those New Class individuals through whom government "poverty money" was channeled ... there can be no doubt about the New Class interests in the resultant networks of bureaucracy.[19]

Questions logically arise: to what degree will the "victims of injustice" be content to play the

202

role of the "foot soldier" for the New Catholic Knowledge Class? Under what situations will such a coalition remain viable or untenable?

Caveats to our discussion of the New Catholic Knowledge Class are in order. First of all, while it is perhaps true that the Catholic Church has, at least vis-a-vis the other American denominations, a well-developed (and growing) organizational and bureaucratic structure, it pales when compared to the enormous government apparatus presently in operation. Secondly, by no means is there any necessary innuendo to the effect that the various Call to Action proposals that were espoused are uncalled for. Thirdly, neither does this imply that the motives of the new class are purely selfish. Suffice it to say here that the motivation of the proposals must be distinguished from their impact. In terms of motivation, in many cases, without doubt, the question of a gain in power and privilege is quite remote from the mental horizon. A great deal of the Bicentennial advocates are individuals who are moved into sacramental this-worldly activity that is derived out of their sense of their religious calling. David Riesman's observation to the effect that "most people believe their own propaganda", while perhaps an unflattering insight, nonetheless correctly perceives the fact that most people are sincere most of the time. In perhaps even more instances, the empirical case may be that motives are "mixed". One can help mankind in the name of God and simultaneously acquire a respected position within one's frame of reference. But the fact remains that the proposals possess an "objective" reality or "impact" that must be contended with at both a social-structural and social-psychological level. The impact in the former case involves certain proposed changes in both the social and formal organization of the American Catholic Church. The impact in the latter case involves the change in personality that an increase in the power and privilege coordinates of one's social location encourages. This insight is partially conveyed through the famous quote of Lord Acton, to the effect "that power corrupts, and absolute power corrupts absolutely".

Another qualification is to make clear that not all of the ideas or proposals of the New Catholic Knowledge Class can be easily fit under the rubric of class-specific ideologies. The point here is that it is precisely the kind of abstract, generalized, and rationalized thinking characteristic of at least the higher levels of the New Catholic Knowledge Class that is capable of critically reflecting on and transcending narrowly defined "interests" and the exigencies of specific occasions. The point here is to acknowledge that certain individuals do possess a greater ability than most for critical thought, skepticism, and logical discourse, whether out of considerations of differing social structural or biographical backgrounds, or differing linguistic or educational training.

There is, then, basically two ideal-typical modes from which to view the new class from the question of their "objectivity". The first extreme case would posit that this new class of Catholic is as "particularistic", as grounded in immediacy, as any other sub-division of the Catholic population-at-large. The only difference here is that these "public sphere" particularists, due to both their ability to manipulate imagery and control over the means of the implementation of that imagery throughout society, have a greater ability to effect change within the American Catholic Church than do other American Catholic groupings. Enough has previously been said to make this assertion at least partially plausible. The other extreme case would impute a magical detachment and objectivity to the new class stressing the justifiable authority that accrues to this class due to their professionalism and expertise.

The point in contrasting these two interpretations is not to choose one over the other; the truth, as usual, is a mixed bag. Rather the point is to qualify and modify one in the light of the other. Simply put, if the possibility of detachment and objectivity lies anywhere, it is with the New Catholic Knowledge Class for the aforementioned reasons. As a matter of fact, a few of the proposals indicate that the delegate and writing committee members did demonstrate at least some empathetic ability and would propose at least some legislation and social policy respecting both the cognitive and normative social definitions of a very complex and pluralistic Church. A few of these are calls for:

--shared responsibility in policy making and administration

--promotion of multilingual and multi-cultural values and education policy

--support for Church movements or small groups which unite persons of any persuasion in either worship/prayer, study, evangelization and apostolic study

--creation of environments in which each person can recognize his or her own vocation, whether married, single, religious or ordained clergy, as a divine call or Christ. Furthermore those calls, by God, to vocation are recognized as equal in dignity

--increased awareness on the part of the parishes of the social, economic, and political realities in which it is enmeshed

--the creation of a Call to Action implementation task-force that reflects accurately the actual racial, ethnic, cultural and sexual makeup of the Church in the U.S.

--the N.C.C.B. to publically communicate its desire to respond to proposals for action which come from ethnic, racial, and cultural organizations; commit itself to facilitate and encourage efforts of such groups to formulate pastoral and social action programs to meet their needs; communicate their needs to the whole Church; and assist in developing the resources to meet those needs

--diocesan and national liturgical commissions and agencies to guarantee adequate representation of all ethnic, racial, and cultural groups

--the facilitation for seminary and other training for ministeries of multilingual and multicultural education

--a recognition on the part of the Church leadership at all levels to clearly assert

its commitment to a unity of faith in
pluralism which recognizes the rights
of diverse ethnic, racial, and cultural
groups to maintain and develop their
traditional cultures.[20]

A final question "holds constant" the question
of whether or not the New Catholic Knowledge Class
constitutes an ideological or detached intelligentsia.
The question, instead, involves the analysis of just
how effective is this new class as a vehicle for
institutionalizing important social change, whether
self-serving or not. Does this class represent a
"prophetic" element within the Church? And, if so,
in what way? Or, is this leading wing of Catholic
professionals and specialists actually in the process
of being coopted by a Church with a long and distinguished record--minus the 16th century exception,
the Reformation--of "containing" its most charismatically
endowed individuals?

The indicators, while far from completely
decisive, point to some important gains for the New
Catholic Knowledge Class. An examination of the
syllabi of many Catholic colleges and certainly all
Catholic universities today would indicate far more
freedom from a narrowly circumscribed Catholic tradition than was the case just prior to the Second
Vatican Council. As but one example of this increased
autonomy from Catholic tradition as shaped by ecclesiastical authority, it is fair to say that, in the battle
between those forces pushing for a distinctly
"Catholic" sociology versus those in favor of a more
ostensibly "value-free" sociology of Catholicism, the
latter camp has emerged victorious.

The related issue of academic versus
ecclesiastical authority in Catholic institutions of
higher education, bitterly contested during the 1960's
at the Catholic University, St. John's University,
Duquesne University, and the University of Dayton among
many others, have generally been won by the advocates
of the former.

Yet another sign of the increased influence
of the new class is the emergence of religious and
intellectual magazines and journals that allow for
severe criticism of the activities of the Church. Of
specific relevance here is the creation of such

"liberal" magazines, newspapers and journals as National Catholic Reporter, America, Commonweal, and Cross-Currents. Another indicator suggesting the successful institutionalization of the vision of the new class is the decreased use, and less effective use, of the Catholic index and other such "lists" which censure "free-thinking" (and "free participation") in the realms of intellectual, moral, and aesthetic discourse.

Regarding the question of the ability to institutionalize social change within the American Catholic Church, the impressive literature in the sociology of organized religion can be of invaluable assistance. Liston Pope's Millhands and Preachers, for instance, makes the point that religious institutions can be a source of cultural transformation only to the degree that they transcend the immediate surrounding matrix in which they function on a day-to-day basis. The New Catholic Knowledge Class, by virtue of their relatively "structurally free" position, to use Jeffrey Hadden's term, is in a position to push for radical social change within the American Catholic Church and within American society. That the new class is not as "structurally-free" as their Protestant or Jewish comrades is explained by the fact that it operates under the potential veto-power of the Bishops. The fact that two of the principal Call to Action organizers, Dr. Frank Butler and Sister Margaret Cafferty were "contained" by the Bishops during the interval between the end of the Call to Action assembly and the first May meeting of Bishops when the majority of Bishops were frightened that the Bicentennial movement might have been "snowballing", empirically illustrates the point. That, on the other hand, the authority of the Bishops is, for simply practical reasons, less than fully capable of controlling the course of events and activities of the New Catholic Knowledge Class is illustrated, again, through Paul M. Harrison's discussion of "rational pragmatic" authority. Translated into the Catholic case the point is that the overwhelming percentage of American Bishops, for both practical and theological reasons, have their primary responsibility at the local level of the diocese and parish. It is, furthermore, primarily managerial in nature and not concerned with the more theoretical issues of translating Catholic theology into a form of Catholic "praxis". They must rely, then, on staffs of "professionals", "specialists", and bureaucrats to run the day-to-day affairs of the various national level organizations, diocesan level organizations and research institutes. That the "void" in authority left by the Bishops' lack of "expertise" can be quickly filled by the confident members of the New Catholic Knowledge Class can be demonstrated in a grand way to pointing to the simple fact that the activities of an ostensibly "safe" "Bishops' Bicentennial Committee" grew in its largeness, boldness, and vision to the point that one could see evidence of the nervousness and infuriation on the part of many Bishops both at Detroit and in their various post-Detroit "maneuvers".

Demerath and Hammond also note the advantage that the Catholic Church has in implementing its social policy precisely because of its bureaucratic construction:

> even though Catholicism's indirect influence on society through its parishioners may be reduced, considerable direct influence remains. One of the ironies of the Catholic impact . . . is that it may well be greater on society at large than among Catholic parishioners alone. Because Catholics are the largest single denomination in America and because they are especially organized to fight bureaucratic fire with bureaucratic fire, Catholicism has considerable leverage as a pressure group . . . . Insofar as religion organizes to conduct information campaigns, to maintain lobbies in Washington and state capitols, and to carry on fund drives, it will have impact. These activities are obviously more easily carried out regionally than locally, nationally than regionally, and ecumenically than denominationally.[21]

In another sense the New Catholic Knowledge Class is actually in a superior position to many fellow social activists in the other religious denominations: not only does the New Catholic Knowledge Class have the formal organizational support of the Catholic Church to operate out of, but also it has the theological legitimation of many post-Vatican II Papal statements. Simply put, the "socially" oriented statements of the recent Popes have forced even the most non-activist Bishop to take the call for social justice seriously--even if not with a great deal of personal sympathy. The advocates of the "Liberty and Justice for All" program know well that, in many areas, the national and international vision of liberal Catholicism has won the day, at least "officially", and they will use their educational, linguistic, social scientific skill as well as their strategic locations in key Church structures to make sure that even the most intransigent "get the message".

To assert that the social activist, national and international perspective of the New Catholic Knowledge Class has become firmly institutionalized within the Church is not to claim that this position represents the wave of the future for the Church; only that it is "here to stay". In a fascinating sense the Catholic Church has been developing a system of "checks and balances" that includes an intricate relationship between Pope, national episcopal conference, local Bishop, clergy, religious and laity. Such a system guards against the Church "as the people of God" making excessive commitments in any direction, be it along the lines of social activism or spirituality, localism or cosmopolitanism, a belief in reason or historically interpreted messages of Divine Revelation. Vatican II, dramatized in the American case through the reality of the Bicentennial Program, has "stretched" the vision of the Church to allow the entrance of those like the New Catholic Knowledge Class who have accepted at least the brunt of the modern vision.

FOOTNOTES

[1] Andrew Greeley, The Catholic Experience (N.Y.: Doubleday, 1970, pp. 301-2).

[2] Ibid., p. 303.

[3] Ibid., pp. 303-4.

[4] Ibid., p. 304.

[5] Peter L. Berger, "Ethics and the Present Class Struggle", Worldview, April, 1978.

[6] Paul M. Harrison, Authority and Power in the Free Church Tradition (Princeton: Princeton University Press, 1959).

[7] Origins: National Catholic Documentary Service, Vol. 6, Number 20, November 4, 1976 and Vol. 6, Number 21, November 21, 1976.

[8] Avery Dulles, Models of the Church (N.Y.: Doubleday, 1978); Gustavo Gutierrez, A Theology of Liberation (Maryknoll, N.Y.: Orbis Books, 1973).

[9] Indeed, as the latter point implies (and by the way a point that Weber apparently missed), the "idea" of rationality can itself be perceived as charismatic.

[10] Andrew Greeley, op. cit., 1970, p. 302.

[11] Ibid.

[12] Peter L. Berger, The Sacred Canopy (N.Y.: Doubleday, 1967).

[13] Crane Brinton, The Anatomy of a Revolution (N.Y.: Random House, 1960).

[14] This problem is a particularly salient one for a new class characterized by a heightened sense of its own importance for both the future of the Church and of world society.

[15] Andrew Greeley, The Communal Catholic (N.Y.: Seabury Press, 1976).

[16] James Hitchcock, "Age of Renewal?" National Catholic Register, March 4, 1979.

[17] Andrew Greeley, op. cit., 1976, p. ix.

[18] Avery Dulles, "Nationhood" (Washington: N.C.C.B. Committee for the Bicentennial, 1975).

[19] Peter L. Berger, op. cit., April, 1978.

[20] Origins: National Catholic Documentary Service, Vol. 6, Number 20, November 4, 1976 and Vol. 6, Number 21, November 21, 1976.

[21] N.J. Demerath and Phillip Hammond, Religion in Social Context (N.Y.: Random House, 1969, pp. 226-9).

CHAPTER NINE

THE SOCIOLOGICAL SOCIAL-PSYCHOLOGICAL PRESUPPOSITION:
THE AMERICAN CATHOLIC SOCIAL-PSYCHOLOGICAL REVOLUTION

It has previously been argued that the Bicentennial Program has served as the vehicle by which the Catholic left has more firmly situated itself within the American Church. This entrenchment is not, however, just a reflection of the reality of Vatican II theology. Neither is it simply exercised through the burgeoning job networks and career channels of a New Catholic Knowledge Class that dominates the Catholic bureaucracy and its educational, publishing, and media institutions. Simply put, an analysis of the cultural-theological and social-formal organizational revolutions does not exhaust the study of the Bicentennial movement and its implications for both the present and future of the Church. There is another revolution which must be discussed in order to complete our portrait. It is the "social psychological" revolution that is taking place in numerous ways and with varying degrees of intensity within the hearts and minds of the different components of the new class.[1]

It is important to point out that the social-psychology of the Bicentennial movement is grounded from a sociological, as compared to psychological, point of view.[2] That is, the discussion of various social psychological orientations in evidence throughout the Bicentennial Program stresses the impact of cultural-theological and social-formal organizational processes on the consciousness of the individual and not, primarily at least, the other way around. Put another way, the emphasis is on personality formation as the intersection of educational, historical, and biographical processes and events. Given such an emphasis, it should be clear that the social psychology of the Bicentennial movement does not paint a picture of like-minded individuals; rather a more accurate portrayal involves a series of partially overlapping distinctions, orientations, and responses that roughly corresponds to differing educational, historical and biographical backgrounds. Such an emphasis on internal differentiation does not preclude certain similarities that cut across the various participants of the movement which, in turn, sets them apart, qua group, from the broader matrix of American Catholicism. A few such regularities would include a this-worldly activistic stance to the cosmos; a desire to be, in some sense, organizationally affiliated to their religion; a belief that a concern for justice is a constitutive part of the religious calling; an openness to change indicative of a fundamental optimism that, in some cases, borders on utopianism; and a belief that a well-grounded use of human reason and the inspirational call and demands of divine revelation, if not synonomous, are almost always compatible.[3] Put negatively, the movement neither sought out nor encouraged those with a more passive world-rejecting "mystical" Catholicism, typical of the monastery; or those whose religious sensibilities can just as easily be satisfied outside of an ecclesiastically defined structure, as with the Catholic charismatics or the "communal" Catholics as discussed by Andrew Greeley; or those working-class ethnic Catholics indifferent to the systematic and symmetrical vision of a Catholic inspired socialism; or, finally, those "hard-line" intransigent conservatives fearing change or any embrace with the outer culture and who find any independent reliance on human reason to be sinful and in fundamental error. This last option runs the gamut from those who form a powerful conservative faction within the Church to those, like the Catholic Traditional Movement, which border on a heresy-of-the-right.

Given these basic regularities, however, a proper analysis of the social psychology of the Bicentennial involves the awareness of a variety of responses on the part of the movement's advocates in light of the exaggerated processes of social change affecting the Church today. This social psychological revolution finds its origins in an exceedingly complex interplay of factors. On the one hand, there is the underlying propensity, engendered for the most part by formal training, of the more intellectual components of the new class--Catholic or otherwise--for abstract thought and the corresponding "need" for neat, rational, logical, systematic, theoretical constructions.[4] The Catholic Church has never lacked historically for such overarching, comprehensive explanations of reality. A fascinating project, far beyond both the scope of this work and the competency of its author, would be to trace the history of these overarching "official" Church explanations of reality and the conditions under which one is supplanted for another. This call, paraphrasing Thomas Kuhn, is for an analysis of "the structure of Catholic revolutions".[5] The concern here, however, is far less ambitious. It entails a brief discussion of (1) the Catholic paradigm that formed the background matrix from which the present social psychological revolution is operating over and against; (2) some general factors that have led to the smashing of this taken-for-granted worldview; (3) the leading contender for paradigmatic ascension in the minds of the New Catholic Knowledge Class; and (4) the relationship of the varied strata of the new class to this social construction which is in the process of gaining theoretical ascension.

The given worldview for the American Catholic intellectual prior to the Second Vatican Council was constructed and molded out of the reality of a Vatican I inspired theology, exemplified quintessentially in the documents of Piux IX, The Dogma of Papal Infallibility and The Syllabus of Errors as well as in Pius XI's Pascendi Dominici and that of his Inquisition, Lamentabile Sane. Enough has previously been said to make clear that the paradigmatic status of this theoretical construction was anything but unchallenged in the United States by the historically ever-present wing of liberal Catholicism. Nonetheless it is reasonably clear that such an inwardly-looking perspective ruled the day, at least "officially". This inwardly-looking worldview was reinforced, again, by the realities of an outer American culture permeated with strong elements of nativism, the concrete needs of a pragmatic immigrant population, and an ad hoc formal organizational structure in which the respective units were in poor communication and were isolated from each other. Such a discontinuous relationship between the Catholic "centre" and "periphery" both among and between parishes and dioceses added to the stabilizing of the Vatican I worldview. Such a worldview stressed that the Catholic intellectual display obedience and piety in respect to a heavily circumscribed Catholic tradition.

It is also important to point out that this Vatican I worldview--as with all worldviews--operates in a "dialectical" fashion at the independent yet interdependent levels of "culture" and "personality".[6]

At the level of culture this system of symbols is capable of attaining a level of perfection, of incontrovertible "logic" and "system". At the individual level of personality, i.e., within the "cognitive map" that outlines the day-to-day thought and activity of the individual such consistency is, however, impossible.[7] It is precisely the intellectual, however, who constantly strives to minimize the inconsistency between the "ideal" cultural symbol system and his own mental action blueprint. The religious virtuosi, following Weber, is capable of reaching the level of a quite rational, ethnically-infused "world-religion". The mass of humanity, in contradistinction, may be characterized by a religiosity and form of rationalism that is more economically-oriented, pragmatic, and "primitive".[8]

The underlying propensity and need for symmetry and consistency of the intellectual comes into play for our analysis of the social psychological revolution given the exaggerated processes of social change operant both within and outside of the Church that have disrupted the hitherto given and taken-for-granted post-Vatican I worldview.[9] The smashing of this worldview finds its cause in many factors. A few of these factors include the development of a more inclusive "civil religion", the reality of the Second Vatican Council itself, the middle-classification of the American Catholic population and a professionalization concomitant with the enormous spread of the Church bureaucracy. These factors have fostered a sense of "irrelevance", "error", or using Thomas Kuhn's phrase, "anomaly" regarding the post Vatican I worldview, at least among the more intellectual segment which feels compelled to synthesize or incorporate the latest ideas or currents within the boundaries of its cognitive map. It is just this ability and need for synthesis that characterizes modern day religiosity as indicated through the impressive formulations of "mysticism", as discussed by Troeltsch, and the "mature religious personality" as developed by Allport.[10] While a certain degree of "irrelevance" is tolerated--that is, considered "normal"--within the mental apparatus of any individual, the "tolerance" degree is apt to be much lower for those intellectuals who yearn so much for a sense of "mental closure".[11] This sense of urgency regarding the "evening out" of "anomalies" is a presupposition of the "paradigmatic revolutions"--scientific or, in this case, religious--of which Thomas Kuhn has spoken.[12]

Interestingly enough, the very factors that have fostered a sense of obsolescence regarding Vatican I worldview have lead to an unusual search for paradigmatic reconstruction, at least from the historic frame of reference of the Catholic Church. The "unusualness" of the search lies in the width of its scope, a scope including many Catholic intellectuals--lay and clergy--only recently emancipated from their previously "contained" role within the Church. The search for paradigmatic reconstruction is operant within no less inclusive an attachment than what Edward Shils has referred to as civil society. Correspondingly, it is the case that many Catholic liberals have redefined for themselves the definition of the "Magisterium", or "teaching authority" of the Church, to include input from the laity. Again, theological conceptions such as the "Church as the people of God" and the "priesthood of all believers" provide the legitimation sought for by many Catholic intellectuals.

This dispersion of charisma coupled with the propensity and the need of the Catholic intellectual to follow, and when needed create, some clear-cut symbolic and cognitive construction has fostered a situation in which the Catholic intellectual is openly involved in the shopping for and modifying of alternative religious, or quasi-religious, paradigmatic constructions. The leading contender in the struggle for supreme paradigmatic status for the New Catholic Knowledge Class is that of the Latin-American inspired "theology of liberation" in some mildly watered down form fitting the needs of an upper-middle class religiosity.[13] At first, this assertion may seem contradictory to the heavy emphasis previously placed on the role of the "American Civil Religion" as providing the theological-cultural presupposition for the Bicentennial process. Very simply, it was argued that the latter non-denominational religious dimension, following the work of Parsons and Bellah, has captured the hearts and minds of a middle-class, professional American segment whose "frame of reference" is that of the nation-state. Again, it is important to recall the conceptual framework previously developed to the effect that one's religiosity is "mediated", i.e., made real in thought and praxis, through frames of reference of varying inclusiveness (e.g., family, neighborhood, ethnicity, denomination, nation, world community). The argument here is that there is no actual contradiction in the simultaneous assertions of the importance of both the American Civil Religion and that of the "theology of liberation". Any possible contradiction is explained through an understanding that, at very best, the American Civil Religion is the "unofficial" religious dimension of the new class. As attractive as the civil religion as filtered through a selective reading of the theology of Vatican II is to this new class, it cannot vie for ultimate paradigmatic status simply because of its avowedly non-denominational, non-Catholic character. It is, as such, not located within the Catholic educational/theological organizational matrix where ideas are created distributed and disseminated throughout Catholic America and across Catholic generations. In addition the civil religion is, again, presently a very vague and contentless social construction. Its dogma is as yet uncodified and its prophets are not unquestionably agreed upon. This is not the case with the "theology of liberation" which, despite its present peripheral status from the viewpoint of the official Church, can make the argument--questionable perhaps--that it is a quite "Catholic" piece of theology. Despite its longer association with the American republic and with American Catholic liberalism, and its far greater impact on the well-educated American Catholic populace (as subtle as that impact may be), the American Civil Religion cannot make this same claim.

The "theology of liberation", as clearly evidenced through the Justice Hearing material, constitutes part of the "core" curriculum for many Catholic seminaries and other Catholic institutes that stress a heavy concern for social justice through social activism. In this regard, Andrew Greeley has previously pointed out to us that the theology of liberation has saturated such important idea generating and distributing centers as the U.S.C.C., the Center for Concern, and C.C.U.M. As a matter of fact, the annual summer institute held at Notre Dame by the Catholic Committee on Urban Ministry--perhaps the most important yearly convention of Catholic liberals and social activists in the U.S.--is unquestionably colored by this perspective. Unlike the situation of the civil religion, the meaning and implications of the theology of liberation have become clearer as the amount of material written on it, the number of advocates it commands, and the years that have allowed for its dissemination have accrued. And finally, even its most vehement detractors would clearly agree that this synthesis is attractive given that the enormously charismatic figures of Jesus Christ and Karl Marx share the prophetic spotlight.

Just why is it that this Christian-Marxist synthesis, and not some other combinations of ideas, is so attractive to the New Catholic Knowledge Class? The appeal, I would argue, finds its source not in the uniqueness of any one element of the synthesis, but in the uniqueness of its combined elements. First of all, like all successful religious paradigms--and perhaps even for all successful scientific ones--it successfully combines the proper "mix" of supernatural and natural, of reality and myth, of modernity and tradition.[14] In the case of a modern day religiousity suited for those avant-garde new class types who have felt the brunt of what Max Weber has termed the "disenchantment of the world", a successful paradigm must be ostensibly "scientific" and "rational" and at the same time be infused with the necessary elements of the non-rational, of the purely religious. The theology of liberation derives much of its power from its capacity to synthesize the rational and the non-rational, the allegedly "scientific socialism" of Marx with the Gospel of the God-man, Jesus Christ, who on the third day rose from the dead. Secondly, it is a religious interpretation of immanence that posits salvation in terms of the this-worldly institutionalization of justice. As previously pointed out, the 1971 Synod of Bishops statement, Justice in the World, comes close to endorsing this basic tenet of the theology of liberation. As the Synod put it "action on behalf of justice and participation in the transformation of the world fully appear to us as a constitutive dimension of the preaching of the Gospel, or in other words, of the Church's mission for the redemption of the human race and its liberation from every oppressive situation". (It is extraordinarily interesting and important to point out the interpretation of the Canon Law Society of America to Justice in the World. The Society, while acknowledging the idea that justice is a constitutive concern of the preaching of the Gospel, nonetheless refused to define such a "constitutive" concern as necessarily the sole, primary, or defining element in the preaching of the Gospel. Predictably enough, the Canon Law Society's interpretation "playing down" the Church's role in social activism was blasted by a U.S.C.C. official and theologian at the "mini-call to Action" follow-up held in Washington in March of 1979 at which the author was personally present). Thirdly, such a synthesis deemphasizes the role of the traditional authority of the Magisterium substituting, instead, the authority of those "experts" who can "raise the consciousness" of individuals through quasi-scientific analyses. Fourthly, the theology of liberation through its emphasis on "experience" and "praxis" can more easily accomodate, theoretically at least, the phenomenon of social change than could a more "static" Vatican I theology stressing an "eternal", changeless Church. This is a consideration of utmost importance for a class so bent on the continuous reconstruction of the social order. Fifthly, its allegedly populist leanings provide convenient legitimation for a class claiming to be operating in the interests of society as a whole or, if you will, for "liberty and justice for all". Sixthly, in an interesting sense the socialist vision of such a synthesis shares an affinity with a Catholic vision that similarly emphasizes "community", "togetherness", "fraternity" and an organic relationship between individuals. Put another way, the medieval "analogy of being" stretching as it does from sacred cosmos to lowly peasant finds a formal analogy in a this-worldly utopian vision that has a place for those from the State Committee or the United States Catholic Conference stretching all the way down to the lumpenproletariat or to the "victims of injustice". And finally such a synthesis offers--thus meeting the minimal requirement of any vision aspiring toward ultimate paradigmatic status--a "total" and all-embracing explanation of reality that has "answers" that satisfy all potentially "anomalous" contingencies, at least in the minds of its most zealous advocates.[15] Put another way, and using Leon Festinger's phrase, "when prophecy fails" the theology of liberation zealot is quite capable of coming up with a Rosa Luxemburg-like equivalent of the theory of the "external proletariat". Translated into Max Weber's discussion of "theodicy"[16] the theology of liberation ingeniously combines the two greatest Western explanations of sickness, suffering and death in the form of the Christian and Marxist eschatologies. In an interesting fashion, the advocates of this synthesis find themselves in a position to "have their cake and eat it too". Such an intellectual and psychological "solution" to two explanations of reality--hitherto competing in a zero-sum fashion--is satisfying to those intellectuals with such a tremendous need for mental closure and consistency. Such a solution alleviates what Georges Sorel has aptly termed the malaise of the intellectual par excellence: that of the "torment of the infinite". The theology of liberation alleviates this torment by reconstructing both the cognitive map and "recementing" the symbolic order of which Durkheim has spoken so persuasively.[17] As well as satisfying the need of the intellectual for consistency and closure, it is also clear that such an all-embracing synthesis pays eloquent testimony to the ability of some intellectuals to combine in a clever--and obviously to some, in a satisfying-- fashion the most seemingly incongruous ideas. The point here is not only that ideas neither triumph or fail in history due to their "intrinsic" truth or falsity but also that just about any constellation of ideas can share a supposedly "logical" affinity with each other given what Peter Berger has aptly termed an appropriate "plausibility structure".[18] The argument here is that the increasingly more modern "rational", this-worldly, ascetic, bureaucratic social contexts or plausibility structures that the New Catholic Knowledge Class increasingly operates from have found a congenial interpretation in the theology of liberation.

Not all, of course, of the New Catholic Knowledge Class share equally in either (a) their need for mental closure or (b) their ability for abstract, rational, logical, systematic thought or (c) their consistency between thought and activity as they themselves define it, i.e., "subjectively" or (d) their consistency between thought and activity as an outside observer would see it, i.e., "objectively".[19] A fifth variable--previously bracketed in Chapter 8-- that of the "motivation" of the new class is added. This dimension attempts to delineate whether the motivation of the individual involved in the Bicentennial Program was primarily "religious" or "material" in origin. Again, as previously argued, the new class is stratified within itself. This stratification can be clearly delineated through the use of five criteria or dimensions just outlined. Differing emphases on these five criteria produce a four-fold division within the new class. The four emerging ideal-typical constructions will be labeled (a) the ideological-intellectual (II), (b) the lower-echelon pragmatist (LEP), (c) the bureaucrat-intellectual (BI) and (d) the detached-intellectual (DI) (Cf. Chart).

DIMENSIONS	NEW CATHOLIC KNOWLEDGE CLASS TYPES			
	II	LEP	BI	DI
Ability to think abstractly	YES	NO	YES	YES
Need for mental closure	YES	NO	NO	NO
Consistency between thought & activity subjectively defined	YES	YES	NO	YES
Consistency between thought & activity objectively defined	YES	NO	YES	NO
Motivation--primarily religious not material	YES	YES	NO	YES

The first two types come, more or less, directly out of Andrew Greeley's previous discussion of, respectively, the "new social actionist" and the "old social actionist".[20] The third type is one that Greeley has hitherto completely ignored within the Church: increasing numbers of non-ideological, highly articulate bureaucrats who have mastered what Karl Mannheim has labeled a "functional rational" social orientation to the world.[21] The final category, while not explicitly mentioned, is perhaps implicit within Greeley's intellectual corpus. This is the development of a detached intellectual stratum that arises out of the priestly-prophetic exchange primarily between, but certainly not necessarily excluding all other segments of the Church, the "old" and "new" social action.[22] In terms of status it is clear that the ideological-intellectual and the bureaucrat-intellectual represent the higher echelon of the new class; the former primarily out of its ability to create and manipulate ideas, the latter out of its ability to create and manipulate social policy and programming that emanate from the former. The lower-echelon pragmatist constitutes clearly the bulk of the new class and holds a "first-line" position within the liberal social activist camp, mostly at the local level. It was the lower-echelon pragmatist who represented just about the social activist element in toto in the American Catholic Church prior to Vatican II. It is precisely the theological-and-cultural and formal-social organizational developments that explain the ascendancy of the ideologue and bureaucrat, respectively, over that of the pragmatist's role in the Church's commitment to questions of social justice. The "detached" intellectual is the most recent variation of the development of the new class within the Church. This is so if for no other reason that the very possibility of detachment presupposes some prior development to be detached from. This segment arises precisely as a response of clear heads to the conflict both within the new class and between the new class and the "old" class of Bishops and their various supporters. Ironically enough, the very "detached" and "objective" nature of this segment almost necessarily guarantees for itself political impotency. As Vilfredo Pareto might put it, in the ruthless "circulation of elites", he who tries to "tightwalk the fence" or "play the middle" is almost certain to be eventually crushed.[23]

The ideological-intellectual represents the extreme left of the New Catholic Knowledge Class; indeed he embodies the endpoint from which other segments of the new class are measured. The ideological-intellectual scores "high" on all five dimensions. He has both the need and the ability, respectively, for mental closure and abstract thought. He is an intellectual version of what Eric Hoffer has aptly termed "the true believer". He is characterized by his moralism, utopianism, dreams of a neat and perfect world, criticisms at the system-wide level and projections of system-wide reforms. For better or worse, his daily activity follows as humanly possible from his internalized belief system. He is consistent from both his own perspective as well as that of the external observer. He is a "purist" from the viewpoint of the latter and a "saint" from that of his own. He is a practicing advocate of what Max Weber has termed the "ethics of absolute ends".[24] In terms of the previous question of "motivation", there is little doubt of the sincerity of his convictions and of the negligible role that material interests play. The "radicalness" of the Bicentennial movement for the ideologue is a reflection of the very radicalness of the Christian commitment in a pristine form. He is a clear example of what Edward Shils has termed "authoritarianism of the left".[25] And he is living proof, at least in terms of motivation if not effect, that contrary to Nietzsche, it is not true "that the only true Christian died on the cross".[26]

The lower-echelon pragmatist is so named for several reasons. On the one hand, he is "lower-echelon" in that he most likely comes from that stratum of liberal Catholicism neither in control of nor concerned with the manipulation of imagery and the theoretical construction of various social policies and programming in a direct way. As a group this segment is the least powerful although by far the most populated of the liberal wing. They constitute the "bulk" of those individuals oriented to questions of social justice at the more local levels. As a group they represented the population base--the "clay" so to speak--from which the ideological and bureaucratic intellectuals who dominate the United States Catholic Conference and the Bicentennial Committee fashioned the Call to Action program. Empirically the pragmatist tends to be older than either the ideologue or bureaucrat; this is a reflection of the fact that he is heavily overrepresented in the pre-Vatican II modal approach to social justice termed by Greeley that of the "old social action". He is an individual who is "simply" concerned with the alleviation of social injustice in the name of God. That is, his approach, vis-a-vis the other more "theoretical" segments of the new class, is at a seemingly more "instinctive" level.

On the other hand, this segment of the New Catholic Knowledge Class deserves the title "pragmatist" for several reasons. He is far more concerned with seeing his concrete goals and programs concerned with the alleviation of social justice actualized than either with the particular means used in the process or the overall aesthetic quality of the procedure. He is flexible, prone to compromise, and always open to coalition with the most ideologically opposed factions (short of allegiance with the devil himself). In most cases, due in large part to educational, historical, biographical background, there is no great evidence of an ability or inclination for abstract theorizing. Neither is there any great need for mental closure. This segment of the new class is quite capable of living peacefully--at least in a social-psychological sense--in a world of imperfection. It is a world that the pragmatist realizes will always be imperfect despite his best efforts; only he hopes, a little less imperfect due to his efforts. As a group, this segment is much more accepting--in a practical as compared to theoretical manner--of the American society in which they live as compared to the ideologue. All systems, the pragmatist rationalizes, are imperfect; the "trick" is to be able to make systems more humane and liveable.

In a very real sense, this segment of the new class operates in a disarticulate (at least vis-a-vis the other three ideal-typical types) relationship with any overarching comprehensive paradigm, whether Catholic or otherwise. For the pragmatist it is the everyday demands of alleviating the plight of the poor that dictates what theoretical legitimation, if any, is applied. Consciously or unselfconsciously, the pragmatist chooses, in an ad hoc fashion, elements and components from various ideational systems as an explanation for his social activity. In a matter of fact way, the pragmatist is a practitioner, if not theoretical defender, of Max Weber's discussion (and advocacy) of the "ethics of responsibility".[27] The ad hoc, less-than-systematic, traditional, "incremental" manner in which they pursue their concerns for social justice gives the external observer--justifiable, in a strict sense--a picture of inconsistency between the thought and practice of such defacto pragmatists. Such a depiction, however, is not shared by the pragmatist himself. When made aware of such "contradictory" thought and activity, the pragmatist simply shrugs his shoulders and replies something to the effect that "I live in a messy world of contradictions. I just do what I think best at any given time and place and let the chips fall where they may".

In terms of the question of "motivation" it is clear that material factors do not greatly enter into the social psychological portrait. Of perhaps some interest, however, is the at times bitter sentiments expressed by this segment toward their conservative

critics. This rancor can most probably be explained
in great part through the recognition that the
Bicentennial Program represented a major "status"
victory for these historically suppressed--many times
in an unthinkingly cruel and offensive fashion--
generations of the old time, old style social
activists. Simply put, the Bicentennial Program
allowed this type of social activist--the modal pre-
Vatican II type--to blow off some of the steam that
had been gathering in intensity since the turn of
the century.[28] While the motivation of both the
ideologue and the pragmatist eschew materialism and
is primarily altruistic and "religious" in nature,
the latter is mitigated by elements of what Gusfield
has termed a "symbolic" or "status" crusade.

The third modal response in evidence during
the Bicentennial Program is that of the bureaucrat-
intellectual. This development in the personality
typology of the American Church is a relatively
recent one. On one hand, the American Catholic
Church has historically been noted for its pragmatism
regarding its stance to all issues, those of social
justice included. Hence, this explains the development of our second modal response. And while the
"ideologically" oriented intellectual has recently
gained a great deal of strength through a variety
of factors, it is clear that there was always some
place--albeit a more limited one--in the American
Church for such zealous theoreticians. The development of the bureaucrat-intellectual, however, finds
its origin clearly in the recent formal and bureaucratic revolution taking place within the Church.
Simply put, once again, as the Church becomes more
bureaucratic and systematic in its approach toward an
ever more bureaucratic and rationalized surrounding
society, an increasing number of influential positions
open up for the professional Catholic bureaucrat.

Regarding the possible combinations of our
dimensions, it is clear that the bureaucrat stands
apart from either the ideologue or the pragmatist.
Like the ideologue, the bureaucrat gives evidence of
a great deal of formal education, although, perhaps
more practical than theological-humanistic in orientation. Like that of the ideologue, the bureaucrat has
the ability to think abstractly, systematically,
logically, and rationally. In this the bureaucrat
disassociates himself from the pragmatist. Unlike

the ideologue, however, the bureaucrat's form of rationality is more "functional" than "substantive", more "goal-rational" than "value-rational".[29] His intellectualizing is more apt to be used for purposes of constructing concrete and "applied" social policy and programming. This is in contradistinction to the ideologue's propensity for formulating absolute, eternal, utopian statements not easily translated into more specific applications. In an interesting sense, in this latter concern with "that which is capable of being done", the bureaucrat stands closer to the pragmatist than the ideologue. The bureaucrat, again, shares an affinity with the pragmatist in that neither have any great need for "mental closure". For the latter, this absence is intimately tied to his lack of an ability to think in the abstract. For the bureaucrat, however, this lack of a need for mental closure has a more intellectual origin. It derives from his theoretical understanding of the difference between the ideal and the real, between the normative and the cognitive, between "what ought to be" and "what is". The bureaucrat, as compared to the ideologue, is more fully aware of the given restraints of fiscal realities and political climates and has learned to adapt himself accordingly. Despite differing backgrounds, orientations, and capabilities, both the pragmatist and bureaucrat aim for the possible. What separates the bureaucrat and the pragmatist on this issue is the motivation for the "adaptability". In the former, the adaptability finds its cause in the self-interest of one's career; in the latter the cause is a concern for social justice.

Subjectively, the bureaucrat realizes, perhaps only willing to admit this privately, that there are many inconsistencies between what he believes and what he does. There is in evidence a sharp parceling out of morality from his public activity; morality is held "privately", to "oneself". In this he stands apart from both the pragmatist and the ideologue. The bureaucrat is quite "calculating", for instance, in both his relationship to the Bishops and in his advocacy of the "theology of liberation". In the latter case, the ideologue feels "morally compelled" to assert the righteousness of this theological possibility. The pragmatist's relationship with the "theology of liberation", while not as articulate or "pure" as that of the ideologue, is such that he is willing to incur the wrath of the Bishops (as he had done historically) by embracing it if convinced that such theological legitimation will be of practical benefit to any one of a number of programs he is involved with. The bureaucrat, in contradistinction, is more careful. He has learned the art of what Erving Goffman has termed "role-distance"--the ability to keep tongue-in-cheek--as a self-survival mechanism.[30] When in the company of powerful enemies of the "theology of liberation" one "shuts up"; when in more private groupings with his fellow liberal social activists his advocacy suddenly waxes strongly. Discretion is always the better part of valor for the bureaucrat.

In the case of his relationship with the Bishops in general, it is clear that no one Bishop is viewed, publicly at least, as "automatically" a friend or foe. This is certainly not the case for the ideologue, given his belief in the power of his own charisma. Neither is it the case for the pragmatist, given the suppression he perceives has incurred against him historically by many of the Bishops. For the bureaucrat the Bishop is always viewed--in a distinctly non-ideological manner--as a potential vote for any one of his possible social programs. Politics, in this case at least, is quite capable of making strange bedfellows. The bureaucrat approximates best and "ethic of moral-neutrality". The union of theory and praxis, while understood clearly as a theoretical option, is quite simply rejected. Interestingly enough, however, the external observer might be quite likely to consider the relationship between the thought and praxis of the bureaucrat to be consistent-- given an understanding of the matrix from which the bureaucrat-intellectual operates.

The bureaucrat-intellectual is most suspect when it comes to the matter of the motivation for his involvement in the Bicentennial movement. His "value-free" pragmatism, his talent in constructing applied programs that would benefit himself both materially and in terms of status, his ability to manipulate words and language, and his uncanny talent in his everyday presentation of self, make the bureaucrat the most likely candidate for involvement that is least "altruistic" or "religious" in nature. Both the pragmatist and ideologue hold the bureaucrat in low esteem as, at best, a "necessary evil" to, at worst, a potential "traitor in the ranks".[31] The

Bishops--especially of a conservative stripe--on the other hand, while perhaps having no personal liking for this type, seem far more able to appreciate the "containable", "suppressable", and "predictable" personality of the bureaucrat. In contradistinction, such Bishops seem to fear the ideologue and tolerate the pragmatist.

Our social-psychological portrait of the American Catholic Bicentennial movement comes to a close with the introduction of our final character type, that of the detached Catholic intellectual. In terms of our five variables, the detached intellec- again forms a unique combination. Indeed the de- tached intellectual, understanding the limitations inherent with any one stance, consciously tries to incorporate the virtues of all the other types. This constant "balancing" procedure precludes any total, pure, unadulterated, immutable, "absolute" allegiances. He is a defender--at both the level of theory and praxis--of Max Weber's advocacy of the "ethics of responsibility".

Like both the bureaucrat and the ideologue, and unlike the pragmatist, the detached intellectual has the ability to think abstractly. As a matter of fact, in a certain sense, he possesses a superior ability vis-a-vis the rest of the new class in this regard. Unlike the bureaucrat who uses this ability for rather applied programs or the ideologue who concerns himself with the social construction of utopian visions, the detached intellectual is con- stantly in a dialogue attempting to mediate the existence of both realities. He does not allow himself the social-psychological "luxury" of various "shortcuts" at both the level of thought and praxis. In the ideologue's case, such a short-cut is the "convenient" ignoring of everyday "messy" contingencies and the reality of given parameters of action. In the bureaucrat's case, such a short-cut might involve the preempting of long-run plans that many times require a "dangerous", uphill, and immediately unprofitable political fight.

Furthermore, the detached intellectual gives little evidence of succumbing to the need for mental closure. In this he clearly stands apart from the ideologue who, as Sorel appropriately enough notes, is most plagued by the open-endedness of life, by the "torment of infinity". In this the detached intellectual shares a similarity with the pragmatist and bureaucrat. However the similarity is quite superficial. For the pragmatist this "open-endedness" derives from his general indifference to highly rationalized and systematic paradigmatic constructions; he is, again, following Weber, characterized by a relatively higher degree of a "primitive rationalism". In the case of the bureaucrat, the cause of this "open-endedness" arises not out of indifference but out of a calculated machiavellian sense of the politically possible and the politically dangerous. In the case of the detached intellectuals, this rejection of succumbing to the symmetry of mental closure arises out of his realization that paradigms (or any other symbolic constructions, for that matter) blind and inhibit as well as enable and allow one to perceive the truth. It is important to point out that, unlike the bureaucrat and pragmatist, this rejection exacts a great social-psychological price; like the ideologue, the detached intellectual feels the need for closure. Unlike the ideologue, however, the detached intellectual's need for intellectual honesty is greater than the need for closure.

It is at this point that our previous discussion on the shifting "frames of reference" through which one's religiosity--and total worldview--is mediated, i.e., is made real in both thought and action, becomes crucial once again. Simply put, the detached intellectual understands the nature of what Werner Stark has aptly termed the "socially conditioned" nature of thought (and hence of subsequent activity).[32] Stark contrasts "socially conditioned" thought with "ideological" thought, i.e., the latter being those ideas directly tied to one's class/material interests. For Stark it is much easier for one to transcend the latter than the former more totally encompassing form of conditioning. Simply put, the fact that both our cognitive and normative conceptions of the world are intimately tied to our biographical and historical experience and to what Emile Durkheim has termed the "collective consciousness" of society[33] constitutes the fundamental problem in the area of the sociology of knowledge and truth.[34] Given the inevitability of a "provincial" outlook linked to the conditions determining thought and activity, the detached intellectual understands that to "settle" for any one system of thought--and to claim that that system of thought is, or should be perceived to be, immutable is to surrender what to him is the calling of the intellectual: the relentless and, in a literal sense, "ruthless" pursuit of truth. The detached intellectual is, then, forced as such not merely to constantly add to his existing stock of knowledge, but to broaden his understanding of how "facts" are shaped by symbolic constructions, to investigate the regularities underlying socially-conditioned thought, to increase his emphathetic abilities in the understanding of just how and why certain forms of knowledge are conceived to be "real" or "unreal" under certain situations, and to determine the relative "truth content" of various symbolic constructions. The detached intellectual, betraying his fundamental humanity, utilizes and needs paradigmatic constructions. But his embrace is always provisional and subject to modification, synthesis, and or abandonment in light of information and insight that warrant such. The detached intellectual is the character type within the new class who accepts fully the challenge of relativity and refuses to succumb to the "leap of faith" of those, who like the "true believer", the ideologue, retreat from its potentially paralyzing effects.[35]

In essence a great deal of the effort of the detached intellectual is spent attempting to constantly "cross-cut" existing ideological and theoretical lines and conventional crystallizations of thought. At the same time that he is attempting to cross-cut existing taken-for-granted positions, he must be careful to avoid any overidentification with the newly emerging social construction. Much like Max Weber's discussion of charisma,[36] his "objective" insights are always in statu crescendi, in the act of becoming. Once created, the detached intellectual must watch the inevitability of the routinization process in which the insight itself becomes taken-for-granted in the mind of its creator, the latter thus becoming less "detached" and "objective" about the insight. Again, it is the intellectual honesty and openness of the detached intellectual that constantly pushes himself to be a critical observer of the symbolic constructions of others as well as of his own.

A few examples from Catholic/social thought can be offered that, at the time of their creation, represented such cross-cutting maneuvers. Regarding existing economic/philosophical systems of thought, a statement of Pius XI is relevant. In <u>Quadragesimo Anno</u> the attempt was made to tread a line between an unbridled economic liberalism and the transcendent-lessness and the totalism of socialism. An example of an ostensibly "value-free" social scientific analysis along shockingly similar lines would be Peter Berger's <u>Pyramids of Sacrifice</u>.[37] Regarding an attempt to cross-cut so-called "conservative-liberal" lines regarding the role and scope of the State in society stands, again, <u>Quadragesimo Anno</u> through its development of the concept of "subsidiarity". Similarly, Peter Berger and Richard Neuhaus' elaboration of Emile Durkheim's discussion of "intermediate institutions" in their <u>To Empower People</u> provides a strikingly compatible analysis.[38] Pope Paul VI's qualified defense of the democratic age in <u>Popularum Progressio</u> and Edward Shils' critique of the exponents of "mass society" theory in his <u>Centre and Periphery</u>[39] provide an indispensible balance wheel to the various assorted "prophets of doom" of contemporary civilization whether theologically or humanistically-inspired. Both Andrew Greeley and Peter Berger have, in similar ways, been presently engaged in attempting to cross-cut lines of "elitism" and "populism" in the area of social policy making. In his <u>The Communal Catholic</u> Greeley makes a plea for combining elements of both authority attitudes.[40] Peter Berger's plea in his <u>Pyramids of Sacrifice</u> for some "cognitive respect" for those not in powerful positions in the business of defining reality in society is here also relevant.[41]

The detached intellectual stands apart from our other types in other ways. From the viewpoint of the external observer, there seems to be a lack of consistency between belief and practice on his part. He shares this apparent inconsistency with the pragmatist. For the latter this is a result of an actual ad hoc, unsystematic relationship. For the detached intellectual this asymmetry results from his perception that it is the world, not he, which is not logically ordered. This asymmetry, again, is not evidenced in the case of the ideologue who orders life in a straight line with his embraced worldview, or with the organizational logic of life within bureaucratic settings that captures the commitment of the bureaucrat-intellectual. Subjectively, however, the detached intellectual shares with the pragmatist and ideologue an internal perception of honesty and consistency. His motivation is as uncontaminated with material interests as any. And unlike the ideologue and the pragmatist, the detached intellectual is more able to eliminate considerations of status from distorting his worldview.

In an interesting way consistent with Max Weber's discussion of "elective affinity", the Bicentennial Program attracted somewhat disparate groupings together. As the thrust of the Bicentennial routinizes itself into the very fabric of American Catholicism, some very important questions will develop. What will be the future relationship between these ideal-typical character types? As the general homogenizing processes of modernity continue, will they merge together forming a sort of "one-dimensionality"? If so, what will the liberal social activist of the future look like? In the probable event that no such blending will result in the near future, which ideal-typical segment will gain ascendancy over the New Catholic Knowledge Class and with what result? If no one faction takes a commanding position within the new class, what are the consequences for the class as a whole in its relationship with the American Bishops and the Pope?

The concluding chapter will interpret--in light of our previous analysis--the meaning of the Bicentennial Program and movement for the future of American Catholicism. Crucial here will be the idea of a developing system of "checks and balances" that protects the autonomy, and encourages a plurality, of forms through which one's Catholicism can be expressed. The argument to be developed is that this peculiar system allows a "dispersion of charisma", a fundamental democratization away from a purely ecclesiastical Catholicism, to take place without destroying the reality of the latter. The American Catholic Bicentennial movement is viewed as only one--albeit a very important one--in which this dispersion is occurring within the Church today.

FOOTNOTES

[1] The general orientation of this chapter is indebted to the following essays: Peter L. Berger, "Ethics and the Present Class Struggle", Worldview; "The Socialist Myth", The Public Interest; and Edward A. Shils, "Introduction" to Georges Sorel, Reflections on Violence (London: Collier, 1961).

[2] Examples of such sociological social-psychological approaches would include Peter Berger and Thomas Luckmann's The Social Construction of Reality (N.Y.: Doubleday 1966) and C.W. Mills, The Sociological Imagination (N.Y.: Oxford University Press, 1959).

[3] Very useful discussions of the general social-psychological orientations of American Catholic liberalism can be found in Andrew Greeley, The Catholic Experience (N.Y.: Doubleday, 1969) and Robert Cross, The Emergence of Liberal Catholicism in America (Chicago: University of Chicago Press, 1958).

[4] I am following the general thrust of the work of Edward A. Shils on the subject of intellectuals. Cf. The Intellectuals and the Powers and Other Essays (Chicago: University of Chicago Press, 1975).

[5] The reference here is to Thomas Kuhn's The Structure of Scientific Revolutions (Chicago: University of Chicago Press, 1970).

[6] In a most general sense, I am following the "dialectical" analysis between "objective" and "subjective" reality as discussed by Berger and Luckmann in their The Social Construction of Reality.

[7] A useful discussion of the "cognitive map" of the individual can be found in Edward Shils' essay, "Deference" in J.A. Jackson, Social Stratification (Cambridge: Cambridge University Press, 1970) and in Clifford Geertz's essay "Ideology as a Cultural System" in his The Interpretation of Cultures (N.Y.: Basic Books, 1973). Berger and Luckmann's application of Alfred Schutz's discussion of the "paramount reality of everyday life" in their The Social Construction of Reality is also relevant.

[8] Max Weber, The Sociology of Religion (Boston: Beacon Press, 1963).

[9] Most generally, I am in agreement with Andrew Greeley's argument as put forth in his The Communal Catholic (N.Y.: Seabury Press, 1976).

[10] Compare Ernest Troeltsch's discussion of a synthetic "mysticism" in the second volume of The Social Teachings of the Christian Churches with Gordon Allport's discussion of "mature religiosity" in his The Individual and His Religion (N.Y.: MacMillan, 1950).

[11] The intellectual's need for "mental closure" is brilliantly discussed in the previously cited work of Georges Sorel, Reflections on Violence.

[12] Thomas Kuhn, op. cit., 1970.

[13] My understanding of the "theology of liberation" is heavily indebted to Gustavo Gutierrez, A Theology of Liberation (Maryknoll, N.Y.: Orbis Books, 1973).

[14] Georges Sorel's discussion of the "general strike" as necessarily infused with a mythic quality is here relevant. Again, cf. Reflections on Violence.

[15] Indeed, a "micro" analysis that reflects Thomas Kuhn's "macro" analysis is that of Leon Festinger, Henry W. Riecken and Stanley Schachter, When Prophecy Fails (N.Y.: Harper and Row, 1964).

[16] Max Weber, op. cit., 1963.

[17] Emile Durkheim, The Elementary Forms of the Religious Life (N.Y.: Free Press, 1948).

[18] Peter Berger has developed this idea to great fruition in the area of the sociology of religion. Cf. The Sacred Canopy (N.Y.: Doubleday, 1967).

[19] This "objective-subjective" discussion of social psychological consistency roughly parallels the Pareto-Weber alternative definitions of "rationality".

[20] Andrew M. Greeley, "Catholic Social Activism-- Real or Rad/Chic?" The National Catholic Reporter

(February 7, 1975).

[21] Karl Mannheim, *Man and Society in an Age of Reconstruction* (London: Routledge and Kegan Paul, 1940).

[22] A reading of Greeley's *The Communal Catholic* suggests that perhaps he is advocating the development--along American Catholic lines--of what Karl Mannheim in his *Ideology and Utopia* (Routledge and Kegan Paul, 1936) has referred to as a "detached intelligentsia".

[23] Vilfredo Pareto, *The Mind and the Society* (N.Y.: Dover, 1963).

[24] Max Weber, *From Max Weber* (editors, H.H. Gerth and C.W. Mills) (N.Y.: Oxford University Press, 1946).

[25] Edward Shils, *Center and Periphery* (Chicago: University of Chicago Press, 1975).

[26] Nietzsche's cynicism in this matter was pronounced in his *Anti-Christ*. *Cf.* Walter Kaufman (editor) *Religion from Tolstoy to Camus* (N.Y.: Harper and Row, 1961).

[27] Max Weber, op. cit. 1946.

[28] This perception is derived from my interviewing and casual observation of the many Bicentennial participants who fit into this particular category. Joseph Gusfield's *Symbolic Crusade* is relevant through his discussion of Weber's "status" politics.

[29] The references here are from the similar analyses of Karl Mannheim in his *Man and Society in an Age of Reconstruction* and Max Weber, *The Theory of Social and Economic Organization* (N.Y.: Free Press, 1947).

[30] Erving Goffman, *Encounters* (N.Y.: Bobbs-Merrill, 1963).

[31] This conclusion was reached through numerous interviews, phone calls, and general evesdropping over conversations with Bicentennial participants and advocates.

[32] Werner Stark, *The Sociology of Knowledge* (Chicago: Free Press of Glencoe, 1958).

[33] Emile Durkheim op. cit. 1948.

[34] Put another way, it is this author's contention that the sociology of knowledge is rooted fundamentally in Durkheim's perspective. The Marxian concern for ideology is then to be treated as a sub-theme of a Durkheimian based sociology of knowledge. Berger and Luckmann's approach in The Social Construction of Reality is, I would argue, quite compatible with a Durkheimian one. My point of departure with the latter approach can be summed up simply: one starts with Durkheim and "works down" to Mead and Schutz and not, as Berger and Luckmann would have it, the other way around. Put another way, "internalization" precedes "externalization".

[35] Compare here the work of Eric Hoffer, The True Believer (N.Y.: Harper and Row, 1966).

[36] Max Weber, From Max Weber.

[37] Peter L. Berger, Pyramids of Sacrifice (N.Y.: Basic Books, 1974).

[38] Peter L. Berger and Richard Neuhaus, To Empower People (Washington: The American Enterprise Institute, 1977).

[39] Edward Shils, Centre and Periphery (Chicago: University of Chicago, 1975).

[40] Andrew Greeley, op. cit., 1976.

[41] Peter L. Berger, op. cit., 1974.

PART IV

CONCLUSION AND EVALUATION

CHAPTER TEN

THE INSTITUTIONALIZATION OF THE
LIBERAL CATHOLIC PERSPECTIVE IN AMERICA:
A "SYSTEM OF CHECKS AND BALANCES",
A THEOLOGICAL PLURALISM, AND
A DEVELOPING THEOLOGY OF PLURALISM

This concluding section will attempt to enhance our previous interpretation of the American Catholic Bicentennial movement by "demagnifying" it and placing it in its "proper perspective" within the overall matrix of the swirling forces of the contemporary religious scene. One can say that the Bicentennial movement which has hitherto been pushed to the "foreground" of our attention, will now be pushed to the "background" as the previously bracketed background matrix is now propelled forward for consideration.[1]

The idea of "demagnifying" the Bicentennial movement and interpreting it in light of the overall matrix of American and world Catholicism necessarily entails making explicit some fundamental assumptions and observations about the state of religion in modern contexts like the United States. The taken-for-granted position on the part of most experts in the sociology of religion is that secularization is occurring at a reasonably rapid rate, especially in middle-class and intellectual milieus.[2] Secularization is here being defined as the waning of religious, i.e., "supernatural", definitions of reality at the level of both human consciousness and everyday activity.[3] Such a position is not the one taken by this author. The author finds it much more useful, instead, to posit the existence of a quantum amount of religious sensibility in any given society. This quantum amount of "charisma" or "sacredness" is dispersed unevenly throughout society in terms of its intensity and degree.[4] That is, one can posit a continuum labeled "access to the sacred" with a relatively minor segment of individuals at each endpoint characterized as either religious virtuosi or as devoid completely of some "spark of divinity". Furthermore, this basic religious sensibility--akin, again, to what Rudolf Otto has referred to as the

241

"numinous"--can be actualized in social life in various ways.[5]

The multidimensional approaches of Gerhard Lenski in The Religious Factor[6] and Charles Glock and Rodney Stark in their Religion and Society in Tension[7] are relevant in this regards. For Lenski, modern day religiosity can be expressed in four different modes, the associative (e.g. Church attendance and parish participation); the communal (e.g. spouse and significant others of the same religion); doctrinal orthodoxy (e.g. assent to the doctrines and social policies of one's church); and devotionalism (e.g. frequency of private prayer and supernatural experience). In their quite compatible endeavor, Glock and Stark identify five ways in which an individual can express his/her religiosity. These modes are labeled the ritualistic, the ideological, the experimental, the intellectualistic, and the consequential. Glock and Stark's "ideological" and "experiential" mirror Lenski's discussion, respectively, of "doctrinal orthodoxy" and "devotionalism" and as such requires no further consideration. Furthermore, this is also the case with Glock and Stark's discussion of "ritualism" which needlessly collapses together Lenski's "associational" and "devotional" forms. However, the last two categories of Glock and Stark represent authentic additions to Lenski's approach. The "intellectualistic" mode may be defined as "knowledge about the basic tenets of one's faith and sacred scripture and how they relate to other ideational belief systems, whether religious or secular". And, finally, the "consequential" may be defined as the "social consequences that arise out of one's religious commitments".

As previously argued, the fact remains that differing conceptual frameworks "carve up" reality in different ways. Given this, it must be pointed out that the author's acceptance of a multidimensional approach has a significance over and beyond the reasonably obvious assertion that the religious numinous can be mediated differentially. One implication of such a conceptual framework is that the proper emphasis of the sociology of religion is not on the analysis of the loss of religion in the modern world but on its changing manifestations and on the factors encouraging such. It is, then, in this light, I argue, that the American Catholic Bicentennial movement must be analyzed.

Modern day existence, as argued previously, can be explained in large part through the pervasive spread of three interrelated social processes, that of pluralism, civility, and democracy. The impact of all this on American Catholicism translates itself into a weakening--although by no means a liquidation--of its organizationally or ecclesiastically defined self. Joseph Ficter's unidimensional analysis in his Southern Parish is here relevant.[8] In this work, Ficter classified Catholics as either nuclear, modal, marginal, or dormant depending upon their participation in such prescribed rituals as mass, confession, parochial education for children, etc., in the various organizations of the Church, and in their extent of interest in the parish in general. This conceptual apparatus has usefulness only in describing the relative weakening of what has previously been termed as "associative" and "doctrinal orthodox" Catholicism; it leaves unaddressed the possibility that the Church has gained in other modes. A multidimensional approach would clearly be more open to an interpretation that sees the Bicentennial movement as a waxing of an "intellectualistic" and "consequential" Catholicism.

In this emphasis away from defining religious sensibilities solely in terms of ecclesiastical definitions, the author points to the groundbreaking work of Thomas Luckmann in his The Invisible Religion.[9] Where Luckmann, however, goes astray is through his only partially correct discussion of the "privatization of the religious experience". Luckmann equates such privatization with the increasing autonomy of the individual in modern life. In this he is correct. However, he is fundamentally in error when he asserts that this autonomy actualizes itself religiously only in the "private sphere" institutions like that of the family and other institutions fostering expressive displays of intimacy and that can generate a positive sense of identity. Luckmann clearly misses a trend capable of generating a positive sense of identity that is a constitutive feature of modern life. At the same time that the religious autonomy of the individual is increasing, so is his/her capacity for an articulate, continuous, vital, and abstract relationship with the social constructions of the public sphere, most notably the nation-state. Our previous discussion of the

American Civil Religion is here relevant.[10] So too is Talcott Parsons' discussion of "value generalization" which so brilliantly captures the double movement of increasing autonomy and abstraction.[11] This latter development--the publitization of the religious experience--clearly fosters the more "intellectualistic" and "consequential" (in this case, "political") forms of expression that were constitutive features of the American Catholic Bicentennial movement.

On the other hand, the very sources of modernity that are producing a publitization of religion is simultaneously producing a backlash in the form of anti-intellectual and anti-political Catholic expressions. The impressive growth of the Catholic charismatic movement among a middle-class constituency is indicative of this "privatization of religion". Going back to our previously delineated multidimensional approach, such a movement is an example of an increase in what Lenski has referred to as "devotionalism". Various forms of monasticism as exemplified in the influential works of Thomas Merton are also relevant here.[12] It is interesting to point out here that theorists accepting the secularization thesis would not necessarily agree with this interpretation; for such a theorist the charismatic movement is part of the same cultural matrix that fosters such other purely secular "experiential" groups as "encounter" and "sensitivity training" groups. A sense of religious transcendence, for such a thinker, is "watered down" as the religious sensibility is reinterpreted into something more modern and contemporaneous. In this case, the alleged reduction takes place in terms of psychological categories; the 'Bicentennial movement" would similarly represent to such a thinker a political reduction.[13] From the anti-secularization thesis posited here, however, one could construct a continuum of publicness and privateness in terms of the varied expressions that religious sensibilities can manifest themselves. Examples of intermediate positions on the continuum would include the various "communal" expressions of Catholicism. One of these would clearly be those forms of Catholic expression made real in both thought and activity through ethnic attachments. This is, of course, the main theme of Andrew Greeley's The Denominational Society.[14] It is also quite consistent with the emphasis that Edward Shils has historically placed in his various essays on "primary groups" as mediating the existence of more public, "secondary" symbols. At the same time that many Catholics are moving away from an ecclesiastically defined Catholicism in both public and private directions, it may also be true that certain segments of the overall American Catholic population are actually moving toward such an allegiance. This is clearly the position taken by Will Herberg through his "triple melting pot" hypothesis in his Protestant, Catholic, Jew; by Moynihan and Glaser in their Beyond the Melting Pot; and by Lenski in his The Religious Factor.[15] Using Weber's[16] and Lenski's terminology such a movement entails a strengthening of at least an "associative" Catholicism. It may also mean a strengthening of "doctrinal orthodoxy". Again, it should be pointed out that the secularization theorist, while agreeing on certain features of the above depiction in a formal sense, would nonetheless disagree with the overall interpretation of the significance of the movement. This is made clear through Herberg's claim of what might be called a "social" or "communal" reduction of religious belief through his discussion of the "American Way of Life".[17] Gibson Winter's book entitled, The Surburban Captivity of the Churches, is another one of a host of influential secularization theses that focus on the idea of a "social" reduction.[18]

It is also important to point out that the acceptance of the multidimensional perspective has implications for any analysis of so-called "religious revivals". Very simply put, a multidimensional approach, with its underlying assumption of a quantum amount of societal charisma, doesn't allow for the phenomenon to occur. Rather, what others call a religious revival is interpreted as a shift of emphasis from one form of religious expression to another. The Bicentennial movement, again, from the perspective offered here, was clearly a funneling of religious energy away from an "associative"/"doctrinal orthodox" form of Catholicism and towards the direction of "intellectualistic" and "consequential"/ political channels. The charismatic movement is also a movement away from an "associative"/"doctrinal orthodox" Catholicism and towards an "experiential" or "devotional" mode. Likewise, the recent "ethnic revival", documented and prophecized by such Bicentennial participants and "white ethnic" advocates as Michael Novak and Monsignor Geno Baroni[19], would be analyzed as the waxing of a "communal" expression at the expense of the waning of the "associative".

On the one hand, it is generally true that the pluralization of Catholic religious dimensions entails a move away from an "associative/doctrinal orthodox" Catholicism.[20] On the other hand, for others the contemporary forces of pluralism--in a sense similar to the Counter-Reformation period in Spain--have encouraged an in-group reaction back toward an "associative"/"doctrinal orthodox" or ecclesiastically defined Catholicism. The spirit, although ironically in light of Vatican II not the law, of the Catholic Traditional Movement is relevant in this regards. And, once again, an ecclesiastical Catholicism is being fostered as a once immigrant, ethnic population is being transformed into a middle-class, surburban, "bourgeoise" Catholic base.[21]

Given this pluralization of Catholic religious manifestations, the question logically arises, "just how much diversity can a Church stand without losing its unity?" On one hand, it is clear that no religion can exist without some minimal consensus in evidence. Given this minimal consensus, however, the degree to which pluralism is, or can be, tolerated varies widely.

Regarding the first question it seems fairly obvious that some minimal consensus does exist within the contemporary Catholic Church. This consensus clearly includes the idea that the hierarchy has some special place within a Church defined now as "the people of God". Just exactly what are the parameters of its authority is a question that is widely debated. In this regard, an ecclesiastically defined Catholicism is anything but rejected totally. That this is the case for the "charismatic renewal" is precisely the reason why Joseph Fichter in his The Catholic Cult of the Paraclete[22] labels the phenomenon a "cult" and not a "sect". That the political activism of the Bicentennial movement has not rejected the ecclesia is made obvious by the simple recalling of the facts that the overall process was originated, monitored, and implemented through the organizational Church. Regarding the "monastic renewal", Thomas Merton through his essays in his Contemplation in a World of Action[23] makes

246

clear that, for better or worse, those monasteries attempting their own "aggiornamento" represent no serious threat to the ecclesiastical authorities. (That this minimal consensus on the need for some ecclesiastical authority need not be met "automatically" can be illustrated no less dramatically than by reference to the Reformation.) This present day consensus also includes the idea that within the history and tradition of the Church lies many answers to the questions of truth and eternal salvation. Again, just what elements or aspects of Church history and tradition are to be emphasized and just how inclusive are the answers to these questions to such a tradition and history are both disputable and disputed.

Regarding the latter question, the degree of pluralism varies according to the stance a religious entity takes vis-a-vis the world. This is, of course, the central theme that concerned Ernest Troeltsch in his The Social Teachings of the Christian Churches.[24] His threefold typology of "sect", "church", and "mysticism" leaves a great deal to be desired in terms of conceptual exhaustiveness in the modern situation. None of his categories, in and by themselves, describes adequately the contemporary Catholic Church. Obviously, the radically individualized religious expression of mysticism, by very definition, has no large place in an entity that is clearly, in some sense, a community of worshippers. Neither, and especially since the destruction of the Vatican I "ghetto" existence of the Church, does the category "sect" apply. Given that the days of a compulsory religious allegiance have ended since the destruction of the Catholic hegemony of the Middle Ages, it is clear that Troeltsch's definition of "church" is also outdated. The term, at a most superficial level, that most seems to apply to the question of American religiosity in general is that of "denomination" with its implications of both voluntariness and community. But this term tells one nothing about the degree of pluralism within any one denomination. One can, perhaps, utilize Troeltsch by stating that the American Catholic Church is a denomination that exhibits all three elements of his typology. Vatican II's concern for "conscience" legitimated the typically modern day "liberal protestant" mystical dimension into the Catholic Church. The Catholic Church clearly is tolerant of its various "sects" which strive for purity and set themselves off against those who compromise with the outer society. These "sects" may be "right-wing" ones (e.g. The Traditional Catholic Movement), "left-wing" ones (e.g. the "ideological" component of the Bicentennial movement), or simply apolitical (e.g. the monastic life of the Trappists). And finally the Church clearly exhibits the "church-like" ascetic orientation of an organization attempting to construct God's Kingdom here on earth with its inevitable implications of at least a partial routinization of charisma and a partial accomodation to this-worldly concerns.

It is perhaps this last point, i.e., the "church-like" tendencies of the contemporary Catholic Church, that tells us most about its capacity for tolerating pluralism. Simply put, the Church, in attempting to keep pace with the rationalizing, pluralizing, democratizing, civilizing tendencies of the outer world, finds herself mirroring, to a degree of at least, these tendencies. In this sense, the Catholic Church is clearly as "catholic" as any religious body can conceivably be. Such "catholicity", again, today includes the incorporation of "sect-like" and "individualistic" religious dimensions. Put crudely, the Church, in attempting to throw a rope around an ever-more complex and pluralized world, finds herself in a situation with a great deal of internal differentiation.

Of course, to a certain degree this has always been the case with the Catholic Church. A key aspect in the development of the Church from a struggling sect to a one time society-wide institution has been its ability to maximize the heterogeneity of its groupings and its ability to avoid an over-identification with any one particular group. The Church has kept pace with the world by ingeniously recombining elements in differing proportions in light of changing circumstances but without abandoning any one particular element in toto. Regarding its various social classes, one would be able to trace the changing emphasis on the theodicies of "escape", "dominance", and "mobility" as discussed by Weber in light of the changing social location that the Church finds herself in. Regarding Weber's "authority patterns", likewise, it is clear that there has been a gradual evolution from "charismatic", to "traditional" to "legal-rational" authority.[25] And, finally, in terms of Troeltsch's "church-sect" distinction, it is fascinating to note how successful the Church has historically been in maintaining its universalistic thrust through the incorporation, as distinctive religious orders, of various sects one time bordering on out-and-out insurrection. Generally speaking, the Catholic Church has weathered the storms of urbanization, industrialism, and nationalism by the increasing emphasis she has placed on the rational. Again, the one outstanding historical failure of the Church Universal to straddle these distinctions produced by the increasing presence of rationalization has been the Protestant Reformation. The closest analogy to a possible "American Reformation" centered on the turn of the century battles between the "Americanizers" (pro-rationalization) and "anti-Americanizers" (anti-rationalization). As Emile Durkheim might put it, such cases are ones in which the Church's attempt to "sacretize" the profane backfired (in the American case, almost backfiring) as the profane retaliated by contaminating the sacred itself. What marks the contemporary situation that the Church finds herself in from previous epochs is the degree of pluralism, civility, democracy, rationalism, and complexity that she confronts.

For the Church to attempt to keep pace with the contemporary social situation today precisely entails her emphasizing, without mirroring exactly, certain developments consistent with the overall process of rationalization as discussed by Max Weber. In terms of the Bicentennial movement, it is clear that a theodicy of "mobility" most approximates the religious needs of a New Catholic Knowledge Class itself a product of the dispersion of charisma and democratizing tendencies of the outer society. Likewise the new class finds itself located within formal and bureaucratic organizations in which legal-rational procedures and criteria extend increasingly down from the high clergy through to its lay membership. Given the pluralizing tendencies concomitant with modernity as discussed by Berger, the religiosity of the new class finds itself one confronting disparate ideational systems. The choice here is twofold. One could, like our "ideological" Catholic intellectual, attempt to synthesize these disparate elements into something akin to the "theology of liberation" or the "American Civil Religion". The "detached" Catholic intellectual, on the other hand, might find cause to celebrate such a pluralism for the opportunity it affords, in and by itself, in the search for truth. Either way, however, the fact remains that pluralism must be confronted. And finally, the dispersion of civility and of democracy that is constitutive of modernity adds a positive, as compared to its historically more pragmatic and negative reasoning, force for the appreciation of such a de facto pluralism.

Perhaps the most significant factor in explaining the contemporary Church's toleration/appreciation of plural definitions of religious reality lies in its very <u>entrapment</u> within a modern, ever more bureaucratic, rationalized, and technocratic world. While Max Weber's anguished cry in the last pages of <u>The Protestant Ethic and the Spirit of Capitalism</u>[27] to the effect that modern man was "trapped in an iron cage of mechanized petrification" may constitute something of an overstatement, there nonetheless lies <u>in nuce</u> an insight of profound importance for the Catholic Church. Simply put, it is this: the modern world both encourages intellectualistic and consequential-political expressions of religiosity. In <u>The Homeless Mind</u>[28] Peter Berger et. al. makes the argument, following Weber, that given modern man's dependency on technology and bureaucracy, any modern day plans for reconstructing society operate within parameters that preclude a return to a "gemeinschaft" or "traditional" setting, pure and simple. This theme, willy nilly, has implications for a Catholic Church that by her very nature refuses to accept a sect-like posture in the world. Very simply, whatever the future of Catholic religiosity will be, it most certainly will contain strong elements of the more "modern" religious expressions empirically available within the contemporary scene.

Interestingly enough, the very fact that the Church bounds the rationalizing expressions of religiosity within a vital Church tradition infused with a strong sense of the charismatic/sacred/numinous, simultaneously allows the Church to provide a place in the modern world for what Peter Berger has aptly termed the various "discontents of modernity"--for those rejecting the more modern religious dimensions. The "discontented" may find solace in numerous ways, whether through an "associative"/"orthodox" Catholicism, an "experiential"/"devotional" Catholicism or a "communal"/"social" Catholicism. Crudely put, the Catholic Church can (and does) accommodate religious expressions which typify every epoch. In order to guarantee the institutionalization across time of such a "civil" posture, the Church requires the crystallization of two developments. They are the creation of, as discussed previously, a "detached" Catholic intelligentsia which can serve as the mediators and arbitrators of the various groupings of the Church Universal and, secondly, the crystallization of a "theology of pluralism" that is openly and unabashedly in praise of the concept. The overwhelmingly positive reception that Avery Dulles' <u>Models of the Church</u> and David Tracy's essay on "The Church"[29] have received on the part of many may be indicative of such a possible development. What is clear, however, is that such a possible crystallization--if and when it occurs--will owe much more to the structural situation that the Church finds herself in than to any "positive" theological endeavor that would, in and by itself, have a significant causal influence.

 The situation that the Church finds herself in has fostered a system of checks and balances with a concomitant orientation of tolerance, caution, and a purposeful "structured ambiguity". The argument is that the "qualified acceptance" on the part of both the Roman and United States ecclesiastical hierarchy towards the American Bicentennial movement, or for that matter towards the "charismatic renewal", can best be seen in light of a development that is occurring within the Church at a world wide level. This is a development that disperses authority throughout the Church defined as "the people of God". This dispersion is, of course, differential in intent, and to a lesser degree, in effect. It by no means intentionally "flattens out" the hierarchial authority of the Magisterium; rather it makes the lay-religious-priestly-Bishop-Papal relationship a more articulate and reciprocal one. This is consistent with the major document of Vatican II, <u>Lumen Gentium</u>, in its declaration that each of the above groupings have both specific callings or roles and, simultaneously, more general commitments to the Catholic whole. The former is stressed through the traditional concept of the different functions of the Church hierarchy that stretch from Pope to laity reaffirmed in Vatican II's <u>Declaration on the Laity</u>; the latter through the

concept of "collegiality". Such a system is quite
analogous to Durkheim's discussion of an "organic"
solidarity based on the needs of an ever increasingly
diversified, specialized, and interdependent population which is given moral cohension through a series
of "non-contractual elements of contract".[30] The
latter point can perhaps be made clearer through
reference to Alvin Gouldner's assertion that increased
human interaction breeds "norms of reciprocity".[31]
Edward Shils' observation that modern life is
characterized by an attenuation of primordial and
sacred ties and the development of civility is also
quite relevant in our analysis of this development at
the level of a worldwide Catholicism.[32] The "de-
Italianization" of the Papacy on the one hand, and the
"internationalization" of the College of Cardinals with
its concomitant recognition of a so-called "Third World"
Catholicism on the other, represent dramatic illustra-
tions of this spread of civility. At anything less
inclusive a frame of reference than that of world
Catholicism, the effect or impact of the spread of
civility and democracy is quite uneven. At a national
level Catholicism, for instance, Spain and the Nether-
lands might well represent the left and right endpoints
on a continuum labeled "increasing democratization
within the Church", with the United States anchored
somewhere in the middle. Within any one nation, the
unevenness of the democratization process can be
illustrated nicely by our previous discussion of the
partial institutionalization, in terms of both law
and spirit, of the priests' senates and pastoral
councils in the United States mandated by Vatican II.

It is important to point out that this
development is, for the most part, unplanned by the
leaders of the Church. It is certainly, to a large
degree, out of the practical, if not theoretical,
control of the Hierarchy. This development of a
system of checks and balances can perhaps best be
seen as a de facto, very practical, and somewhat
desperate response of the Church to legitimate as
"Catholic" changes that have their origin outside
the Church in world-transforming social forces. The
"people of God" imagery instituted by Vatican II has,
in large part, been invoked because it stands in an
elective affinity with the general rationalizing
trend since the eighteenth century toward democratization, pluralism, and civility in the world dominating

Western hemisphere. (Conversely, it may very well be
the case that the growing perception of increasing
weakness in the West, militarily, morally, and
spiritually, on the part of the various leaders and
observers of the contemporary world may increasingly
encourage Pope John Paul II to attempt to shift the
imagery of the Church, at least in part, "to the
East" and away from, to some degree, these Western
themes). Viewed either way, Pareto's discussion of
"rationalization"--that things happen first and
then legitimations for such are concocted, that
"men first act and then think"--is here, a useful--if
somewhat overexaggerated--insight.[33] As of now,
however, what the Church leadership seems to be
doing is to allow--within rather broad limits--the
regional, national, and local Church to define its
own mission given the realities of the temperment of
the various regional/national episcopal conferences,
the diocesan Bishops, clergy, religious and laity as
they are influenced by the surrounding social-cultural
matrix. Important here, once again, are the questions
of just how much consensus exists between the various
elements at each level and the degree of organizational
and "interest group" strength that each component
commands. A theoretical pluralism, "at the top",
obviously, need not be mirrored empirically at a
more local level. In such cases, conflict and rancor
will ensue. In this regards, however, one must note,
again, the historically verifiable and overall tendency
of the Catholic Church to turn potential disaster into
relative success, to "snatch victory from the jaws of
defeat". The argument here is that, despite the
undeniable amount of disequilibrium and disagreement
within the Church today, there is, nonetheless,
evident a minimal consensus that is supported by an
increasing display of civility. This strain towards
equilibrium is primarily being fostered by the demands
of "interest group" politics; nonetheless it may very
well be true that the Church is presently in the
process of developing an overarching framework of
pluralism, which praises the idea, as well as the
given reality, of pluralism within the Church.

What would such a framework constitute? It
might very well, by recognizing a multitude of partial
truths, constantly push the Church towards "la via
media". Following the logic of Avery Dulles' Models
of the Church it would not be a paradigm in the strict

sense of a seemless symbolic construction that guides but also inhibits the search for truth or denies the "mysterious" nature of the Church. As previously argued, symbolic constructions "channel off" the "numinous" inherent within it in one specific direction, at the expense of other possible avenues. A framework of pluralism, on the other hand, makes no attempt to integrate in a synthetic whole the various dimensions or aspects that are part of a Church tradition that, as Chesterton has put it, "has spanned the ages". Put another way, the numinous inherent within a variety of hierophanies--both physical and more importantly, symbolic--are respected, are granted what Peter Berger has referred to as "cognitive respect". Such a framework respects well the adage of the Papal historian, Ranke, to the effect that "each age is immediate unto God". Such a framework recognizes that within the living tradition(s) of the Church lies a vast depository of partial truths that must be recognized in their own right as such.

In this, the framework is to be sharply contrasted to the "modal" thrusts of both the "American Civil Religion" and the "theology of liberation" or, for that matter, the great synthesis of Thomas Acquinas. It can be argued that all of the latter do a basic injustice to the varieties of both Catholic and religious-in-general experience in that they either do not recognize elements not included in the overall synthesis or that they insufficiently recognize the basic integrity of any one dimension that forms part of the newly created whole. As Avery Dulles puts it, "in order to do justice to the various aspects of the Church, as a complex reality, we must work simultaneously with the different models. By a kind of mental juggling act, we have to keep several models in the air at once". Such a framework--one that sociologist Robert Merton might call that of "disciplined eclecticism" and one that rules out proceeding theologically from a "closed" theological construction--is consonant with Pope Paul VI's opening words at the second session of Vatican II. As Pope Paul put it, "The Church is a mystery. It is a reality imbued with the hidden presence of God. It lies, therefore, within the very nature of the Church to always be open to new and ever greater exploration". Furthermore, such an eclectic framework stands in opposition to the pre-Vatican II preeminence afforded to Thomism. Indeed, as late as 1950, Pope Pius XII, in Humani Generis attacked the critics of the great Catholic-Aristotlian merger as follows:

> They say that this philosophy upholds the erroneous notion that there can be a metaphysic that is absolutely true; whereas in fact, they say, reality, especially transcendent reality, cannot better be expressed than by disparate teachings, which mutually complete each other, although they are in a way mutually opposed. Our traditional philosophy, then, with this clear exposition of solution of questions, its accurate definition of terms, its clearcut distinctions, can be, they concede, useful as a preparation for scholastic theology, a preparation quite in accord with medieval mentality; but his philosophy hardly offers a method of philosophizing suited to the needs of modern culture . . . they seem to imply that any kind of philosophy or theory, with a few additions or corrections, if need be, can be reconciled with Catholic dogma.[34]

This overarching theology of pluralism is precisely one that is open to the idea of "disparate teachings, which mutually complete each other". Such a position fosters, either consciously or unselfconsciously, what Peter Berger et al. in The Homeless Mind[35] has referred to as "cognitive bargaining", that is, compromises at the level of human consciousness between traditional and more modern patterns of thought. While such a theology makes every attempt to respect the "partial truths" that are incarnate within the Catholic tradition and is wary of identifying the Catholic faith solely with modern expressions of religiosity, it is nonetheless, in a certain sense, a constitutively "modern" theology. Simply put, the very idea of "cognitive bargaining", i.e., that theologians can be selective, is modern, indeed is modernizing in itself. One of the most pervasive characteristics of pre-Vatican II theologies is the notion that there is no choice but to accept the dogma in toto, that the theological construction is inevitable, "a once and forever" phenomenon, rooted in human nature, and part and parcel of the very essence of the cosmos. The Syllabus of Errors, again, is exemplary in this regards.

A "theology of pluralism" is aided no doubt by what may be termed our present day "age of sociology" in which the imagination and consciousness of individuals are increasingly becoming sensitive to the historical and social roots of contemporary normative and cognitive conceptions of the universe. It can be asserted that the relativizing of both the religious and ethical considerations that arise out of this "age of sociology" stand in an affinity with the spread of our previously mentioned social forces. While the "age of sociology" might be relativizing knowledge, one cannot overlook the relatively more obvious, but by no means less crucial, fact that knowledge is more evenly distributed in contemporary, especially Western, society. In this regards the dispersion of a mass education system, the increasing access of the mass to library facilities, and the growing sophistication of technology in the publication of inexpensive "paperback" editions which make the stored knowledge of recorded Catholic history reasonably available to most, have fostered a situation in which a "theology of pluralism" becomes a viable and plausible proposition. While such a development would have a more theoretical significance for the "knowledge class", especially for its more detached segment, and for the "post-Vatican II" members of the hierarchy, it would by no means necessarily be of significance only to these groups. Simply put, such a framework of pluralism is quite capable of being dispersed downwards to the mass of moderately educated Catholics, only of course, in a "watered down" fashion with a more "pragmatic" impact on the thought and activity of "everyday" citizens. In the case of the knowledge class and the Church hierarchy, the "cognitive bargaining" between the various elements of Catholic tradition is self-consciously theoretical; in the latter case it is performed at a more lower level of self-conscious awareness indicative of the general spread of the idea and practice of civility.

Biblically, such a framework of pluralism finds support in I Corinthians 12: 4-7,

> and now there are varieties of gifts, but
> the same Spirit, and there are varieties
> of service, but the same Lord; and there
> are varieties of working; but it is the
> same God who inspires them all in everyone.
> To each is given a manifestation of the
> Spirit for the common good.

And such a framework would require the tolerance called forth by Thomas Kempis in his The Imitation of Christ. As he put it,

> it is certainly true that many a person in
> religion is disposed to act after his own
> will and can agree best with those who
> follow his own ways (however, it is
> necessary) if we desire that God be among
> us, to sometimes set aside our own will
> though it seems good so that we have love
> and peace with others. Who is so wise that
> he can fully know all things? No one,
> surely.[36]

That, theologically speaking, such a framework is already in the beginning stages of its development is made clear through the following passage in one of Vatican II's more important documents, Gaudium et Spes ("Pastoral Constitution on the Church in the Modern World"):

> They also have a claim on our respect and
> charity who think and act differently from
> us in social, political, and religious
> matters. In fact the more deeply we
> come to understand their ways of thinking
> through good will and love, the more
> easily we will be able to undertake
> dialogue with them.[37]

It is also, in a very real sense, compatible with the recent theological endeavors of Peter L. Berger, especially as evidenced by his A Rumor of Angels and The Heretical Imperative.[38] For Berger, a sense of the theologically possible must emanate from an understanding of the relativizing implications of the sociology of knowledge. The compatibility of his work with a Catholic framework of pluralism lies in the openness of his search for various "signals of

257

transcendence" within society and throughout history. The framework that Catholic theologians, however, must develop out of various "disparate teachings which mutually complete each other" is bounded, for the most part at least, by her own history. The work of Avery Dulles, Models of the Church, is exemplary in this regards. For Berger, who is apparently unwilling to make any "leap of faith" whatsoever, there is an all-important difference: the intellectual search is across all time and space. Put crudely, while both Dulles' and Berger's endeavors are, literally speaking, "heretical", i.e., they involve "choice", Dulles' decision involves a leap of faith which regards the Catholic tradition as the primary, if not certainly sole, vehicle of eternal salvation. It is in Dulles', and not Berger's, direction that a Catholic "theology of pluralism" must follow.

The dispersion of authority that is concomitant with the crystallization of this framework of "disciplined ecclecticism" moves various Catholic groupings centrifugally away from an ecclesiastically or organizationally defined Catholicism in multidimensional space. The American Bicentennial movement is seen as only one direction that this is taking place within the United States and throughout world Catholicism. Simply put, once again, a systematic concern for the implementation of social justice is now officially and legitimately seen as constitutive of the Catholic calling. It is a central and institutionalized concern of the United States Catholic Church. In this regards, the first major encyclical of Pope John Paul II, Redemptor Hominis ("The Redeemer of Man"), is supportive of this contention. But the Church cannot, for John Paul II, simply define its mission solely in terms of a commitment to implement social justice. Such a commitment falls far short of exhausting the idea of an ever-changing Church, of the "Church as mystery". On the one hand, it is true that the calling of the Church entails the attempt to discover "new truths" about the nature of the relationship of what Vico called "civil society" to God. The relatively recent, in terms of human history, "discovery" of the "fundamental dignity of the everyday man" by both theologians and humanists may be cited there as a case in point and quite consistent with the underlying philosophical anthropology of recent Catholic theology and the Bicentennial movement.

On the other hand, "that men have made the civil world, can understand it, and subsequently can and should change it" (to do some injustice to Vico's famous dictum) is only part of the Catholic vision. Certain Catholics might argue that much more fundamental is the call to ancient truths about the relationship of man to God. Specifically, the basic awareness centers around the overwhelming reality that God sent his Son to die so that men could live life ever lasting. The Church is not just Servant, but perhaps most importantly for such Catholics, Herald of the Word.

FOOTNOTES

[1] The "foreground-background" metaphor is central to the work of Gehlen. Cf. Berger and Luckmann, The Social Construction of Reality (N.Y.: Doubleday, 1966).

[2] The question of "secularization" is a terribly difficult and complex one. It is equally as difficult to attempt to dichotomize authors as either "secularization" or "anti-secularization" theorists. With qualifications however, I would list Parsons, Shils, Greeley, Bellah, and Martin as foremost among the anti-secularization theorists. Berger, Luckmann, and Herberg represent the most eloquent of the secularization theorists.

[3] The definition offered here is basically Berger's in his The Sacred Canopy (N.Y.: Doubleday, 1967).

[4] Edward Shils, Center and Periphery (Chicago: University of Chicago Press, 1975).

[5] Rudolph Otto, The Idea of the Holy (N.Y.: Oxford University Press, 1950).

[6] Gerhard Lenski, The Religious Factor (N.Y.: Doubleday, 1961).

[7] Charles Glock and Rodney Stark, Religion and Society in Tension (Chicago: Rand McNally 1965).

[8] Joseph Fichter, Southern Parish (Chicago: University of Chicago Press, 1951.

[9] Thomas Luckmann, The Invisible Religion (N.Y.: Macmillan, 1963).

[10] Robert Bellah, "Civil Religion in America", Daedalus 96 Winter 1967.

[11] Refer back to Chapter 6 for the author's application of Parsons' concept to the American Catholic case.

[12] Thomas Merton, Contemplation in a World of Action (N.Y.: Doubleday, 1973).

[13] Cf. Peter Berger's article in U.S. News and World Report, April 11, 1977.

[14] Andrew Greeley, The Denominational Society (Glencoe, Illinois: Scott, Foresman and Co., 1972).

[15] Will Herberg, Protestant, Catholic, Jew (N.Y.: Doubleday, 1955);Daniel Moynihan and Nathan Glaser, Beyond the Melting Pot (Boston: M.I.T. Press); Gerhard Lenski, op. cit., 1961.

[16] Max Weber, The Theory of Economic and Social Organization (N.Y.: Free Press, 1947).

[17] Will Herberg, op. cit., 1955.

[18] Gibson Winter, The Suburban Captivity of the Churches (N.Y.: Doubleday, 1961).

[19] Refer here to Liberty and Justice for All: A Discussion Guide (1975) discussed in Chapter four and to the contributions of these two authors. Of course, Novak's The Rise of the Unmeltable Ethnics (N.Y.: McMillan, 1971), is relevant here.

[20] Gerhard Lenski, op. cit., 1961.

[21] Interestingly enough, this is one trend that Greeley is completely unaware of as evidenced by his writings to date.

[22] Joseph Fichter, The Catholic Cult of the Paraclete (N.Y.: Sheed and Ward, 1975).

[23] Thomas Merton, op. cit., 1973.

[24] Ernest Troeltsch, The Social Teachings of the Christian Churches (N.Y.: Harper Torchbooks, 1960.

[25] Max Weber, The Sociology of Religion (Boston: Beacon Press, 1963).

[26] Emile Durkheim, The Elementary Forms of the Religious Life (N.Y.: Free Press, 1954).

[27] Max Weber, The Protestant Ethic and the Spirit of Capitalism (N.Y.: Charles Scribner's Sons, 1958).

[28] Berger, Peter, Brigette Berger and Hansfried Kellner, The Homeless Mind (N.Y.: Random House, 1973).

[29] Avery Dulles, Models of the Church (N.Y.: Doubleday, 1978), David Tracy "The Church" in Liberty and Justice for All: Discussion Guide (Washington: N.C.C.B. Committee for the Bicentennial, 1975).

[30] Emile Durkheim, The Division of Labor in Society (N.Y.: Free Press, 1964).

[31] Alvin Gouldner, "The Norm of Reciprocity" in the American Sociological Review, 1963.

[32] Edward Shils, op. cit., 1975.

[33] Vilfredo Pareto, The Mind and the Society (N.Y.: Dover, 1963).

[34] Pope Pius XII, Humani Generis 1950 (Boston: St. Paul Editions).

[35] Peter Berger et al., op. cit., 1973.

[36] Thomas a Kempis, The Imitation of Christ (N.Y.: Doubleday 1955).

[37] Gaudium et Spes in (editor Walter Abbott) The Documents of Vatican II (Washington: America Press, 1966.

[38] Peter L. Berger, A Rumor of Angels (N.Y.: Doubleday, 1970); The Heretical Imperative (N.Y.: Doubleday, 1979).

APPENDIX A

What follows is a listing of the 182 proposals that emanated from the Call to Action assembly. The proposals have been divided along the eight sub-themes or headings of "Church", "Ethnicity and Race", "Family", "Humankind", "Nationhood", "Neighborhood", "Personkind", and "Work". The proposals have previously been published in Origins: Catholic Documentary Service Vol. 6 Number 20, November 4, 1976 and Volume 6, Number 21, November 21, 1976. Included along with each proposal, proposal number, and sub-theme heading is the "directive" assigned to each proposal by the National Conference of Catholic Bishops. Each proposal was given a directive either (1) to be given further study, (2) to be acted immediately on, (3) to be supported through strengthening existing activity or (4) to be "responded to in light of the universal law of the Church". (Cf. Final Committee Evaluations of the Call to Action Recommendations, Washington: N.C.C.B. Committee for the Call to Action Plan, February 13, 1978). The information is as follows:

RESOLUTION NUMBER   HEADING   DIRECTIVE

1   Church   3

That Church authorities on all levels should hold themselves accountable for their financial policies and practices to the larger Catholic population through the creation of parish and diocesan pastoral councils.

2   Church   1

That a National Review Board, composed of members of the Church (Bishops, clergy, religious and laity) be established to address itself aggressively to the issue of due process by initiating procedures of appeal, redress and reconciliation.

263

RESOLUTION NUMBER	HEADING	DIRECTIVE
3	Church	3

That the Church must eliminate the "geographic morality" which allows for matrimonial nullity to be granted in one place and not another.

| 4 | Church | 4 |

That the Local Church must be involved in the selection of Bishops and Pastors.

| 5 | Church | 3 |

That Church leaders ought to extend to the Catholic population a shared responsibility in both social policy making and the administration of that social policy.

| 6 | Church | 2, 3 |

That responsible Church officials and committees should establish policies designed to eliminate every form of discrimination on the basis of race, language, sexual orientation, culture, nationality and mere physical considerations within the Church.

| 7 | Church | 2, 3 |

That, given that the Catholic community has the right to competent pastoral care, professional training should be provided in seminaries or special programs for men and women--lay, religious, or clergy-- preparing for or assigned to particular ministries.

| 8 | Church | 2 |

That the preparation, continuing education, and evaluation of the clergy should receive priority attention.

| 9 | Church | 3 |

That the Bishops insure that the faithful receive competent theological guidance by endeavoring to provide greater clarity in theological teaching, upholding the unity of faith while accepting differences of opinion on theological matters, insofar as these represent legitimate theological pluralism.

10   Church   2

That all members of the Church earnestly and prayerfully seek to foster vocations to the priesthood.

11   Church   3, 4

That the Church should recognize the right of those who have been laicized from the priesthood to function in non-sacramental ministries.

12   Church   4

That the N.C.C.B. take affirmative action to respectfully petition the Holy Father to change the present discipline in the Western Rite of the Roman Catholic Church to allow married men to be ordained to the priesthood.

13   Church   4

That the N.C.C.B. initiate dialogue with Rome to change the present discipline in the Western Rite of the Roman Catholic Church to allow women to be ordained to the diaconate and priesthood.

14   Church   4

That the N.C.C.B. assign to an appropriate committee the task of studying the possibility of changing the present discipline of the Roman Catholic Church to allow priests to exercise the right to marry and remain in or resume the active priesthood.

15   Church   1

That the N.C.C.B., in consultation with a body of representatives of each of the National Catholic Organizations of Women, establish within the N.C.C.B./U.S.C.C. an effectively staffed structure to promote the full participation of women in the Church.

| 16 | Church | 4 |

That the N.C.C.B. offer leadership in justice to the universal Church by providing a process which facilitates the formation of a more fully developed position on the ordination of women to sacred orders.

| 17 | Church | 1 |

That an Affirmative Action Plan be developed by the N.C.C.B. and local ordinaries, together with representative women, to assure the equal status of women in the Church.

| 18 | Church | 1 |

That the N.C.C.B. and Catholic publishing houses act to insure that sexist language and imagery be eliminated from all official Church documents.

| 19 | Church | 1, 2, 3 |

That the Church identify and formally authenticate and expand ministries being performed by women.

| 20 | Church | 4 |

That female children be granted the right and opportunity to serve at the altar in the role traditionally allowed to altar boys.

| 21 | Church | 2, 3 |

That structures to insure participative decision-making by the Catholic community (including parents, students and educators) be established or strengthened to determine total Catholic educational policy at the local and diocesan level.

| 22 | Church | 1, 2 |

That the Church support independent, competent research to evaluate the present educational programs of the Church.

| 23 | Church | 2 |

That the diocesan Church affirm the value and continue to support, philosophically and financially, Catholic schools.

| 24 | Church | 2 |

That the local Church acting through pastoral councils (diocesan and parish) and boards of education should determine the priorities of Catholic schools in their areas.

| 25 | Church | 1 |

That the Church should take the initiative in founding a national organization representative of racially nondiscriminatory Protestant, Catholic, Jewish and nondenominational private schools for the purpose of working through the democratic processes for the enactment of state and/or federal legislation to provide tax funds to parents to enable them to exercise their religious freedom rights in the education of their children in the schools of their choice.

| 26 | Church | 1, 2 |

That the Church must be actively concerned and involved with public education.

| 27 | Church | 2 |

That Church leaders, educators, and laity move to achieve racial integration and move to promote multi-cultural values in Catholic Schools.

| 28 | Church | 2 |

That dioceses provide opportunities for their clergy to take part in programs in the academic, spiritual and pastoral areas of the ministerial life.

| 29 | Church | 2 |

That Catholic institutions of higher education which demonstrate a commitment to the Church's teaching on social justice be supported.

| 30 | Church | 1 |

That the Call to Action Conference support the efforts of the National Catechetical Directory to reiterate and concretize the Synod of Bishops' statement that "action on behalf of justice is a constitutive element of the preaching of the Gospel".

| 31 | Ethnicity & Race | 2 |

That the N.C.C.B. must acknowledge that its efforts to address the problem of racism are not subsumed or diluted by applying remedies appropriate to cure problems of ethnicity which are often insufficient to address the problem of racism.

| 32 | Ethnicity & Race | 1 |

That the N.C.C.B. within itself should bring about a proportional representation of racial, ethnic and cultural groups in the formation and implementation of Church policy which will reflect the national make-up of the Church.

| 33 | Ethnicity & Race | 2 |

That each diocese, parish and all Church-related agencies establish Affirmative Action Plans.

| 34 | Ethnicity & Race | 2 |

That in every aspect of the allocation of human material and financial resources and the preparation of budgets, the Church acts to combat racism and discrimination and promote justice.

| 35 | Ethnicity & Race | 2 |

That the Church avoid those investment institutions and service agencies which refuse to take Affirmative action to achieve equal opportunity.

| 36 | Ethnicity & Race | 2 |

That Church leadership at all levels clearly assert its commitment to a unity of faith in a pluralism which recognizes and appreciates the right of diverse, ethnic, racial and cultural groups to maintain and develop their traditional culture.

37   Ethnicity & Race   1

That the N.C.C.B. should commit itself to facilitate and encourage efforts of ethnic, racial, and cultural organizations to formulate pastoral and social action programs.

38   Ethnicity & Race   2

That facilities for seminary and other training for ministries among ethnic, racial and cultural groups should include multilingual and multicultural education, and intensive inservice training in relation to the specific ethnic, racial and cultural communities they will serve.

39   Ethnicity & Race   2

That Catholic communications and media experts in both national and diocesan offices take deliberate, positive action to understand and affirm the values of cultural, ethnic and racial diversity.

40   Ethnicity & Race   2

That scholars in college and seminaries study the many peoples in the U.S. to assist in documenting ethnic, racial and cultural diversity.

41   Ethnicity & Race   1

That the Church should establish a multi-ethnic office under the N.C.C.B. to promote appreciation of ethnic values within the Catholic Church.

42   Ethnicity & Race   1

That the Church should expand the Spanish-speaking Secretariat of the N.C.C.B. and establish a National Hispanic Research Center.

43   Ethnicity & Race   2

That diocesan and national liturgical commissions and agencies should insure adequate representation of all ethnic, racial and cultural groups.

44   Ethnicity & Race   4

That the N.C.C.B. take immediate action to secure a larger membership in the hierarchy from the ethnic, racial and cultural community in the U.S.

45   Ethnicity & Race   3

That the Church commit itself to the American Indian people in matters of land disposition, educational policies, health care, direct financial assistance, individual liberties and inherent tribal sovereignty.

46   Ethnicity & Race   1

That the Bishops ought to create an American Indian Secretariat within the N.C.C.B./U.S.C.C.

47   Ethnicity & Race   2

That the Church strongly support quality Indian education--spiritual academic and vocational--both on and off reservations, by direct financial assistance, insisting that the control of education be in the hands of the Indian people.

48   Ethnicity & Race   1

That the Church admit American Indian liturgies.

49   Ethnicity & Race   1

That the N.C.C.B. include, in the prescribed curriculum for seminaries in the U.S., courses in American Indian spirituality.

50   Ethnicity & Race   3

That the N.C.C.B. recognize, study, and implement the pastoral letter, A New Beginning, now being implemented by the Bishops of Minnesota.

51   Ethnicity & Race   4

That the ordination of Indian Bishops take place as soon as possible, depending upon the human resources available.

270

52   Ethnicity & Race   4

   That the Catholic Bishops support a realistic policy for an Indian diaconate program, carried on at the local community under the direction of the local director, revising current policy on sex, age requirement, celibacy, and permanency, which at present hinder development of the Indian diaconate.

53   Ethnicity & Race   3

   That the Church ought to increase Catholic awareness of the American Indian peoples' cultural contribution towards the humanization of this nation.

54   Ethnicity & Race   2

   To develop and support a special ministry to non-reservation Indians, especially in any and all areas where jurisdiction, tradition, poverty and paternalism have perpetuated grave injustices in law enforcement, medical care, education, worship and community acceptance and leadership.

55   Ethnicity & Race   3

   That the Call to Action Assembly require the N.C.C.B./U.S.C.C., especially through the Social Development Office of the U.S.C.C., to commit itself to the National Office for Black Catholics, the secretariat for the Spanish-speaking and the Catholic Conference of Ethnic and Neighborhood Affairs, and the proposed American Indian secretariat by providing the human and financial resources necessary for the development and implementation of national pastoral and social action plans for their respective communities.

56   Ethnicity & Race   3

   That the N.C.C.B. establish a task force, with representation from the National Office of Black Catholics and the American Indian communities, to evaluate the work of the Commission for Catholic Missions.

57   Ethnicity & Race   3

   That the N.C.C.B., the Campaign for Human Development and other appropriate organizations sponsor or advocate research and action to meet the social and economic needs of the urban and rural poor whites who comprise two thirds of the urban poor.

58   Ethnicity & Race   1, 3

That the needs of the millions of Appalachian and Puerto Rican migrants, as well as their empowerment and self-development in Appalachia and Puerto Rico, deserve a special consideration in pastoral research and action.

59   Ethnicity & Race   1, 2

That all official and semi-official agencies of the Church dealing with education join together to make a public report on the educational needs of Black, Spanish-speaking, American Indian, Asian-American, and other ethnic groups.

60   Ethnicity & Race   2

That each diocese should give very high priority to the continued operation of parochial schools already existing in poor urban and rural areas as a service to the poor on the part of the entire diocese and not that of the parish alone.

61   Ethnicity & Race   3

That the Church in the United States, acting through its established agencies for social and legislative action, make every effort to bring to an end all forms of racism and discrimination, particularly in such public policy areas as housing, education, neighborhood development, job opportunities, health care and nutrition.

62   Ethnicity & Race   1

That the N.C.C.B. produce a pastoral letter on the sin and evil of racism in American life.

63   Ethnicity & Race   1

That the N.C.C.B., through the U.S.C.C. give higher priority to the study of the problem of the alienation of our black, Hispanic and Indian youth and develop appropriate policies and programs.

| 64 | Ethnicity & Race | 2 |

That the American Church use whatever means available to it to see that freedom of the press and the media is upheld and not utilized as a central mechanism to foster more discrimination and racism.

| 65 | Ethnicity & Race | 2 |

That every diocese have a specifically designated task force, racially mixed and representative, to make a Christian response to all acts of racism and discrimination within the diocese, including cooperation with existing public agencies committed to respond to such actions.

| 66 | Ethnicity & Race | 1 |

That each diocese establish a Black, Hispanic, Indian and Ethnic Secretariat to keep Bishops informed on the needs and feelings of these racial and ethnic groups.

| 67 | Ethnicity & Race | 1 |

That the N.C.C.B. recommend that the local and national Church groups withdraw any monies deposited in financial institutions which are complicit in redlining, hiring discrimination, or which make clear profits from racism and other forms of exploitation, either in the U.S. or abroad.

| 68 | Ethnicity & Race | 3 |

That the proper Church agencies and the media at our disposal be used to fight discrimination in the U.S. immigration policy and to promote just legislation in this area, as well as promote generous amnesty for undocumented aliens already residing in the U.S.

| 69 | Family | 3 |

That the Church recognize the special need for theologians to collaborate in developing further the theology of matrimony based on an appropriate understanding of sexuality.

70	Family	1

That the Church, with the leadership of the Bishops, develop a comprehensive pastoral plan for family ministry based upon a continuing process of dialogue between families and competent authorities.

71	Family	1

That the Bishops should move to establish a standing committee within the N.C.C.B. with responsibility for marriage and family life and, furthermore, enlarge and support the existing National Family Life Office.

72	Family	2

That the Church establish diocesan family life offices with appropriate diocesan, vicariate, deanery and parish committees.

73	Family	3

That the Church recognize the special competency of permanent deacons and lay people, especially married couples, in family ministry by seeking them out and assuring them roles of leadership and authority.

74	Family	1, 2

That the Church recognize the need for appropriate training for all those involved in leadership positions in family ministry.

75	Family	2

That all Church programs dealing in family life will work with other social justice agencies to create environments and develop programs which encourage families to get involved in an action and reflection process in the service of others and the attainment of justice.

76	Family	1

That the entire Catholic community, through the establishment of pastoral councils on the national, regional diocesan, district, parish and neighborhood levels and in conjunction with State Catholic conferences and the U.S.C.C., should systematically participate in the development of a clear position on the role of the family in public policy.

77   Family   1, 3

That families, in cooperation with parish and diocesan life commissions, with diocesan communications offices, with the U.S.C.C. Department of Communications, with the Catholic Association of Broadcasters and Allied Communications, with the Catholic Press Association and with their religious and civic organizations, work to support programming which reinforces family values.

78   Family   1, 2, 4

That the Church (1) extend pastoral care to separated, divorced and divorced/remarried Catholics, (2) put an immediate end to practices which brand separated, divorced and divorced/remarried Catholics as failures and discriminate against them; and (3) publicly address the request of the divorced who have remarried to receive, under certain conditions, the sacraments of the Church.

79   Family   1

That the Church invest in serious study the causes of marital breakdown with particular attention to the impact of cultural conditions on marriage and family life.

80   Family   3

That the Bishops of the U.S. take the action required to repeal the penalty of automatic excommunication decreed by the Third Council of Baltimore for those Catholics who "dare to remarry after divorce".

81   Humankind   1

That the N.C.C.B. strongly urge the establishment in each diocese an office for justice and peace.

| 82 | Humankind | 2, 3 |

That the Office of International Justice and Peace of the U.S.C.C. be encouraged and supported in its work.

| 83 | Humankind | 1 |

That the U.S.C.C., through its Office of International Justice and Peace, establish and maintain in New York an office with professional staff as a center of information and laison with the United Nations.

| 84 | Humankind | 1 |

That the U.S.C.C., through its Office of International Justice and Peace, collaborate with other National ecclesial communities, the National Council of Churches, the Jewish community and with other religions and that it enter into dialogue with other world religions on the issues of justice and peace.

| 85 | Humankind | 3 |

That the Office of International Justice and Peace and the Department of Education of the U.S.C.C. begin immediately to build on and support present efforts (U.S.C.C., N.C.E.A., etc.) to develop models of justice education at all levels affirmative of the different cultures among us, and stimulate research and evaluation in regions throughout the country (e.g. Catholic) educational institutions, universities, etc.

| 86 | Humankind | 1 |

That the N.C.C.B. should invite all scholars to participate in the ministry of justice and peace by collaborative research into questions of global justice, including the relation of Catholic and other (e.g. socialist, Gandhian) traditions to contemporary situations.

| 87 | Humankind | 1 |

That the Bishops make a renewed attempt to focus in their communications with each other and with the faithful on issues of justice and peace, including regular evaluation of the effectiveness of their communication on these subjects.

88   Humankind   3

That active efforts be made in every diocese to initiate on a parish level the development of the education for justice process.

89   Humankind   1

That the Bishops and missionary societies should (1) invite indigenous representatives of the Third World to "raise the critical consciousness" of the people of the U.S. regarding their situation, and (2) utilize, more advantageously, returning missionaries for American Catholic justice and peace education programs.

90   Humankind   1

That the Catholic Church should use television, radio, press, and other means of social communication as vehicles for bringing a larger and more comprehensive view of global justice before the public.

91   Humankind   1

That the role of small intentional communities, such as Catholic worker and other ecumenical grass-roots groups, be recognized and promoted in the work of education and formation for justice.

92   Humankind   1

That the N.C.C.B., the U.S.C.C., and the Catholic community of the U.S. advocate before their government a foreign policy that is in keeping with the defense of human rights as stipulated in the U.N. Universal Declaration of Rights.

Also, that the N.C.C.B./U.S.C.C. continue to examine the moral dimensions of the policies of our government and to address particular attention to the operation effects of multinational corporations with large investments in third world countries.

93 Humankind 3

   That all Catholics and Catholic institutions review their purchases and investments, applying moral and ethical criteria suggested in the "guidelines" published by such groups as the National Federation of Priests' Councils, the Justice and Peace Center in Milwaukee, and the National Council of Churches.

94 Humankind 3

   That the Church in America, as a way of affirming the right of every person to an adequate diet, institutionalize "Operation Rice Bowl" as a regular element of the Lenten season.

95 Humankind 2

   That parishes promote enrollment in organizations such as Bread for the World, the Christian Citizens Organization, enlisting members who, in turn, contact government leaders on policy matters that have a direct bearing on world hunger, and that maximum use be made of its publications in parish bulletins and other available media.

96 Humankind 1

   That the Bishops responsible for Catholic Relief Services evaluate the policies, programs, activities and structures of Catholic Relief Services toward making it an even more effective instrument for the integral development of people, including the promotion of human rights, and to insure that this humanitarian assistance to the needy transcends government priorities and national security policies.

97 Humankind 2, 3

   That the Bishops educate Catholics to a sense of moral responsibility to share the world's goods and that the Catholic community, on all levels, examine its lifestyle and reduce its unnecessary consumption of goods.

98   Humankind   2, 3

That the N.C.C.B., through the offices of Justice and Peace and other appropriate groups available to them, urge individual Catholics and other citizens to convince their local political representatives to urge the U.S. to ratify the U.N. Covenants on <u>Civil and Political Rights</u> and <u>Social and Economic Rights</u>.

99   Humankind   1

That the N.C.C.B. advocate adequate and accessible health care as a human right, by the issuance of a pastoral letter.

100   Humankind   2

That the Church recognize that the issue of undocumented immigration into the U.S. is an international question and that undocumented immigrants have the basic human right to be free from economic and physical abuse from the U.S. government and private employers and that, furthermore, the Church should encourage legislation granting amnesty to all undocumented workers in the U.S.

101   Humankind   1

That the N.C.C.B., the U.S.C.C. and other appropriate organizations actively support and critically challenge both U.S. and corporations with regard to their promotion of human rights.

102   Humankind   1

That the Office of International Justice and Peace of the U.S.C.C. encourage implementation of the U.S. Commission to monitor the Helsinki accord, and focus the attention of U.S. Catholics and other citizens on the continuing suppression of the religious, political, cultural and other human rights of the oppressed nations of Eastern Europe, including the right to emigrate.

103   Humankind   1

That the N.C.C.B. and the U.S.C.C. mobilize the international conscience on behalf of all political prisoners under repressive governments in any country of the world who are subject to torture, disappearance and assassination without respect for their basic human rights to life and liberty.

104   Humankind   1

That, in light of consistent Church teaching on modern warfare, the U.S. Catholic Community condemn, and be among those who lead in resisting, the production, possession, proliferation and threatened use of nuclear weapons.

105   Humankind   2, 3

That peace education programs at every level of Church life emphasize the dangers and evils of the arms race and an aggressive military posture because of the threat they pose to all humanity.

106   Humankind   1

That the Church in the U.S. give support to those, who on grounds of conscience, refuse to serve in war or preparation for war and that Catholics support legal provision for selective and general conscientious objection to military service and to the payment of war or military taxes.

107   Humankind   1

That the Catholic Community do all in its power to halt the sale or transfer of arms overseas and make the U.S. convert to a peace-based economy.

108   Humankind   2

That services of reconciliation between people and nations be encouraged so that the world community can face in prayer the fact that large numbers of people have already perished through the use of indiscriminate weaponry.

109   Humankind   2

That Pope Paul's theme for the 1977 World Day of Peace, "If you want peace, defend life", be explored throughout the Catholic community in various forums for study and discussion with the intent of linking the concern for the right to life with efforts to end the wanton destruction of life by modern warfare.

110 Humankind 2

That the Catholic community continue to press all governments for full disclosure of information concerning prisoners of war and those missing in action in all conflicts and that such information not be withheld for political or economic reasons.

111 Humankind 1

That the National Catholic Community Service explore forms of ministry to the military alternative to the current system in which chaplains are officers in the armed services; that special attention be given to Church-paid salaries other than government paid salaries; that the recommendations be considered by the Bishops.

112 Humankind 3

That Catholics be encouraged to support movements for freedom, justice and reconciliation in other nations and to identify with the oppressed peoples in such countries as South Africa, Chile, those countries under Communist domination, Korea, the Philippines, Northern Ireland, and Lebanon, to name a few.

113 Nationhood 2

That committees for political responsibility be designated at parish, diocesan, state and national levels to establish priorities for public policy, define the major issues at stake in elections, be representative of the poor and powerless, educate Church members and the public regarding the moral dimensions of public issues and work with other churches and civic groups to implement these goals.

114 Nationhood 1

That the Church promote the following goals for public policy: (a) disarmament, (b) right to life,

(c) elimination of poverty, (d) full employment, (e) redistribution of income through tax reform, (f) National Health Care, (g) conservation of natural resources and protection of the environment, (h) guaranteed housing, (i) institutionalization of human rights, (j) commitment to end racism, (k) guaranteed education , (l) support of equal rights amendment, (m) liberalization of immigration laws, (n) unconditional amnesty to all draft, military and civilian resisters to the Vietnam War, (o) Welfare reform.

    115   Nationhood   3

  That the Church support research exploring alternatives in innovative economic structures that will distribute power more equitably.

    116   Nationhood   3

  That the Catholic Communications Organization (UNDA), other coalitions and religious communicators, make citizens aware of present efforts to influence the human and aesthetic quality of network and local programming and advertising so that citizens can cooperate with these efforts.

    117   Nationhood   1, 2, 3

  That the process of consultation (listening, responding, implementing) becomes a regular element of U.S. Catholic life and that there be established local structures to enable people to participate in the decision-making processes so that trust can grow between the Bishop and the people; the pastor and the people; and the powerful and the powerless.

    118   Nationhood   1

  That the N.C.C.B., through the Bicentennial Office, establish a representative task force to dialogue with the Bishops concerning plans for the ongoing implementation of the Call to Action recommendations and, furthermore, that the American Church leadership commit adequate resources of money and personnel for the ongoing implementation of the Liberty and Justice for All process.

119   Nationhood   1

That each diocese and religious order, in order to implement the words of Pope Paul VI that "no one is justified in keeping for his exclusive use what he does not need, when others lack necessities . . . in a word, the right to property must never be exercised to the detriment of the common good", divest themselves of that which is unnecessary or not in keeping with "institutional simplicity".

120   Neighborhood   2

That parish liturgies must be celebrations of community life; that the sacramental life of the neighborhood church should reflect the relationship between Christian commitment and community realities; that the parish personalize its outreach into the neighborhood community; that the parish community educate itself in its role of "neighborhood servant", and that in the selection and tenure of parish personnel great consideration should be given to the needs of the neighborhood.

121   Neighborhood   2

That the neighborhood parish ought to make available to competent neighborhood action groups needed facilities and resources; that a budgetary item of every parish to financially support competent neighborhood action groups be considered a necessary investment; that the Church should initiate and be actively involved in the development of community organizing projects among all peoples; that each diocese shall establish an office for community affairs or shall expand its existing office; that the Church should commit itself to the concept of "open neighborhoods", whereby new residents of any race, ethnic group, cultural background or religious faith would be welcomed as brothers and sisters in Christ; and that the urgent need in the inner-city situations mandates that the Church recognize inner-city neighborhoods as territories demanding priority attention.

122   Neighborhood   2

That each diocese recognize the vital responsibility of ministry to Catholics and other persons who ask for our ministry at colleges and universities and allocate a fixed portion of its personnel and resources to assist those people in effective Christian action in their collegiate neighborhoods.

123 Neighborhood 1, 2

That the Church develop an urban social policy that is based on the concept of equality of persons, races, ethnic and culturally diverse groups, and recognize the commitment in every diocese that community development must flow from the needs of the people as identified by the people.

124 Neighborhood 1

That social justice courses in the area of neighborhood parish community development, community organization and multi-cultural education be mandatory in the training of seminaries and in the continuing education of clergy and religious.

125 Neighborhood 2

That in each diocese the decision whether or not to close parishes and schools should include the involvement of the neighborhood community.

126 Neighborhood 2

That each diocese and state conference should develop a staff position whose major responsibility shall consist of the monitoring and reporting of local, state and federal policy and program initiatives which have impact on the parish/neighborhood community.

127 Neighborhood 3

That the U.S.C.C. establish a similar office to coordinate the actions on behalf of social justice and community development of all organizations and institutions of the Church, with special emphasis on housing and employment needs.

| 128 | Neighborhood | 3 |

That there be initiation and continued development of effective advocacy with the poor through the support and expansion of the Campaign for Human Development.

| 129 | Neighborhood | 3 |

That the N.C.C.B. continue its support of the National Rural Life Conference as the American Church's voice for land, town and country related concerns, and that it urge grassroots support adequate for carrying out this role.

| 130 | Neighborhood | 1 |

That there should be an evaluation of Church structures and programs of ministry to the rural community in the light of the present needs for social action, religious education and social services.

| 131 | Neighborhood | 2, 3 |

That the Bishops reevaluate their policies, disbursements of funds and personnel placement in rural communities.

| 132 | Neighborhood | 1 |

That our Bishops be encouraged to address a pastoral letter to the people of their diocese on the dignity of rural life for Christian living.

| 133 | Neighborhood | 1 |

That the Bishops, in consultation with the larger Catholic population, develop new structures and ministries appropriate to the needs of rural communities, such as mobile teams of resource persons and new forms of lay leadership and ministry.

| 134 | Neighborhood | 1 |

That national Church organizations consider the needs of more rural dioceses in the location of meetings and allotment of funds.

135   Neighborhood   2

That a special task force be set up through the National Catholic Rural Life Conference to address and develop legislative action relative to the problems of rural poverty, rural health and housing; land use and theology of stewardship; estate, property, and income tax reform; rural financing (redlining); corporate tax deduction (loss) farming; use of food products as a national and international political tool.

136   Neighborhood   3

That the Church support the God-given rights of the poor rural wage earners, immigrants, sharecroppers, and family farmers, and the rights of small and independent businessmen; and that the Church recognize and encourage their rights to organize.

137   Neighborhood   1

That the N.C.C.B. through the Bicentennial Office establish a representative task force to sustain the Call to Action momentum; to promote the implementation of all the recommendations; and to set in motion another consultation within five years to evaluate the results of this program and to suggest goals for the next period.

138   Personhood   1

That the N.C.C.B. should give priority to the development of community especially at the parish level.

139   Personhood   2, 3

That all Catholics foster an awareness of, and create an environment in which each person can recognize his or her vocation, whether married, single, religious or ordained clergy, as a divine call of Christ and that these vocations are recognized as equal in dignity and essential to the building of a Christian Community.

140   Personhood   1

    That the N.C.C.B. reconsider policies and Church structure that exclude persons from ministry and establish policies and structures that support persons in their shared responsibility for carrying out the mission of the Church.

141   Personhood   4

    That the N.C.C.B. should initiate or open the office of preaching to women and that consideration should be given to unordained men, married couples, laicized priests who also could make a valuable contribution to the community through this office.

142   Personhood   2, 3

    That the Catholic Church in the United States of America foster diocesan, parochial, intentional and familial environments in which all persons can respond fully to the universal call to holiness.

143   Personhood   1

    That the N.C.C.B. exercise the option given by the Holy Father to permit reception of holy communion in the hand as a sign of adult Christian commitment and human dignity.

144   Personhood   3

    That the Church seek to promote personal dignity by advocating the rights of the aging in the areas of housing, health, employment, transportation and economics.

145   Personhood   3

    That Catholics endorse and work to implement the 1975 Bishops' <u>Pastoral Plan for Pro-Life Activities</u>.

146   Personhood   3

    That the Catholic Church in the U.S., recognizing the teaching of Vatican II that "every type of discrimination . . . based on sex . . . is to be overcome and eradicated as contrary to God's intent", work to achieve full equality under the law for men and women in the U.S., and full economic justice for women in all sectors of American society.

    147   Personhood   1

  That the American Church ought to endorse and support the Equal Rights Amendment to the Constitution.

    148   Personhood   2, 3

  That the Bishops initiate, implement and evaluate pastoral plans for and with and by youth.

    149   Personhood   2, 3

  That the Church support the physically and mentally handicapped by providing appropriate educational and rehabilitation programs; providing and advocating necessary architectural modifications; advocating adequate governmental funding to the handicapped person and family so that, whenever possible, the handicapped may remain in the family, advocating the rights and principle of normalization so that the handicapped can find housing, employment, social life, educational opportunities and valuable spiritual and parish life.

    150   Personhood   1

  That the N.C.C.B./U.S.C.C. study the feasibility of establishing a National Catholic Office for the Handicapped to develop at the national level the Church's ministry to the handicapped.

    151   Personhood   2

  That diocesan Catholic Social Service Agencies offer leadership to all appropriate lay diocesan groups in planning and coordinating the various church and community social service efforts on behalf of clients.

    152   Personhood   2

  That Catholic social action agencies and

offices look closely at what is commonly perceived to be institutionalized racism and oppression in our society and they closely examine the structures which racial minorities experience to be threatening.

153　　　　　Personhood　　　　2

That the Church call for (1) the extension of civil rights to all prisoners; (2) the creation of community alternatives to present patterns of incarceration; (3) the development of parish outreach programs to inmates, ex-offenders and their families to facilitate reentry into the community; and (4) elimination of so-called status offenses for 18 year olds and younger, which are discriminatory and unnecessarily introduce teenagers into the criminal justice system.

154　　　　　Personhood　　　　1

That dialogue, coupled with serious inter-disciplinary research, should be initiated that can assist all persons in the Church to inform their consciences more fully on the moral dimensions of human sexuality.

155　　　　　Personhood　　　　1

That the American Bishops should use their present pastoral leadership to affirm more clearly the right and responsibility of married people to form their own consciences and to discover what is morally appropriate regarding contraception within the context of their marriage in view of historical Church teaching, including <u>HUMANAE VITAE</u>, and contemporary theological reflection, biological and social scientific research; and those factors influencing the spiritual and emotional quality of their marital and family lives.

156　　　　　Personhood　　　　2

That educational programs in sexuality for the young should begin at an early age and be developed with the cooperation of parents, teachers, pastors and include as well the experience of young adults.

| 157 | Personhood | 2, 3 |

That the Church actively seek to serve the pastoral needs of those persons with a homosexual orientation, to root out those structures and attitudes which discriminate against homosexuals as persons and to join the struggle by homosexual men and women for their basic constitutional rights to employment and housing.

| 158 | Work | 1 |

That the Bishops of the U.S., in consultation with canon lawyers, theologians and other scholars, and in cooperation with representatives of the entire Church, prepare a bill of rights for Catholics in the U.S., which would ultimately be included within canon law.

| 159 | Work | 1 |

That the U.S.C.C., through its Department of Social Development, call upon all Catholic ordinaries to establish in their dioceses a plan for equal opportunity.

| 160 | Work | 1 |

That the Church should commit significant economic resources and personnel, especially in social action agencies and offices, to achieve speedy ratification of the Equal Rights Amendment.

| 161 | Work | 3 |

That the Bishops of the U.S. shall work toward promotion of full employment for all people.

| 162 | Work | 1 |

That an equal employment opportunity program be implemented immediately by the U.S.C.C.

| 163 | Work | 1 |

That the Church, at its headquarters, college universities, and in each diocese, immediately launch a continual survey of its employees in its chanceries, schools, hospitals, parishes and in its other institutions so that the Church can determine how it can attain equal employment through affirmative action.

164   Work   1

That a pastoral letter be sent to Catholic institutions, groups and individuals affirming the responsibility of Catholics to promote equal opportunity and affirmative action to insure justice to all groups in American society.

165   Work   2

That the Bishops direct every Catholic institution which has financial investments in multi-national corporations to use their power as shareholders to assure economic and social justice for all concerned, especially in Latin American and other Third World countries.

166   Work   1

That a commission on economic justice, with voluntary representation from each diocese and from national organizations, dealing with business, economic, labor and social issues be established.

167   Work   2

That in support of the Commission on Economic Justice, committees with grass-roots representatives should be established on the diocesan level, in religious orders and in various Catholic organizations and parishes.

168   Work   2

That the N.C.C.B. mandate the preaching and teaching of Catholic social doctrine at all levels of the Church.

169   Work   2

That the Church actively support the repeal of "right to work" laws as they now exist in 20 states in the U.S.

| 170 | Work | 1 |

That the Church should support the Equal Rights Amendment to the U.S. Constitution.

| 171 | Work | 2 |

That the social doctrine of Pope John XXIII, Paul VI, Vatican II, the U.S. Bishops and the social teachings of the Church, in their historical developments since 1891 be taught, respected, and implemented in parishes, seminaries and other Catholic institutions.

| 172 | Work | 2 |

That Catholics encourage and assist unemployed and unorganized workers, regardless of immigrant status, to join or form unions to represent their common interests and support legislation which encourages such organization.

| 173 | Work | 2, 3 |

That the Catholic community recognize and support the rights of its employees, including documented and undocumented in the Church or Church-related institutions, to form and/or join unions and other appropriate organizations of their own choosing to represent their collective interests and concerns.

| 174 | Work | 2, 3 |

That the Church should encourage efforts at labor-management cooperation including research and prudent experimentation on profit sharing, ownership of capital by employees, and participative management in business and industry, especially those in which the Church has an economic interest.

| 175 | Work | 2, 3 |

That the Church help to reform working conditions and assist farmworkers to help themselves by the formation of cooperatives, credit unions, health centers, etc.

| 176 | Work | 1, 2, 3 |

That the Church support amnesty for undocumented immigrants whose departure from the U.S. would impose upon them or their families any hardship.

| 177 | Work | 2 |

That the Church encourage the private and public business sectors to adopt an affirmative action policy on the hiring of Vietnam era veterans.

| 178 | Work | 1 |

That a local commission on economic justice be established in every diocese whose specific task it is to monitor and report annually on the implementation of the "work" resolutions.

| 179 | Work | 1, 2 |

That the Bishops and all people in pastoral work should have adequate training in Catholic social science and spirituality.

| 180 | Work | 2 |

That Catholic educational programs at appropriate levels incorporate vocational and career counseling.

| 181 | Work | 1 |

That Catholic scholars, especially theologians and social scientists, commissioned by the U.S.C.C., utilizing the resources of Catholic tradition, contemporary research and the experience of working people, develop a theology of work and leisure, critique and evaluate economic life, and identify alternatives to our present system of economic organization.

| 182 | Work | 3 |

That the U.S.C.C. should stimulate, either through new or existing organizations, dialogue with groups such as labor unions, professional societies, business organizations, cooperative movements and citizens groups to translate the implications of justice into practical norms of action.

APPENDIX B

CALL TO ACTION DELEGATE PROFILE
ENTIRE SAMPLE

Item	Response	No.	Percent
1. Sex			
(1)	Female	469	40.0
(2)	Male	703	60.0
2. Age			
(1)	15-17	12	1.0
(2)	18-25	42	3.6
(3)	26-40	377	32.2
(4)	41-60	632	53.9
(5)	Over 60	109	9.3
3. Income			
( )	No Response	29	2.5
(1)	0-3,499	233	19.9
(2)	3,500-6,999	347	29.6
(3)	7,800-9,999	134	11.4
(4)	10,000-14,999	124	10.6
(5)	15,000-24,999	173	14.8
(6)	25,000 or more	132	11.3
4. Type			
( )	No Response	13	1.1
(1)	Laity	555	47.4
(2)	Clergy	400	34.1
(3)	Religious Women	196	16.7
(4)	Religious Brothers	8	.7
5. Living Area			
( )	No Response	5	.4
(1)	Urban	426	36.3
(2)	Inner City	190	16.2
(3)	Suburban	194	16.6
(4)	Small City (pop. 20,000-50,000)	142	12.1
(5)	Small Town (pop. less than 20,000)	104	8.9
(6)	Rural	111	9.5

Item	Response	No.	Percent
6.	Race		
	( ) No Response	1	.1
	(1) White	940	80.2
	(2) Black	87	7.4
	(3) Hispanic	108	9.2
	(4) American Indian	16	1.4
	(5) Asian	6	.5
	(6) Other	14	1.2
7.	Liberty and Justice For All Discussion		
	( ) No Response	9	.8
	(1) Yes	650	55.5
	(2) No	513	43.8
8.	National Hearings		
	( ) No Response	8	.7
	(1) Yes	236	20.1
	(2) No	928	79.2
9.	Work Classification		
	( ) No Response	17	1.5
	(1) Armed Service	15	1.3
	(2) Business or Industry	118	10.1
	(3) Church	754	64.3
	(4) Government (Federal, State, Local)	76	6.5
	(5) Homemaker	97	8.3
	(6) Self-Employed	50	4.3
	(7) Student	34	2.9
	(8) Unemployed	11	.9
10.	Church Work Area		
	( ) No Response	420	35.8
	(1) Administration	285	24.3
	(2) Education	178	15.2
	(3) Health	10	.9
	(4) Social Justice	169	14.4
	(5) Social Services	110	9.4
11.	Group Representation		
	( ) No Response	74	6.3
	(1) Diocesan Administration	435	37.1
	(2) Parish Life	464	39.6
	(3) Affected by Injustice	199	17.0

Item	Response	No.	Percent
12.	Parish Identification		
	( ) No Response	22	1.9
	(1) Territorial Parish	604	51.5
	(2) Alternative or Non Geographic	93	7.9
	(3) Community Institution	185	15.8
	(4) National Parish	53	4.5
	(5) Other Relationship to Parish	147	12.5
	(6) No Relationship to Parish	68	5.8
13.	Involvement		
	( ) No Response	23	2.0
	(1) Parish Committee	139	11.9
	(2) Diocesan Committee or Commission	437	37.3
	(3) Church Movement	218	18.6
	(4) Local Church Organization	143	12.2
	(5) National Church Organization	121	10.3
	(6) None of These	91	7.8
14.	Section Worked On		
	( ) No Response	12	1.0
	(1) Church	180	15.4
	(2) Ethnicity and Race	146	12.5
	(3) Family	150	12.8
	(4) Humankind	137	11.7
	(5) Nationhood	132	11.3
	(6) Neighborhood	144	12.3
	(7) Personhood	151	12.9
	(8) Work	120	10.2
15.	Release Address		
	( ) No Response	21	1.8
	(1) Yes	880	75.1
	(2) No	271	23.1

TOTAL NUMBER OF RESPONSES 1,172

BIBLIOGRAPHY

The Bibliography is divided into five sections. They are as follows: (I) "Books"; (II) "Articles"; (III) "Unpublished Material on the Call to Action"; (IV) "Material on the Call to Action from the N.C.C.B./U.S.C.C."; and (V) "Catholic Theology".

I. BOOKS

Abell, Aaron I., American Catholicism and Social Action: A Search for Social Justice, 1865-1900. N.Y.: Doubleday, 1960.

_____. The Urban Impact on American Protestantism 1965-1900. Cambridge: Harvard Historical Studies 1945.

Allport, Gordon. The Individual and His Religion. N.Y.: MacMillan, 1960.

Aron, Raymond. Main Currents of Sociological Thought Vol. II. N.Y.: Basic Books, 1970.

Berger, Peter L., Facing Up to Modernity. N.Y.: Basic Books, 1977.

_____. The Heretical Imperative. N.Y.: Basic Books, 1979.

_____. Invitation to Sociology. N.Y.: Doubleday, 1963.

_____. Pyramids of Sacrifice. N.Y.: Basic Books, 1974.

_____. A Rumor of Angels. N.Y.: Doubleday, 1970.

_____. The Sacred Canopy. N.Y.: Doubldeay, 1967.

Berger, Peter L. and Brigette Berger. Sociology: A Biographical Approach. N.Y.: Basic Books, 1975.

Berger, Peter L., Brigitte Berger and Hansfried Kellner. The Homeless Mind. N.Y.: Random House, 1975.

Berger, Peter and Thomas Luckmann. *The Social Construction of Reality*. N.Y.: Doubleday, 1966.

Berger, Peter L. and Richard Neuhaus. *To Empower People: The Role of Mediating Structures in Public Policy*. Washington: American Enterprise Institute, 1978.

Brinton, Crane. *The Anatomy of A Revolution*. N.Y.: Random House, 1960.

Browne, H. J., *The Catholic Church and the Knights of Labor*. N.Y.: Arno Press, 1975.

Caporale, Rocco and Antonio Grumelli (editors). *The Culture of Unbelief*. Berkeley: University of California Press, 1971.

Cogley, John. *Catholic America*. N.Y.: Dial Press, 1973.

Coser, Lewis. *The Functions of Conflict*. Glencoe, Illinois Free Press, 1956.

Cross, Robert. *The Emergence of Liberal Catholicism in America*. Chicago: Quadrangle Books, 1958.

De Coulanges, Fustel. *The Ancient City*. N.Y.: Doubleday, 1976.

Demerath, N. J. and Phillip Hammond. *Religion in Social Context*. N.Y.: Random House, 1969.

Demerath, Jay and Gerald Marwell. *Sociology*. N.Y.: Harper and Row, 1976.

Dolan, John P., *Catholicism*. N.Y.: Barron, 1968.

Durkheim, Emile. *The Division of Labor in Society*. N.Y.: Free Press, 1964.

_____. *The Elementary Forms of the Religious Life*. N.Y. Free Press, 1947.

Dulles, Avery. *Models of the Church*. N.Y.: Doubleday, 1978.

Eliade, Mircea. *The Sacred and the Profane*. N.Y.: Harcourt Brace and World, 1959.

Ellis, John Tracy. *American Catholicism*. Chicago: University of Chicago Press, 1969.

Festinger, Leon and Henry W. Riecken and Stanley Schacter. *When Prophecy Fails*. N.Y.: Harper and Row, 1964.

Fichter, Joseph. *Southern Parish*. Chicago: University of Chicago Press, 1951.

_____. *The Catholic Cult of the Paraclete*. N.Y.: Sheed and Ward, 1975.

Freud, Sigmund. *The Future of an Illusion*. N.Y.: Anchor Books.

Gambino, Richard. *Blood of My Blood*. N.Y.: Doubleday, 1974.

Geertz, Clifford. *The Interpretation of Cultures*. N.Y.: Basic Books, 1973.

Glock, Charles and Rodney Stark. *Religion and Society in Tension*. Chicago: Rand McNally, 1965.

Goffman, Erving. *Encounters*. N.Y.: Bobbs-Merrill, 1965.

_____. *Interaction Ritual*. N.Y.: Doubleday, 1967.

Greeley, Andrew. *The American Catholic*. N.Y.: Basic Books, 1977.

_____. *The Catholic Experience*. N.Y.: Doubleday, 1970.

_____. *The Communal Catholic*. N.Y.: Seabury Press, 1976.

_____. *The Denominational Society*. Glencoe, Illinois: Scott, Foresman, and Company, 1972.

_____. *Unsecular Man*. N.Y.: Delta, 1972.

_____. *Why Can't They Be Like Us?* N.Y.: E.F. Dutton, 1975.

Gusfield, Joseph. *Symbolic Crusade*. Chicago University of Illinois Press, 1976.

Gutierrez, Gustavo. *A Theology of Liberation*. Maryknoll, N.Y.: Orbis Books, 1973.

Hadden, Jeffrey. *The Gathering Storm in the Churches*. N.Y.: Doubleday, 1969.

Hammond, Phillip. *The Campus Clergyman*. N.Y.: Basic Books, 1966.

Harrison, Paul M., *Authority and Power in the Free Church Tradition*. Princeton: Princeton University Press, 1959.

Herberg, Will. *Protestant, Catholic, Jew*. N.Y.: Doubleday, 1955.

Hitchcock, James. *The Decline and Fall of Radical Catholicism*. N.Y.: Doubleday, 1972.

Hoffer, Eric. *The True Believer*. N.Y.: Harper and Row, 1966.

Hofstadter, Richard. *The Age of Reason*. N.Y.: A. A. Knopf, 1955.

Hughes, Philip. *A Popular History of The Catholic Church*. N.Y.: MacMillan, 1947.

Jackson, J. A., *Social Stratification*. Cambridge: Cambridge University Press, 1970.

Kaufman, Walter (editor). *Religion from Tolstoy to Camus*. N.Y.: Harper and Row, 1964.

Kempis, Thomas A., *The Imitation of Christ*. N.Y.: Doubleday, 1955.

Kuhn, Thomas. *The Structure of Scientific Revolutions*. Chicago: University of Chicago Press, 1970.

Lenski, Gerhard. *The Religious Factor*. N.Y.: Doubleday, 1961.

Luckmann, Thomas. *The Invisible Religion*. N.Y.: MacMillan, 1963.

Mannheim, Karl. *Ideology and Utopia*. Routledge and Kegan Paul, 1936.

———. *Man and Society in an Age of Reconstruction*. London: Routledge and Kegan Paul, 1940.

Marx, Karl. *Selected Writings in Sociology and Social Philosophy* (editors T.B. Bottomore and Maximillian Rubel). Baltimore: Penguin, 1967.

Mead, George Herbert. *On Social Psychology*. Chicago: University of Chicago Press, 1964.

Merton, Thomas. *Contemplation in a World of Action*. N.Y.: Doubleday, 1973.

McAvoy, Thomas T., *A History of the Catholic Church in the United States*. Notre Dame: University of Notre Dame Press, 1969.

Mills, C. W., *The Sociological Imagination*. N.Y.: Oxford University Press, 1959.

Moynihan, Daniel and Nathan Glaser. *Beyond the Melting Pot*. Boston: M.I.T. Press, 1966.

Murray, John Courtney. *We Hold These Truths*. N.Y.: Doubleday, 1964.

Otto, Rudolph. *The Idea of The Holy*. N.Y.: Oxford University Press, 1950.

Pareto, Vilfredo. *The Mind and the Society*. N.Y.: Dover, 1965.

Parsons, Talcott. *The Social System*. N.Y.: Free Press, 1951.

Riesman, David. *The Lonely Crowd*. New Haven: Yale University Press, 1961.

Roche, Douglas J., *The Catholic Revolution*. N.Y.: McKay, 1968.

Schoenherr, Richard A. and Eleanor P. Simpson. *The Political Economy of Diocesan Advisory Councils: A Report of the Comparative Religious Organization Studies*. University of Wisconsin, Madison, 1978.

Shils, Edward. *Center and Periphery*. Chicago: University of Chicago Press, 1975.

_____. *The Intellectuals and the Powers and Other Essays*. Chicago: University of Chicago Press, 1972.

Sorel, Georges. *Reflections on Violence*. London: Collier, 1961.

Stark, Werner. *The Sociology of Knowledge*. Chicago: Free Press of Glencoe, 1958.

Tiryakian, Edward A. (editor). *Sociological Theory, Values and Sociocultural Change*. New York: Free Press, 1963.

Troeltsch, Ernest. *The Social Teachings of the Christian Churches*. N.Y.: Harper Torchbooks, 1960.

Weber, Max. *From Max Weber* (editors, H. H. Gerth and C. W. Mills). N.Y.: Oxford University Press, 1946.

_____. *The Protestant Ethic and the Spirit of Capitalism*. N.Y.: Scribner, 1958.

_____. *The Religion of China*. N.Y.: Free Press, 1951.

_____. *The Sociology of Religion*. Boston: Beacon Press, 1963.

_____. *The Theory of Economic and Social Organization*. N.Y.: Free Press, 1947.

Winter, Gibson. *The Suburban Captivity of the Churches*. N.Y.: Doubleday, 1961.

II. ARTICLES

Bellah, Robert. "Civil Religion in America" in *Daedulus*, 96, Winter, 1967.

Berger, Peter L., "Interview on Religious Revival in U.S." in *U.S. News and World Report*, April 1, 1977.

_____. "Ethics and the Present Class Struggle" in *Worldview*, April, 1978.

Briggs, Kenneth, A., "Catholic Bishops Give Positive Reply to Call to Action, *The New York Times*, May 5, 1977.

"A Chicago Declaration of Concern", *Commonweal*, December, 1977.

Coleman, John. "The Worldly Calling", *Commonweal*, February 17, 1978.

Coston, Carol. "Call to Action", *Network Quarterly*, Vol. 6 Number 8, October 1978.

Detroit and Beyond: The Continuing Quest for Social Justice, Washington, Center of Concern, 1976.

"Editorial", "Call to Action", *Christian Century*, November 17, 1976.

"Editorial", "Bishops Pastoral", *America*, November 27, 1976.

"Editorial", "No Need for the Great Wait", *America*, March 19, 1977.

"Editorial", "Call to Action", *America*, May 20, 1978.

"Editorial", "A New Social Principle!", *The National Catholic Register*, December 31, 1978.

Finn, James. "Catholics Called to Action", *Worldview*, March, 1977.

_____. "Second Call to Action", *Commonweal*. April 29, 1977.

Five Year Report of the Center of Concern, 1971-76, Washington: Center of Concern, 1967.

Fox, Thomas. "Made In Detroit", Commonweal, November 19, 1977.

Gouldner, Alvin. "The Norm of Reciprocity", The American Sociological Review, 1963.

Greeley, Andrew. "Catholic Social Activism: Real or Rad/Chic?", National Catholic Reporter, February 7, 1975.

Handbook: A Call to Action, Notre Dame: Catholic Committee on Urban Ministry, November 9, 1976.

Hitchcock, James (Dr.). "Age of Renewal?", National Catholic Register, March 4, 1979.

Kirk, Russell. "The Mice That Roared", The National Review, December 10, 1976.

Klauser, Alfred, P. "Editorial Correspondence", The Christian Century, May 25, 1977.

Marshner, William. "Bicentennial Alert", The Wanderer, February 20, 1975.

Mantagno, Margaret and Sylvester Monroe. "Call to Action", Newsweek, May, 1977.

McCarthy, Abigail. "Laity and Church: II", Commonweal July 21, 1978.

O'Brien, David. "Lifeboat Ethics", National Catholic Reporter, July 14, 1978.

_____. "Toward An American Catholic Church", Cross Currents, Vol. XXI, # 4, Winter, 1981.

"The National Catholic Welfare Conference" in The New Catholic Encyclopedia, 1959.

"The National Conference of Catholic Bishops/United States Catholic Conference" in The Kenedy Directory 1977.

Quixote Center, Agenda for Justice: Basic Documents of the U.S. Church's Social Policy, 1973-83, 1979.

"Report on the Call to Action, Time, November 8, 1976.

Spaeth, Robert L., "Network", in The St. Cloud Visitor, October 26, 1978.

Stahel, Thomas. "More Action Than They Called For", America, November 6, 1976.

Steinfels, Peter. "New Chance for the Bishops" in Commonweal, April 1, 1977.

Winiarski, Mark. "Cardinal Fights to Save Call to Action Process: In-Fighting Follows Task Force Recommendations", The National Catholic Reporter, April 22, 1977.

III. UNPUBLISHED MATERIAL ON THE CALL TO ACTION

Egan, Monsignor John and Sister Peggy Roach. "Catholic Committee on Urban Ministry: Ministry to the Ministers", unpublished paper, September 1977.

Francis, Bishop Joseph. The Diocesan Implementation of "To Do The Work of Justice: A Plan of Action for the Catholic Community in the United States." Bishops Ad Hoc Committee on the Call to Action, September, 1980.

Manning, Frank V., Call to Action: A Review and Assessment, unpublished manuscript, 1977.

O'Brien, David J., A Call to Action: The Church Prepares for the Third Century, unpublished manuscript, July 1978.

"Report of the Bicentennial Committee on the Call to Action", unpublished report, December 1976.

Roach, Archbishop John. "Doing Justice: Some Reflections on The Call to Action Plan", unpublished manuscript, March 1979.

IV. MATERIAL ON THE "CALL TO ACTION" FROM THE
    N.C.C.B./U.S.C.C.

"Bicentennial Convocation on Global Justice", Justice
   Hearing, Number 7, Washington: N.C.C.B., Committee
   for the Bicentennial, 1976.

"A Call to Action: An Agenda for the Catholic
   Community, Washington: N.C.C.B./U.S.C.C., 1979.

"The Call to Action Proposals", Origins: National
   Catholic Documentary Service, Vol. 6, Number 20,
   November 4, 1976 and Vol. 6, Number 21, November 21,
   1976.

"Ethnicity and Race", Justice Hearing, Number 6,
   Washington: N.C.C.B., Committee for the Bicentennial
   1975.

"The Family", Justice Hearing, Number 4, Washington:
   N.C.C.B., Committee for the Bicentennial, 1975.

Final Committee Evaluations of the Call to Action
   Recommendations, Washington: N.C.C.B./U.S.C.C.,
   February 13, 1978.

"Humankind", Justice Hearing, Number 1, Washington:
   N.C.C.B., Committee for the Bicentennial, 1975.

"The Land", Justice Hearing, Number 3, Washington:
   N.C.C.B., Committee for the Bicentennial, 1975.

Liberty and Justice for All: A Discussion Guide,
   Washington: N.C.C.B., Committee for the
   Bicentennial, 1975.

"Nationhood", Justice Hearing, Number 2, Washington:
   N.C.C.B., Committee for the Bicentennial, 1975.

"Work", Justice Hearing, Number 5, Washington:
   N.C.C.B., Committee for the Bicentennial, 1975.

V. CATHOLIC THEOLOGY (IN CHRONOLIGICAL ORDER)

Pope Pius IX, The Syllabus of Errors, in Walter Kaufman (editor), Religion from Tolstoy to Camus, N.Y.: Harper and Row, 1964.

Pope Pius IX, The Dogma of Papal Infallibility, in Walter Kaufman (editor), Religion from Tolstoy to Camus, N.Y.: Harper and Row, 1964.

Pope Pius X, Pascendi Dominici Gregis, September 8, 1907, Boston: St. Paul Editions.

Pope Pius X, Lamentabili Sane, July 3, 1907, Boston: St. Paul Editions.

Pope Leo XIII, Testem Benevolentiae, in John Tracy Ellis (editor), The Documents of American Catholic History, Milwaukee: Bruce, 1956.

Pope Leo XIII, Rerum Novarum, 1891, Boston: St. Paul Editions.

Pope Pius XI, Quadragesimo Anno, 1931, Boston: St. Paul Editions.

Pope Pius XII, Humani Generis, 1950, Boston: St. Paul Editions.

Pope John XXIII, Mater et Magistra, 1961, Boston: St. Paul Editions.

Pope John XXIII, Pacem in Terris, 1963, Boston: St. Paul Editions.

The Documents of Vatican II (Walter Abbott, editor), Washington: America Press, 1966.

Catechism of Vatican II (Franco Peirini, editor), N.Y.: Alba House, 1967.

Pope Paul VI, Popularum Progressio, 1967, Washington, U.S.C.C.

The Church in Our Day, Collective Pastoral Letter of The Most Reverend Bishops of the United States, January 11, 1968, Washington: National Catholic News Service.

Synod of Bishops, *Justice in the World*, Washington: N.C.C.B., 1971.

Pope Paul VI, *A Call to Action*, 1971, Washington: United States Catholic Conference.

Social Justice! The Catholic Position (Vincent Mainelli, editor), Washington: Consortium Press, 1975.

Bishops Pastoral Reply to the Call to Action, Origins National Catholic Documentary Service, May 9, 1977.

To Do the Work of Justice, Washington: U.S.C.C., 197

Pope John Paul II, *Redemptor Homis*, 1979, Boston, St. Pauls Edition.